Though renowned as a theorist, critic and writer of fiction, Hélène Cixous is less known in the English-speaking world for her work in theatre. Yet her playwriting – working mainly with the Théâtre du Soleil and its director Ariane Mnouchkine – establishes her as a participant in some of the most adventurous European theatre-making of the last forty years.

This collection brings together four of Cixous's plays – three of which appear in English for the first time:

- *Portrait of Dora*, translated by Ann Liddle
- *Black Sail White Sail*, translated by Donald Watson
- *The Perjured City*, translated by Bernadette Fort
- *Drums on the Dam*, translated by Judith G. Miller and Brian J. Mallet

Featuring a new interview with Hélène Cixous in which she talks in detail about her experience and practice as a playwright, and a translation of her essay, "Enter the Theatre," *Selected Plays of Hélène Cixous* concludes with a bibliography of her theatre writing and a complete list of premières of her work.

This exciting new collection is a unique and extraordinary resource for scholars, students and theatre-makers alike.

Hélène Cixous is a writer, playwright, theorist and critic. She created the first French doctoral programme in Women's Studies and has published several major plays and theoretical texts, as well as more than thirty works of fiction. Her publications in English translation include *First Days of the Year* (1998), *The Third Body* (1999), *Portrait of Jacques Derrida* (2003) and *Reveries of the Wild Woman* (2003).

Selected Plays of Hélène Cixous

EDITED BY ERIC PRENOWITZ

 Routledge
Taylor & Francis Group

LONDON AND NEW YORK

First published 2004
by Routledge
11 New Fetter Lane, London EC4P 4EE

Simultaneously published in the USA and Canada
by Routledge
29 West 35th Street, New York, NY 10001

Routledge is an imprint of the Taylor & Francis Group

© 2004 Hélène Cixous

"On Theatre," translation; Foreword © 2004 Eric Prenowitz
"Enter the Theatre," translation © 2004 Brian J. Mallet
Portrait of Dora, translation © 2004 Ann Liddle
Black Sail White Sail, translation © 2004 Donald Watson
The Perjured City, translation © 2004 Bernadette Fort
Drums on the Dam, translation © 2004 Judith G. Miller and Brian J. Mallet

Designed and typeset in Janson by
Keystroke, Jacaranda Lodge, Wolverhampton
Printed and bound in Great Britain by
TJ International Ltd, Padstow, Cornwall

British Library Cataloguing in Publication Data
A catalogue record for this book is available from the British Library

Library of Congress Cataloging in Publication Data
Cixous, Hélène, 1937–
     [Plays. Selections]
     Selected plays of Hélène Cixous.
         p. cm.
     I. Title.
     PQ2663.I9A6 2003
     842′.914–dc21   2003001259

ISBN 0–415–23667–3 (hbk)
ISBN 0–415–23668–1 (pbk)

Contents

Foreword

Modernepic Theatre

ERIC PRENOWITZ

This collection of plays by Hélène Cixous is the first of its kind in any language. It contains four plays in previously unpublished English translations which together begin to chart out one of the essential theatrical itineraries of our times: both in Hélène Cixous's long writing career and in the history of contemporary theatre. The volume opens with two additional texts that serve to situate Cixous's involvement with theatre in theoretical, historical and literary terms. The first is an extended interview with the author conducted expressly for this publication, and in which she discusses the "laws" of theatre and retraces her journey as a playwright. The second, "Enter the Theatre," is an essay by Cixous, originally a lecture delivered in 2000, in which she reflects on one of her recent plays and explores the origins (autobiographical, artistic, ethical) and the ends of her theatre. A bibliography of Hélène Cixous's plays and a list of premières complete the book.

Hélène Cixous was born in Oran, Algeria in 1937. She grew up in a multilingual household formed of the North and the South, of European and North African memories, of Ashkenazi and Sephardic Jewish heritages. Although she received French nationality at birth – Algeria was then a French colony – in 1941 her citizenship was revoked by the anti-Jewish laws of the Vichy regime. Her profound mistrust of nationalism and the concept of nationality can be dated to this decisive experience. Her father died when she was ten years old, and in 1955 she moved to France. Her mother remained in Algeria until 1971, well after Independence. As an author of fiction, a playwright, a professor, a theorist and a critic, Hélène Cixous has been a central figure in the profound reassessment of prevailing intellectual paradigms that has swept through virtually every domain of the humanities since the 1960s. She participated in the events of 1968, and was among the founders of the experimental Université de Paris VIII. At this time, Cixous's friends and collaborators included such scholars and artists as Michel Foucault, Gilles Deleuze, Jacques Derrida, Jean Genet and Jacques Lacan, some of whom she recruited to join Paris VIII.

The earliest of Hélène Cixous's plays included here is *Portrait of Dora*, in which a Freudian primal scene is revisited and played out again on a different stage. It originally opened in 1976, although *Portrait du soleil*, the book of fiction on which it was based, had been published in 1973. This was a period during which Cixous had become intensely involved in the women's movement. In 1975 she published "The Laugh of the Medusa" which, along with a number of other theoretical texts, contributed to her reputation, particularly in the English-speaking world, as a "new" French feminist theorist. By the time her next major play, *The Conquest of the School at Madhubaï*, was staged in 1983, many transformations had taken place: in the French political world, with the election of the Socialists in 1981, but particularly in Hélène Cixous's world of writing. In 1977 she had discovered Clarice Lispector, a Brazilian author who was to join Cixous's elected family of vital writers. And above all, in the early 1980s, Ariane Mnouchkine, the director of the Théâtre du Soleil, asked Hélène Cixous to write a play for her troupe.

The result was *The Terrible but Unfinished Story of Norodom Sihanouk, King of Cambodia*, which opened in 1985 and marked a watershed in Cixous's theatrical writing. This "history play" in the Shakespearian tradition seems in retrospect to have obeyed both political and personal imperatives. It develops a critique of Western Cold War and neo-colonial politics and, at the same time, this tragic account of Cambodia's recent history recalls that of another former French colony, Cixous's native Algeria. *The Indiad, or The India of Their Dreams*, Hélène Cixous's second play for the Théâtre du Soleil, opened in 1987. It involved an even more ambitious political-poetical project, in which the story of the Partition of India becomes a metaphor for all the hopes and tragedies of the twentieth and twenty-first centuries. The protagonists of the cruel dismemberments in recent history (former Yugoslavia, Rwanda, Israel–Palestine . . .) find their parts played out in this epic battle between love and hate, between new aspirations to freedom and recourse to divisive delimitations. Each of the succeeding plays – *Black Sail White Sail, The Story (That We'll Never Know), The Perjured City, Drums on the Dam*, to name the major productions – is a radically singular creation, marked at once by Cixous's celebrated audacity in linguistic and textual innovation, and by a complex relationship to the great theatrical traditions (Shakespeare, Aeschylus, Noh . . .), which are simultaneously summoned, reinterpreted and transfigured. Each play in turn has attempted to find a just alliance between the art of the theatre and its political messianicity.[1] *The Perjured City* and *Drums on the Dam*, both included in this volume, are the two most recent works Cixous has written for the Théâtre du Soleil, this unique laboratory of theatrical innovation where Cixous has played a central role for some twenty years.

Although there are more translations of Cixous into English than into any other language, those currently available represent only a small proportion of her prolific and multifaceted oeuvre. There are many reasons for this, including the sheer volume of Hélène Cixous's publications. But one of the most important factors is precisely the resistance to translation for which her texts are known. As Jacques Derrida puts it, Cixous's entire oeuvre is "nearly untranslatable."[2] This does not mean that it is simply untranslatable, but neither is it *simply* translatable. If a text were to offer no resistance whatsoever to translation, the original would have no originality: it would always already be in virtual translation. In other words, the true work of translation is to grapple with the untranslatable: that element of a text that will never (fully) surrender to translation's siege. In this sense a translation is creative in the manner of a reading: it involves an interpretative activity that is necessarily selective, partial. This is particularly true in translating Cixous. She inhabits the French language in non-standard ways, pushing it ever farther in the direction of its idiomatic singularities. She herself has often spoken and written about her intense, complex, "foreign" relationship to the French language.[3] Even in the original, her texts call for a certain intralingual translation, a careful reading capable of interpreting subtle *displacements* of the French language within the French language.

Hélène Cixous's theatrical texts and her poetic fiction are not woven on the same loom. Whereas in her fiction, the signifier, and generally speaking the unconscious forces of the writing subject, are cast in a major role, the theatre demands a different textual economy. But what Cixous holds back in terms of properly poetical textual density she unleashes at another level: the slightest nuances and inflexions of spoken language are pressed into service, minuscule variations on everyday expressions, juxtapositions or omissions, all of which take on life in the body of an actor and in the ear of a spectator. And this leads to another type of difficulty for translation: the need to be particularly attentive to the breath, the phrasing, the musicality of the language, the different levels of discourse – for the vegetable hawker and the king may not have the same turn of phrase – and ultimately to all that is left unsaid when something is said.

The four plays in this collection have been translated by five translators. Each translation is a remarkable achievement in itself, and no attempt has been made to harmonize or to standardize them. A translation of Cixous is never a fixed monument, but a smuggler, a furtive border-crosser, and a witness. This volume is for theatre-goers in the broadest sense of the word, for scholars and readers of Cixous, for those who wish to study – and perform – her plays. But it is also a study in translation, as each of the English texts included here is the result of a unique encounter with Hélène Cixous's inimitable writing.

Notes

1 I am thinking here of what Derrida calls "Messianicity without messianism," as "the openness to the future or to the coming of the other as the advent of justice, but without any horizon of awaiting and without any prophetic prefiguration," *Foi et savoir*, Paris: Seuil, 2000 [1996], p. 30.

2 "H. C. pour la vie, c'est à dire . . . " in *Hélène Cixous, croisées d'une oeuvre*, Paris: Galilée, 2000, p. 17.

3 See, for example, Hélène Cixous, *Rootprints*, Routledge, 1997, p. 84.

On Theatre

An Interview with Hélène Cixous

ERIC PRENOWITZ

PRENOWITZ The plays included here were written between 1974 and 1998. At the beginning of the 1980s, when Ariane Mnouchkine asked you to write for the Théâtre du Soleil, you were already a playwright (*The Pupil, Portrait of Dora, The Name of Oedipus, The Conquest of the School at Madhubaï* . . .): what changed then in your relationship to theatre writing?

CIXOUS In the first place, the feeling that I was beginning to do theatre. Which is to say that what I wrote before embarking on the theatrical adventure and alliance with Ariane Mnouchkine and the Théâtre du Soleil can be thought of as pre-theatrical. As the prehistory of an engagement or an event. A veritable event: the day when *Ariane asked me* to try to write for the Théâtre du Soleil. Because I had a very strong, disturbing, alarming feeling that I was being called, that I was being summoned to respond by the theatre in person, if you will. I do not mean Ariane herself, who was its representative, but the theatre in its eternal figure. I was summoned to answer to the call of an ancient and ever-present world, a quasi-divine world: whether or not I really wanted to do theatre. Why? Because I must say in all humility that I had not considered what had preceded that moment to be theatre, but rather an allusion, a childish game. It was as if I had been going on excursions, practically tourism, on a continent or in a universe, a cosmos which I never thought I would ever really come to inhabit. For many reasons. In some cases, as for *The Pupil*, it consisted in theatralizing a kind of vision of the world which was at once political and rather abstract, as if in an attempt to make it concrete, but this theatralization remained intra-literary. Which is to say that I did not think that *The Pupil* had a properly theatrical destiny, that it would ever be produced. It was an extremely experimental text.

The Accident

The adventures which preceded my entry into the universe of the Soleil were always kinds of accidents for me. I was not looking for the theatre universe, but it was as if without my knowing it "theatricality," more than the theatre, crossed my path and was pointed out to me by others. The case of *Portrait of Dora* is exemplary. In fact *Dora* even made me think that I would never write theatre. It is paradoxical, but here's why: one day Simone Benmussa, who was the assistant, playwright and administrator for Jean-Louis Barrault at the Théâtre d'Orsay, and who read my books, told me that in one of my books of fiction called *Portrait du soleil*, she saw a play. I saw nothing at all. I saw a fiction. And she literally told me "But look hard," as if I had to lean over a river, "and you will see there is a play in there." What Simone Benmussa had sensed was a diffuse theatricality in my texts which is certainly related to the presence of voices in what I write. She must have heard voices which were there, because I have the habit of lending an ear to them.

But I did not think they were emanations of what is called the theatre. Yet I obeyed Simone Benmussa's injunction and I cut and pasted the text. I considered that act to be an artifice, which is to say not at all like a creation but what would now be called an adaptation, for example, a kind of handiwork, a montage. I did not take the act at all seriously, I thought of it as a form of literary tinkering. To my great surprise this little mock-up, which was directed by Simone Benmussa, was an enormous success. I concluded that the audience considered it to be theatre. So if the audience considers it to be theatre, including Lacan himself, who was an enthusiastic spectator, then perhaps I was doing theatre without knowing it, as Mr Jourdain did prose without knowing it. But I was not convinced. I did not think of myself as a theatre writer. I thought of myself as a *theatrical accident*.

I also considered *The Name of Oedipus* not to be theatre. Because there too I had responded to a call: the composer André Bouckereshliev had been commissioned to write an opera, which was later to be performed in the Cour d'Honneur of the Palais des Papes in Avignon (Claude Régy was the director), and he asked me to write the libretto. But here too I felt I was writing poetry, for example, and for me this poetry, which was incantation and which staged characters, was not the work of theatre. I think I also had a memory of what is called "theatre" which led me not to consider these acts which I committed with caution, or on the contrary with recklessness, to be "theatre." This memory was that of my book-knowledge of Shakespeare. I thought that theatre is what Shakespeare did, i.e. to create the universe: it is not only that "All the world's a stage," but his stage was truly the entire world. I felt I was extremely far from this. What I learned later –

THESSIE Mieaoo!

CIXOUS Now the cat has spoken, for example, as I was speaking to you. This intrusion of the cat, who enters into the scene where we are, is precisely a theatrical act. Which is to say that the theatre is itself an action, a drama, and one of the marks of the theatre is the *unexpected intervention*. The fact that at any moment characters enter or events take place which are completely uncalculated. It seems to me that in my first plays I had not opened the door to the *event*. If only in so far as there were no events in *Portrait of Dora* because it was already there. I lifted *Portrait of Dora* from *Portrait du soleil*, and I myself had no surprises, there was no surprise; there was sculpting. For *The Name of Oedipus* it was quite similar, because it involved reanimating or resuscitating the legend of Jocasta and Oedipus, which I did in my own way, but here too I think the element of surprise was textual, aesthetic, and not dramatic.

The Event

It was only later that I had the first moment of temptation, or the first attempt at what I continue to consider to be the theatre, which is to say the great machine of events. It can be said that *the god of theatre is the event*: an event that happens on the stage, but that *happens to the author*. The first time I let events come to me, which is to say the first time I myself engaged in a voluntary exercise in which I said to myself "This time I am going to open my interior space, my interior theatre, to events," was with *The Conquest of the School at Madhubaï*. It was certainly the first time I lent myself to the theatre or that I gave myself over to the theatre (I prefer "lent" because it is more modest). So what is the event? To *create emptiness* in oneself. An emptiness that is not an abyss. It is the *plateau* (in English: stage, platter, plateau). And the *plateau* is not a particular, concrete, referential object. Every time I say *plateau*, and I like this word in French, I am reminded of the plateaux, the high plateaux, for example, what were called the high plateaux in Algeria. Immense, telluric geographic zones, flat like a stage, where storms can erupt, or all of a sudden a nomad can appear, one never knows. At first there is nothing, it is barren, it is deserted, and all of a sudden a camel or a bird arrives, some animate being arrives and becomes the character of this *plateau*. But it is unforeseeable. I had never experienced this unforeseeability, this desertedness which is suddenly animated, which receives the soul of a being. Quite simply because on the contrary I had always been preceded, all the texts I had previously written were preceded and occupied.

The Desert

The non-occupation which is indispensable to what I now consider to be the theatre constitutes the first moment of my practice with the Théâtre du Soleil. Which is to say that everything I do with the Théâtre du Soleil begins with this non-occupation and this desert. But I had never practised it, I had never even thought of thinking of it, and I had never had the thinking and imagining experience of this inaugural state, which is indeed a state. With *The Conquest of the School at Madhubaï* I did it on purpose for the first time. It started with something that was very interesting and entirely new and revolutionary for me – an attempt to answer the question: Is it possible today to imagine or identify in the world someone who has the dimensions, the stature, the mystery of what is called a theatrical character? Because characters and not human beings are what inhabit the theatre. But there are also characters in the world's theatre. And I thought: But are there any today? Is there someone on the earth today like Oedipus? Is there a king who is at once innocent and guilty? Is there a woman who takes up arms to restore justice, or to attack injustice or to make war – is it possible that there exist today heroes or heroines like those we know from the archives of memory and legend? And I thought not, that there are none. Or at least I imagined it would not be easy to find them. And in the end they did exist. I searched, I looked, it was as if I had climbed up a tree or a tower and I was scrutinizing the horizon, I saw nothing, I saw nothing, and then all of a sudden I saw someone, and it was none other than Phoolan Devi, called the Queen of the Bandits. An incredible contemporary Indian character, but whose history and whose every gesture was worthy of the legends, of the Mahabharata. She was a sort of untouchable Joan of Arc, and I realized that she indeed had all the traits of a character, someone who resists the ready-made, or what has already been done, who resists the attribution of a form of life or of destiny that leaves no freedom of invention to the human being. I thought: Here is someone who invents. And from the moment she invents new situations, she also encounters new situations. I found her in a newspaper. And I decided I would see if I could make her live, if I could make her arrive in my desert and have her invent a play – it no longer had to do with me or what I thought or my double, because she became the author – in which fictive events would happen to her. To tell the truth, this was a great shock for me . . .

So I entered into a passiveness, which ought to be comparable to a trance, a passivity, an emptiness, an evacuation of myself, in which I let this character I did not know enter. I had only read a few references in a newspaper and I let entirely fictive events take place as if I were an observer or a witness of events I knew nothing about ahead of time. For example, with *Oedipus*, I knew. For her, I knew nothing. And because I had to be in a state of trance I wrote it without stopping, I think in a single day, and at the end I passed out. I had to undergo such a tension of substitution – in order to let myself be replaced, since I was not there, by someone entirely foreign – that at the end of this experience of trance, of possession, I fainted, I had a terrible and frightening feeling of faintness. I lost myself. At the same time this play was very small. There were only three characters and I lacked the strength, and the *connaissance* – I do not mean the knowledge: the consciousness – necessary to pursue the experience any further. What's more it was quite brief. But I thought: Ah, the theatre must be something like that. And shortly thereafter, a year later perhaps, Ariane asked me: "Would you like to work for the Théâtre du Soleil?"

PRENOWITZ But you already had some sense of the emptiness of the interior *plateau* and this relationship with history, the search for a character in the world who could become an event on your stage?

CIXOUS Yes, of course. But this could have been an isolated experience. What happened next was that Ariane asked me – which was another event because it was totally unexpected, this request that was turned towards me at a time when I had known her for nearly ten years, and we were friends. But I had never had either the idea or the desire to write a play for the Théâtre du Soleil. In fact it was out of the question. For two reasons. A writing reason: my writing, which had nothing to do with Ariane's theatrical practice. And a theatre reason: what Ariane did seemed to me to participate in the great theatrical tradition I believed in – I had faith – but in which I did not at all see myself as a participant. If only because of the immense dimensions of the ambition and the scope of her enterprises. Ariane belonged to that epic dimension of the theatre that is found in the Greeks, in Shakespeare, etc., but at the time I did not feel I was concerned. I watched as a spectator but absolutely not as an agent. I did not at all think I could ever in any way be called by or respond to that space. And so when Ariane proposed that I try, she was very prudent, very just, very wise, she asked me to try and she did not guarantee either that I would succeed or that what I would do would be received by her troupe. And this was very good because it gave both of us great freedom. I did not commit myself, I could not promise, I did not believe in it, and neither did she. It was a possibility. And quite honestly I did not succeed right away. I wandered as I always wander. Which is to say that each time I start off again on a trail with Ariane I go through a period of wandering, of erring and of error before glimpsing in the distance the light of a theatre. Always. It remains for me the *foreign country*. Each time I start off again I go towards a foreign country and don't even know what this country is. All I know is that I'm off. Which is to say that I move away from myself. I move away from the interior in the interior, I move away from my limits, and I take to the open sea.

The Foreign Country

I think that for me, although this is also part of its essence and its mystery, the theatre remains, the theatre will always remain the place of two types of laying bare: the change of country, the un-country, it is an un-country, another country, another world, it is the world but a world that is other, or it is the world that can tear itself away from the world as it is by becoming the sublime form of the world as it is. It is no longer the world as it is; it is the world's world, it is the world par excellence. And it is a world that is a figure. It is entirely transfigured. It is true that in a certain way the theatre as world, the theatre-world exists virtually in the great epics. This is why it was not absolutely impossible for me, because I am someone who has always frequented the epic, it is my childhood imagination, my place of childhood. The Bible is extremely theatrical; nearly all the great stories of the Bible could be staged. All the adventures that are related in the Bible as being historical – whereas they are not at all historical, they are fantastical – have a partner who is none other than God. From time to time the Devil, but rarely, and in fact God. Which is to say the gods. There is no theatre without gods. It is the first thing that becomes clear when you turn to the theatre: there are god(s). In the singular and in the plural. God in all forms, at times the lowly forms, or else sublime forms. They are superior forces. God is what I would call all the superior forces with which we negotiate or which treat us or mistreat us, which we imagine at times to be interior but which we experience as exterior, against which we fight. Sometimes they have names of powerful abstraction like King or Justice or State or Honour, all those sorts of values that precipitate the great theatrical actions, even War, Hate. At the theatre, God or the gods are always blowing, as if in the sails of the theatre, in the theatre's invisible sails; they give to the theatre, they take the theatre, they lift it above the earth, up to the *plateau*, higher still. This is what we see in the Bible: everything is lifted, one is always setting off towards the mountains, further along, higher up, stronger, more terrible. It is more. The theatre is more, always more. It is what the Greeks called enthusiasm, possession by the gods.

PRENOWITZ It is bigger-than-we-are.

Always More

CIXOUS Always more. It can be worse. A "bigger" that transports us, enthusiasm is being transported, it is called transports, to have transports. Something that unglues us, that makes us lift off, that tears us from the earth, from common sense and from identification, from identity, from the self. A moment ago I said there is a change of country; at the same time there is de-selfing. This is something I formulated very quickly when I was at the Théâtre du Soleil, but my first experience of it was *The Conquest of the School at Madhubaï*: it is only possible to enter the theatre *without self*. And in the place where my self had previously been: my place without myself, deserted by the self and left vacant so that all the others can approach, manifest themselves, take place. This is why the theatre is a genre that is mentally, spiritually, physically difficult, and dangerous. Because it requires a temporary but none the less sufficiently long suppression, ablation, confiscation of the usual occupant of the author's head. And because this entering into trance, which happens in many primitive cultures, is no longer practised in the West. We are no longer accustomed to it. In primitive societies the trance has an accompaniment: when these rites take place in Africa or in Asia, they are accompanied by a group of people, by music, by magical incantations . . . All of this must be reconstituted in oneself, in the little European Western head without any means or instruments, and it is very difficult. At the same time it is fascinating, it's a passion in the proper sense of the word: it must be suffered, and when it happens it is an absolutely extraordinary and non-communicable experience. Except that it leaves a trace in the form of the play. But it is also exhausting, and I always enter into this sort of interior temple and give myself over to it with a kind of fear, as I prepare myself for an extreme mental and physical ordeal. This is why I prefer not to repeat the theatrical ordeal too often. Every three years is enough, because it wears me out.

PRENOWITZ Even after becoming the Théâtre du Soleil's playwright, you have also written plays for other companies: for example, *The Story (That We'll Never Know)* for Daniel Mesguich. What is the relationship between these two paths in your theatrical writing since the 1980s? I'm thinking for instance of the fact that you are actively involved in the staging of your plays at the Théâtre du Soleil, reworking your text in response to the obstacles or the possibilities that arise in rehearsals, while *The Story* or *Rouen* were mounted by Mesguich virtually without any modifications.

CIXOUS I have to say to begin with that the trunk and the roots are the Théâtre du Soleil. This is not to suggest that what I do outside the Théâtre du Soleil is only branches, but that the apprenticeship, the vitality, the sap, the nourishment come to me from the Théâtre du Soleil. For many reasons. In the first place because I think it is originative: in its practices, which are those of Ariane, it is at the origins, at the sources. It is at the sources of theatre. I must add, being as they say the house author, that the Théâtre du Soleil represents the *sources*, but also the school. Because I know nothing, I do not have knowledge, and I feel that I always go to the theatre as an apprentice, as a disciple, as a schoolgirl, as a researcher, as a student of this art that I will never have acquired, which I am always only discovering, and searching for, and glimpsing by illumination, but without ever acquiring it as a knowledge. And I believe it will always be thus. It happens that the Théâtre du Soleil is a theatre in exercise; it is also a theatre school. Which begins again every two or three years, which goes back to the sources, which begins again to do theatre from the first elements, which returns to a sort of ignorance that is not a lack and disregard of knowledge but a childhood, which returns to a sort of naiveté, of newborn-ness, and where all the active elements of the theatre are reanimated anew, where initiations are always taking place. At once in the art of acting, in the initiation to mask-work, to the musical instruments, to the different dances from the most ancient theatrical arts. In addition, the Théâtre du Soleil, which is perhaps unique in the world, does not stage a play as it is done almost everywhere else, but *searches for the play*, as the author will have searched, at length. This would be called rehearsal in classical vocabulary, but it is a search and a recreation of the play that can take months and months and months. This is not done elsewhere, for reasons of economy; most theatres cannot treat themselves to such a long period of research and they generally take shortcuts. The Théâtre du Soleil does not take shortcuts; it goes back over the entire path.

Searching for the Play

It happens that from time to time I write for someone else or for another space. It is rare, it has only happened two or three times. But I do not write plays abstractly or in the direction of the unknown. In general these other plays are intended for or turned towards a particular person. I usually address them to Daniel Mesguich. My friendship with Daniel is different from the friendship that links me with Ariane, but it is very familiar, I would say fraternal. I use the word fraternal on purpose, because there are cultural, literary, intellectual connivances and complicities between us, it is perfectly overdetermined. So I address plays to him which are like letters. As if I were writing letters and not plays. They are plays all the same, in so far as they are structured, executed, organized, controlled by the experience with the Théâtre du Soleil. Daniel knows Ariane very well, they are friends, so this stays within a sphere of friendly connections, and Daniel has even said to me: "Write me a play as if it were for the Théâtre du Soleil." Which is to say that he has placed himself within his desire, or placed his desire in a space which remains this antique and primordial space. But Daniel's intellectual and textual structure gives priority to textuality, and much more than for Ariane his referent is the great French texts. The texts Ariane has mounted are the very great texts from Aeschylus to Shakespeare: the great immemorial texts – which of course don't have a wrinkle. Curiously enough, Daniel, who is no more French than I am, is more steeped in, more shaped by the French tradition, the French language, whether Racine or Claudel. And so when I write a letter to Daniel in a sense I write in my-kind-of-French, that is, in poetic French, going back along the path or the course of a grand verbal, linguistic French tradition. Because I know he is a man of letters of that language, as you would say a Chinese man of letters. He knows all its tricks, all its stratagems and all its strangenesses, all its foreignnesses. So in his direction I give free reign to a certain writing which in general I keep for my fiction writing and which is relatively uncommon under the great roof of the theatre. Daniel is the first receptor. But there is not only one receptor, after him there are others, as these plays are taken up again and performed abroad. But the first receptor is essential. This is why the text that I write in his direction will be received as a letter. He reinterprets it of course, because he performs it, he transposes it, he does a reading of it; but he receives it, in the end and without our ever having said this to each other, as one would receive a letter. He does not remove a sentence, because in the relay that is set in motion from the genesis of a theatrical text to its different transpositions on the stage, he places himself within a great tradition of literally – "to the letter" – epistolary reading.

PRENOWITZ   The fact that you write for a real theatre company or troupe, the Théâtre du Soleil, is in itself very important it seems to me, and your relationship with it, the singularity of the theatrical project of this troupe which devotes all its many lives (including yours) to an amazing adventure in "creation," is at once rare and I would think decisive for the theatre it produces. This is what Shakespeare and a certain number of others no doubt did, but there are very few real troupes left today. What is the importance of this relation to a theatre company in the history of your writing, in your plays and for the theatre in general?

CIXOUS   It is indeed decisive. I think the word "adventure" is very important. It is decisive in the first place with regard to the dream. If there is an art that has a structural complicity with the dream, it is the theatre. I mean the dream in the sense that children have grand dreams. Where they dream that they will be a king, or a bandit or a corsair. The theatre company dreams that it will play all the roles and that it is going on an adventure like the great heroes in the epics, or like those who went in search of the golden fleece. It is a treasure hunt. And the treasure is the theatre. It is simultaneously a dream that has an absolutely magnificent goal, which is to do theatre together; and at the same time something very dangerous because to do theatre together is like going in search of India, which became America. The spices, the gold are this art which can only be done together, it is a collective art; and on the other hand no one knows where the country is. Just as they went in the wrong direction, they went to the East in order to find what later turned out to be to the West. It is the same thing with the theatre: you go in one direction and you arrive at another. At the same time what is shared is the sense of adventure without any certainty that the goal will be reached, for it is entirely possible that the company will fail, that it will not find what it is searching for. The adventure is very dangerous because the collection of sixty dreams is always dangerous: it is never sure that all the dreams will hold together in the same boat. What is more, the adventure is heroic in the sense that it is very costly. It comes at a very high social, mental and economic price.

No One Knows

Doing theatre is a question of passion: the reward is not assured at any level. So it involves consciously putting oneself in danger, and by the way one never knows what the extent of the danger is, without a guarantee of any benefit or that anything will be found. What animates the members of a theatre company is also the capacity to take this risk. The people who come to the Théâtre du Soleil are very diverse: there are the actors, the technicians, the painters, the sculptor, the musician, the silk painters . . . Each one goes there in the hopes of satisfying at least his or her artistic taste. And I think that this satisfaction exists. But it must be said that they pay for it "economically," because the salaries are very modest. Everyone earns the same thing. Each of the people engaged in this adventure is paid exactly the same sum; the actors, the technicians, Ariane the director, myself, the musician-composer, we all earn the same thing. The salaries are modest relative to the salaries that are current in the institutional theatres, not to mention in the film industry. All of these people could in fact go in other directions and earn money. But what they want here is not money (*argent*) but art (*art*) and people (*gens*).

At the same time it is fragile: from time to time the company must rely on unemployment benefits, so they earn even less and find themselves in a holding pattern that would be difficult to put up with and even intolerable, impossible, if they thought of themselves as workers. But they are dreamers. Dreamers who have a profession. Professional dreamers. Whose profession is dreaming. But again, it is very dangerous. People's destinies, their lives, their material conditions of existence are all at stake. On the other hand, working together is a pleasure. But it is a trembling happiness. And then there is the moment the play is presented to the audience, and it's double or nothing. Which is to say it will either be a triumph or a failure. Thank God it is generally a triumph. But it is a triumph because everyone has worked for it, with sweat and tears. Has struggled to get to this point. Without any stability ever setting in: one never settles down. No one is a functionary. The reward, when it is achieved, is the relation to the audience, the happiness of sharing an experience with the audience which, at the Théâtre du Soleil, is very large: 600 people a day, and when we give 100 or 150 performances that makes 100,000 people who come. That is a lot of people. This means that we speak the same language, 100,000 people speak the same language for at least a few hours, and share the same dream. This is ethically and politically powerful. This is of course the reward, when there is one. In addition, as with *Drums on the Dam*, when the production ends up going beyond our theatre, when it travels, goes out into the world, to Japan, to Korea, to Canada, to Australia, we have the sense of an extraordinary vision of humanity. The feeling that in the world, in the universe, there are no borders, because of course art passes across everything, that the desire for dreams is shared by a great number of very diverse populations, and that they communicate through a common language which is the language of theatre. This clearly gives immense happiness, but it is a fragile happiness: for *Drums* it will have lasted two or three years, and now we are going to find ourselves once again before the unknown. It means starting off again on an adventure, towards another imaginary country without knowing where we are going, if we will arrive, and who will arrive. Because I must also say that exactly as Ulysses lost men along the way in the *Odyssey*, along the way we also lose members of the crew. For many reasons: since these are very long voyages people can fall ill, and all sorts of accidents can occur. On these magnificent long voyages there is also mourning – and one has to be aware of this.

So it is very important for me to work inside this troupe, in community, in communion. With human beings I know and love, and with whom we all share. Just as people share bread and wine, here we share bread and wine that are sublime, symbolic. My desire, my appetite for sharing and love and friendship and beauty are fulfilled. On the other hand I also pay in my way, which is to say that I am in a dependant relationship to the group. Inside the troupe one does not have the freedom one has alone. There are immense human benefits and they are paid for in restrictions, because there are common laws, common rules, obligations. The other thing that should be noted is that what I do in this case is to adopt the direction of the dreamer which is a direction that I do not command alone. I respond to an order. This order is formulated by Ariane, who must be thought of as herself-plus-the-troupe. The Soleil has its own aesthetics, there are aesthetic and political choices, and if I did not share them, quite simply I could not be the troupe's author. But it happens that we have common visions, we have a relationship to society, to political commitments, to art that is shareable and that has been in place for a long time. We have been in agreement for nearly thirty years. We are in tune, we are musically harmonized.

There is an order. Which is to say that I have never made a proposition to Ariane saying "This is what we must do." She proposes a direction to me, but she proposes it after long discussions between us. We discuss different possible projects. And what orients the choice of a subject – because in the end what we agree on is an initial subject – is in the first place that it must of course correspond to the history of the art of the Théâtre du Soleil, but even more that it should inspire Ariane. She must be able to see, even before I write, she must have the possibility of having a vision in the fullest sense of the word: to have visions, which are visions in space. This has to do with her own art. Her art must be nourished, set ablaze, or else she cannot create. There is a sort of order: when we talk, when we have our discussions, as we always do in these situations, we cannot take an orientation if she has no visions, even for example if I say: Ah! I'd like to go in that direction! Her workshop must be illuminated. This suits me, I can function in a certain number of directions because my functioning is not based on visions but on voices. My visions are auditory, if I can put it that way. I simply have to be able to hear voices.

To Hear Voices

That is what it is to be in a troupe. It is an experience which is not only of being on stage, but one of sharing a certain time which is out of the ordinary. And it is a time that goes on. Twenty years of creation with Ariane. But with the company it is a human time, a prolonged time that overflows the simple stage to go into the kitchen, into the workshops and very often into the particular, intense and subjective moments of each actor. But I would say that it succeeds rather well, because after all it has been twenty years that Ariane and I have been working together unfailingly. It is the same thing with the composer of the company, Jean-Jacques Lemêtre, whom I consider to be absolutely brilliant and with whom from time to time we take little excursions. For example, he recently did the music for another of my plays in a reading directed by Daniel Mesguich, and I know that he has a project for an opera whose libretto he wants me to write. In the end we weave together living and continuous affinities: there are no divisions among us. It is very well orchestrated. It is clearly quite miraculous. And this leaves a mark, this marks everything I write for the Théâtre du Soleil.

PRENOWITZ Is there a chronology, a history, an evolution from play to play in your work with the Théâtre du Soleil? If so, to what extent is it due to the history of this theatre and to what extent does it have to do with an evolution in your works or life as a writer?

CIXOUS It is possible now, twenty years later, to talk in terms of a history. Because there has been a history, there has been time. When you begin, the first play has no history. It is an event, and you do not know what it will lead to. But after twenty years, like all stories that go on for a certain time, if you look back, yes, you can imagine or make out a shape that has emerged, but which was not anticipated. When we began this was not our goal. Each time we have proceeded as if from play to play it was the first time we were working on something. This is not true, because from one play to the next something gains in depth, or appears in a slightly more familiar way. For example, I realized after a few plays that there were elements that returned, types of characters, but this was never planned in advance. It is only with experience that you recognize signs and accents. Going from play to play I noticed that there were recurrent characters. Characters from my own unconscious who come onto the stage. If I had not written a series of plays, in the first place they simply would not have returned, nor would I have noticed them. I spoke of this in "Enter the Theatre": the character who is constantly returning and who is therefore in some sense my signature in the play, is the character of the border-crosser. The one who goes between the living and the dead, between eras, between different circles, between the different "houses." When I was working on *Sihanouk*, we used this word "house," which came from Shakespeare's theatre. In Shakespeare you have this royal house and that royal house, and with *Sihanouk* there were the house of the king, the house of the Americans, the house of the people. These are groups, sorts of microcosms that form a macrocosm. These houses are closed in, they are enclosures, and then there is a character who can pass from one to the other, and who, in this first play, can even go from the house of the dead to the house of the Khmer people, and all the way to Chou En Lai's house in Peking – and the whole way on a bicycle. He is a magic character who crosses through everything. This magic character was Sihanouk's father, who was dead, a dead king who can pass from one house to the other; it is the magic of theatre. At the time I did that, for me it was necessary for the play, I needed someone who could go from one place to another, and it is only very recently that I realized there was always such a character in my plays. That there was always someone who could give passage, like the needle that takes the thread through the tapestry. I did not recognize it myself because the play was what required it. The theatre required it. It was not some recipe I had. Suddenly I noticed that in *The Perjured City* the person who passed from the scene of the Cemetery to the scene of the City, which do not communicate otherwise, or between the living and the dead, was Aeschylus, the guardian of the Cemetery. This little character was also present in *The Indiad*: it was the Baul woman who could cross India on foot, or the bear tamer. These are characters who do not belong to any house, who precisely do not belong, who are not identified with houses and who are the messengers the envoys the border-crossers of theatre, of the spirit of the theatre, of the spirit of humanity, from one place to another. Because there is a path and along this path from one play to the next something is communicated: the spirit, memory. It was not a decision or a calculation, it was not a kind of speculation. It was necessity.

The Border-Crosser

So from play to play: there is certainly something even if, once again, for each play we go back to zero, we start from nothing. We are on the beach, on a sandbank, and we do not know what is before us. Once the work is underway and has developed, in looking back we can say that each play was engendered by the previous one. That *The Indiad* is in a certain sense the child of *Sihanouk*. And one could continue and say that from play to play there is engendering and causality, which we are not able to see when we begin. When we begin, it is really in a state of innocence. We start the world over. The feeling of genesis, of creation *ex nihilo* is always there, otherwise we would do nothing. But after all we are ourselves human beings with memories. I think that if we were to analyse the question, which I don't wish to do or don't have the time to do here, we would see the lineage, where elements of *The Perjured City* come from *Sihanouk* by way of *The Indiad* . . . At times it disturbs me, for example when I was writing *Drums*, at a certain point I said to myself "But there are elements of *The Perjured City* here: the tidal wave." But then I forget. I do not want to know. If we feel we are repeating ourselves or doing something over again then we have to stop.

But these elements that travel in a subterranean fashion and which reappear differently – because when they reappear it is in an altogether different way – probably come from the fact that when I write for the Théâtre du Soleil, I always place things at the root, at the *causes*, what causes the behaviours, the catastrophes, the wars, the destructions in humanity. And here we are in a space that is continuous with the space of engendering, thus of mythologies, of all that caused the first literary works: the epics, etc. There are fundamental structures. In the same way that one talks of the fundamental elements of genealogical ties, there are fundamental elements in the history of humanity, and each time we ask how things happened, where they came from, we find driving elements that are universal. This is why the theatre can travel from continent to continent.

Causes

The one which functioned explicitly in *Drums on the Dam* is auto-immunity. This is a force of self-destruction that is at work in humanity. Take what is going on at this moment, the great drama that is occupying the entire world and which began on 11 September, 2001. We can see it as a play, and who could imagine more of a play: the most symbolic, the most beautiful, the most triumphant place in the universe, the World Trade Center, disappears. It is an extremely spectacular event. Scene 1. And then we discover in Scene 2 that this was done by a character who is the opposite: the towers are as visible, obvious and ostentatious as he is hidden. The metaphors are incredibly powerful. He is in a cave. They are as naked as he is hidden. And the entire world is at the theatre, the tragic theatre. The auto-immunity factor, the self-destruction, is everywhere. Some people have asked: "Is it not the United States that caused this?" which is a perverse question. However, there is auto-immunity in that Bin Laden will come to a bad end. He has already lost the war, he is destroying what he wants to save, he has already lost his power, he risks losing his freedom and his life. We can ask what principle guided him: it was the certainty that he would triumph, that his power would grow enormously. The fantasy that this character could have is to crush the most powerful country in the world, to have his God rule over the earth, his God being the partial God (in both senses of the word) that is the Islamist God. Afterwards we can transport ourselves a bit later in time: if we look at this story we see that he set everything up for his own destruction. Why is it that he brings about his own destruction?

Drums on the Dam is set in an absolutely magnificent kingdom which has always been prosperous and which in the excesses of the exercise of power – it is always the same thing – overturns itself. It turns its power, its beauty, its riches, into absolute destruction. We wonder: Why do people do what will produce their own ruin? But this question exists in Shakespeare. It is a question that is being increasingly described, thought about, philosophized today. It is like the question of globalization: the Americans have refused to sign the Kyoto accords. They ought to protect human life on earth, but they do not want to put a limit on the exercise of their industrial and capitalistic power. They are heading quite simply towards their own suicide. It is at a great distance, it is always the question of the great distance: I am not the one who is going to die, it is my children. This is an enormous question. We think: How can human beings think such a thing? How can human beings say to themselves "I don't care"? In France there is a phrase for this, Louis XV's phrase: "Après moi le déluge," "After me the flood." A king who is the successor to Louis XIV, the greatest king of the French monarchy, who little by little causes the catastrophes of his kingdom, and who, when reprimanded and told that this is not a good policy, says "Après moi le déluge." And the deluge arrives: the death of Louis XVI, the French Revolution . . . We look at this each time and wonder: But what is it that motivates these people? The phrase says that after all I will have lived well and if the deluge comes after me I don't care. It is incredible, and yet this is what rules power. Power thinks it rules, yet it is ruled. And it is ruled over by death.

PRENOWITZ So there are elements that return, continuities such as the border-crosser, the tidal wave, the "causes," the fundamental structures. But you said that on the one hand you have to begin each time at zero and on the other hand that you must not repeat yourself. So what changes? How would you describe the evolution? Where are you going?

CIXOUS First remark: if I look retrospectively – because clearly only retrospectively can one begin to recount the history of a collaboration or of series of works – looking backwards from *Drums* successively to *The Perjured City, The Eumenides, The Indiad, Sihanouk*, I see an evolution I find very interesting, though it was not planned out, towards less and less realism, or fewer and fewer references to existing facts, and more and more inventions. Less and less reliance on immediately readable current affairs, to the point of attaining pure fiction with *Drums on the Dam*. Once again this was not planned by us; it is like a telluric, organic evolution, the natural maturation of a working engagement over time. In the first place because in an obvious way, it is not simply an arbitrary succession: each of the plays can be seen to come out of the previous one. They cause each other, they engender each other, they suggest each other but without there ever being an omniscient project. It is a process.

Less and Less Realism

I think I have already told the story of *Sihanouk*. The first play I wrote for the Théâtre du Soleil was *Sihanouk*, a play of enormous dimensions. Here is what I could say about the prologue to the story of the creation of the play: when Ariane asked me if I wanted to write for the Théâtre du Soleil, although I had known her for a long time by then and had never thought of writing for the Théâtre du Soleil, she asked me very directly to write on India. That was her dream. And I was struck with terror. I was emerging from a chamber; and in this little room or in this little office I had convoked characters like Freud. My dimensions and my imaginary horizon were no greater than that. The most I had done, and it was already in the direction of India, was the little play *The Conquest of the School at Madhubaï*. But even if it took place in India and even if the character was Indian, India was only in the atmosphere, which is to say the rain, the monsoon: everything took place in a cabin, the equivalent of a plain little room. It could be performed in a small theatre, there were no more than three or five characters. I had not gone beyond the dimensions of what I have always called "chamber theatre." When Ariane said India I knew that for her it was the Indian continent. And I truly panicked. I ruled it out right away, I immediately said no, I cannot do it. I saw that I was a little ant before the Himalayas, and I thought: What is she talking about? An ant cannot write the Himalayas. It's impossible. It will take me centuries to climb the Himalayas. I was incapable of *envisaging* India, in the proper meaning of the word. I understood Ariane's desire, but for me it was out of the question. It was a question of proportion, of capacity – and this is very important because it is a question of theatrical art – which is to say that my capacity, what I could contain, was very small. It could not be anything so gigantic. So Ariane conceded to my concerns and we started looking for something else, but in Asia none the less. This is where the Théâtre du Soleil's Asia comes from: Ariane needs to be Asian, and what she wanted was an author who could write something Asian for her, because Asia has always been the cradle of all her images, of all her references.

In the first place *Asia*; in the second place *today*. A today that has never been rigidly tied to current events, but a present – the present being in any case the time of the theatre – making reference to something very close, contemporary, because what she wanted was something contemporary, but which would be valid for all times. I could understand a present that would apply to all times, but not a universal Asia. So I began to look around in the twentieth century which is relatively easy to explore mentally from a historical, political point of view. It is clear that the great events of the twentieth century can be seen in the light of their universal implications: for example the chaos produced by the Vietnam war which affects Asia. I saw all of this. And while searching I read a great deal – I have always done this for the Théâtre du Soleil – I read everything that could be seen to interweave the political and the mythological, the theatrical and the ethnological. All the books that are archives relating to structures of the imagination or of a culture, as well as the narratives of the tragedies of our times. I even think that Ariane must have told me she was looking for the story of a people – the theatre is itself a people – whose tragic destiny could be the image of other tragedies, of other contemporary stories. In this research I was attracted by the tragic history of a little people named the Jarai, a tiny ethnic group between Cambodia and Vietnam that simply disappeared during the Vietnam war because they were bombed, massacred, and nothing was left. A people that has disappeared. I had begun working on this, I began writing a few scenes and when I showed them to Ariane she cried: "What is this? It's much too small. This is the story of a village!" And indeed it took place in a village. "This is not for us. We are a kingdom, you have got the wrong dimensions." I had gone from too big to too small. This woke me up. It was as if I had forgotten the dimensions of the Théâtre du Soleil, which are royal dimensions. So I looked for a kingdom with Ariane, and very quickly, because we only had to take a step to the side, we were either in Vietnam or in Cambodia. So we were in Cambodia, and we found a lot of very good books. The one that acted as a trigger for us was a remarkable book by an American journalist (*Sideshow* by W. Shawcross). The epic dimensions of this universe became clear to me in reading this book. At the same time, and in a way that was enlightening for me, what carried me was the fact that Cambodia resembled Shakespeare's England. Like two peas in a pod. England saw itself as a large kingdom, but it was small, three million inhabitants. The exact dimensions of Cambodia.

The Small for the Large

The first lesson I learned at that time was the small for the large. It is clearly a question of image: just as England saw itself in Shakespeare's time as the greatest kingdom in the world even if France was its rival, Cambodia could see itself as an immense kingdom even if it was very small. And from there we could have taken any other kingdom, we could have turned to Tibet: any small-large kingdom. I understood something about the imaginary dimension that reigns at the theatre, whereas I had been realistic in my first choice. And so I set off on that path. I began to write in a way that was instilled with my epic memory, from Shakespeare. And this gave *Sihanouk*.

But for us, *Sihanouk* was the story of Cambodia. The way we experienced this story was in the first place literary for me, then human. Ariane wanted right away to go to Cambodia. I did not. Which is to say that I am so fearful of the curse of realism, and also of reality; I thought that too much reality would simply crush my capacity to dream. I must be able to dream something. I told her that I had to finish writing first, before going to Cambodia. She left before me and during that time I finished the first part and I began the second part. It was only then, when I was sure of my own inner images and my own dreams, that I joined her in the refugee and resistance camps between Thailand and Cambodia. Because at that point I could support the reality without it destroying the imagination. And in the same way I thought to myself that I did not want to establish relations with real Cambodians before my imaginary Cambodians had taken flesh. And once they existed, based only on the documents and images I had, I began to see the real ones. Real Khmers, either in Cambodia or here in France, where there is an enormous Khmer community. And at the very end, once everything was finished, Sihanouk himself. So that was the first period of practice in the adventure.

PRENOWITZ So the spectral presence of Shakespeare in *Sihanouk* comes first of all from this parallel between the small that sees itself as large . . .

CIXOUS The small-large.

PRENOWITZ . . . the small-large of these kingdoms and the imaginary dimension of the theatre: it had primarily to do with these questions rather than, for example, being a way of giving a form or a frame, that would be recognizable by a Western audience, to a story that is in principle very distant?

CIXOUS Yes. On the other hand the small-large is so important that in *Sihanouk* I am constantly talking about the small and the large. This is my way of inscribing things in the text, both in fiction and in theatre: when I begin to understand the genealogical and genetic roots of a work, they also become a subject of the work itself. Which is to say that there is a reflexivity that I inscribe in the text. So in *Sihanouk* there are reflections on the small and the large just as there are reflections on Shakespeare: these are signatures, genealogical traces. It is a derived form of what could be called intertextuality. It is not intertextual but it's a way of reminding myself and whoever can perceive it that this is a work of theatre or a work of art; it is not something realistic. The genealogy has its sources in the history, in the real events that it formalizes, that it transfigures, and also in the other world which is the world of literary creation. There are always two worlds. There is the political world and the literary world, and I cross-pollinate them.

Then comes *The Indiad*. Curiously enough, *Sihanouk* served as if it were the first stage of a rocket. From the moment I was able to take on a play that had immense proportions, even if the focal point was small, I realized I had discovered the trick that would allow me to undertake what seemed impossible to me, for example a play with fifty characters. I could not write a play with fifty characters all at once: I had to go at it ten times. That is, I did five plus five plus five . . . I shuttled back and forth, as if I were a boat, to bring five characters across each time. I realized that I am a limited being; I could have quintuplets but I could not have fifty children at once. But the obstacle had been removed. So when Ariane and I started off on the second venture, India was no longer impossible. But the lesson was there, i.e. the small for the large, and also the trigger, which is to say a particular emotion, a particular event. What is interesting is that we both had a strong emotional reaction to the death of Indira Gandhi, and we let ourselves be taken in by the seduction of this drama. We thought it's terrible, it's perfectly theatrical: the assassination of this woman who is in charge of the biggest country in the world, so to speak. And we went to India (we had to go there for the archives, the documentation, etc.) with the presupposition that we would work on Indira Gandhi. I worked for months, and the more I worked the more it became impossible. I worked as an academic, as an archivist, I had a great mass of documents, and what increasingly appeared – I was horrified – was what I said to Ariane slowly and then more and more urgently: Indira Gandhi was not an interesting character. She was not a theatrical character. She was a newspaper character, not one that could be transformed to make an epic character. Because with any ordinary character you can make an immense theatrical character on the condition that you be able to invent him or her. But I could not invent Indira Gandhi. She was too close, there were millions of witnesses of her reality, and what she was in reality was not interesting. It was not her fault, most political beings in the world are uninteresting. There are very few who have a transformable dimension. An epicable or saga-able dimension, if you will. They must have an interior greatness. If we look at the world stage now, there are hardly any characters who would lend themselves to transposition.

PRENOWITZ Who is there?

CIXOUS That is the question Ariane and I have always been asking. Sakundeva, who was in fact Phoolan Devi, had an epic dimension. It was not a question of power, because people in power are very often dull, stupid, without imagination, without dreams. You have to find someone who has a dream, a real dream. There was de Gaulle in France; no one since, of course. I do not know. We were obliged to go back to the previous generation. When we discussed it, I said to Ariane "It's too early. In fifty years I could invent Indira Gandhi, but now I cannot: because she exists, so I can't get around her, and I can't do anything with her." At that point, after months of suffering and panic, all of a sudden Ariane said to me "But why are we doing this? We were moved by her death, but since the spectacular theatrical heroes of the history of India are of the previous generation we must simply take a step backwards. It's obvious." We took a leap backwards, which was in fact a leap forwards, and from then on I had no more problems: I had all the great heroes of the twentieth century. They all lived at the same time. And of course this is not an accident: one hero calls forth another. So there was Gandhi, there was Nehru, there was Abdul Ghaffar Khan, the great Pashtun, all the great figures of the history of India up until today were there, including the evil Jinnah, the founder of Pakistan. So we had only made an error in diagnosis, but it was because we were ignorant. We did not know who Indira Gandhi was. Which I discovered in rummaging through the newspapers. I read everything, and each time I came across documents on her political policies or in reading each of her speeches I said to myself "My God it's enough to bore you to death. There is nothing there. There is no vision." She was a woman without vision, a pragmatic woman. And even if people had an embellishing vision of her, she resisted all transfiguration.

Great Heroes of the Twentieth Century

During the Second World War there were dreamers. There was Churchill, it is undeniable. In France there were the heroes of the Resistance. Today we could find a local character here and there, among the Kanaks or something like that, but again this is not enough because we find ourselves back with the Jarai. It is too small and does not bring with it the history of the world. These are local heroes, even if they are heroes. They will not change the world machine. What we need is to find the cog that makes the universe turn. Which is to say that by touching for example on India, and in working on the Partition of India, we were working on all that followed, up until Kosovo. All the disintegrations of all the national, nationalist groupings: when this was happening in Yugoslavia people asked us: "Are you going to do something on Yugoslavia?" But we had just done it, it's in *The Indiad*. It is a metaphor.

PRENOWITZ And why were there theatrical characters on the world stage at that time?

CIXOUS I think it is due to two things. First, these are very old struggles: the struggle for the independence of India began with the twentieth century. Such struggles end up engendering the characters that are necessary to the triumph of the struggle. Here is another character: Mandela. I'll come back to him. And second, once there is a truly great character, as I said, he or she attracts others. The greatest is Gandhi, and by the way it is not an accident that he started out as a young lawyer in South Africa. Gandhi makes Nehru possible. He ends up engendering someone like Nehru, who is younger, who adores him and who has been raised by him. Gandhi raised up the characters around him. But there must be at least one, after which there are two, three, four . . . They form a generation. Then we have Mandela and his world. At one point we thought about working on him. I had written a book on Mandela, called *Manna, to the Mandelstams to the Mandelas*, I have a passion for that man and for that magnificent story. And Ariane was drawn by the beauty of those events, of that struggle. But at the time she said to me "I'm unable to find a theatrical way to stage black people with our troupe which isn't black." It would be necessary to use masks . . . She could not find the necessary theatricality. So we went no further; otherwise I surely would have written something of the sort. Perhaps she could change her mind today, I don't know.

So *The Indiad* came after *Sihanouk* in the same river of research, except that I was less anxious, less terrorized, and that I wasted a year because we had chosen the wrong subject. In that case the problem was not that I was too small for India, it was Indira Gandhi who was too small.

PRENOWITZ You had "discovered the trick" as you said, which was to take the characters across five by five. You also spoke of the character of the border-crosser: can we say that this is another example of how you reinscribe the genesis of the play in the play, that this character in the play repeats metaphorically your posture or the work you do as an author?

CIXOUS Yes, indeed. Although I never planned it because once again it was only long afterwards that I noticed this necessary internal structure. In *The Indiad* there were several of them, but they seemed to me to be the spirits of India. There was Haridasi, the Baul woman who could cross all of India, and since she was a nomad, since she was a detached character, an element that circulates, she came in the place of Sihanouk's father. But I did not realize this. What's more she was not alone: since India is an absolutely gigantic continent I needed her – to be the people, to be the person who could show up anywhere in India at any moment, she is a magic character – and I doubled her up. Since she was Baul, thus leaning in the Hindu, Gandhian, Sufi direction, I also needed her Muslim equivalent, which was the bear trainer and his bear.

The Nomad

Actually, I could say that there is the *border-crosser*, but also the *nomad*, as a double or as another possible incarnation of the travelling flame, of the spirit in the sense of ghost. The one who is unattached, like the ghost, and who, being unattached, is not tied and obliged to belong to this or that house or this or that intrigue because he or she can simply appear. It is the *bearer of apparitions*, who can appear at any moment from behind a curtain, from under the earth . . .

After which Ariane needed to nourish herself on the most ancient models, and perhaps the plays we had done together are what both allowed and required her to go back to the sources. This time they were not at all Shakespearian: up until then she had gone in the direction of Shakespeare, she had staged the Shakespeares just before I began to work with her. Instead, began a kind of re-apprenticeship in the direction of Greece, which she had never tackled. So she staged the *Atreids* in an Asian manner. And in this cycle I translated *The Eumenides*, which was theatrically and textually decisive for me.

But to come back to the place of history in this type of theatre, after *Sihanouk* and *The Indiad*, and before *The Eumenides*, there was the project on the Resistance, our third moment of contemporary political and historical aspiration. It is worth mentioning because it has never left us. We did not succeed in engendering it, but this phantom play is still with us. It is still here with all the characters I had brought onto my stage and also the spirit of the play, that is, the spirit of the Resistance. At once as an ideal and as a reality because Ariane and I spent a year going to see all the surviving members of the Resistance in France. Who have remained our friends; those who are still alive are our friends. The spirit of the Resistance was what we wanted to work on, but it is also the spirit of resistance that animates literature as an art and theatre as a practice in the city. We did not do the play for a thousand reasons, but we were on the road to doing it. I wrote about half of a play. And it remains for us as an indispensable theatrical adventure. There had been a problem of transposition, certain figures had not been found, and so to try to get around the limit we had reached and were unable to cross, Ariane needed to return to a very ancient theatrical tradition. To see how it would be possible to find images for texts of another kind. This led to the *Atreids*.

In this cycle of plays, I had the task of translating *The Eumenides*. And this was decisive, again without our having calculated it. In the first place because *The Eumenides* is an extraordinary play. It is rarely staged because it seems to have a sort of aridity: it is a play on the questions of vengeance, of the law, of justice, of the foundations of democracy. But for me it was absolutely enlightening in theatrical, textual and philosophical terms, although I was not at all expecting that. *The Eumenides* is an eminently political play, in the most ancient sense of the word: it tells of the very foundation of the city, of modern law, by Athena and the invention of the vote, of the election, of choice, of the exercise of citizenship, and even the invention, which Ariane staged in a remarkable way, of the court of justice. All of this touched on my most intense preoccupations concerning this problematic, as I reflect on them and have always reflected on them, at once in theatre, in fiction, in my seminars, etc. And what struck me was to see how Aeschylus gave form to these profound, complex things with an extraordinary verbal economy. But a Greek economy. It was the first time that I had found such a sober verbal garment which was at the same time so poly-semantic, so polysemous, comparable to an economy I would find later in the Noh. But I had not made the connection. Aeschylus writes the way the Noh would later be written. With the same condensation, the same reduction. And these are foreign languages, they are not our languages. Our languages do not have that economy, they are much more dilated, much more luxuriant. Like Japanese, ancient Greek has structures, a grammar that is very lapidary, which our Western languages do not have at this time. And if for example I were to write like Aeschylus, which I did for *The Eumenides* since it was Aeschylus, it would seem artificial, whereas it is indispensable.

Aeschylus – Noh

But that experience was very important for me without my calculating what effects it would have subsequently. After the cycle of the *Atreids*, when we set off again as always in search of a subject that would be at once the most ancient and the most contemporary, the small-in-the-large, this experience immediately came to my aid. But not consciously. We were going in a direction that was as far as could be from *The Perjured City*. We first discussed the fall of the Soviet empire. Then we moved to something smaller, which occupied us for a while: Czechoslovakia with Havel as the main character. And while we were in the process of dreaming in that direction, the story of AIDS-contaminated blood passed before us, as if it were a meteor shooting by. It was something that was not the product of historic events reaching across the twentieth century; it was an accident, but a mortal accident of Western culture.

PRENOWITZ But which reflects the state of Western culture in the twentieth century.

CIXOUS Yes, of course. It is an accident of this culture, which is to say a symptom. But at first I resisted. I resisted for a thousand reasons: this story of contaminated blood was so monstrous that I needed a certain amount of time, perhaps a month, to be sure it was true. That the horror was true. But from the moment this story appeared, and since I belong autobiographically to the medical world, it was overdetermined for me. That is, at once the vile story of the contaminated blood and the story of medicine, within which I have always lived. I know doctors only too well. I am the daughter of a doctor and the sister of a doctor, I have always lived in that world. And always in revolt because, to tell the truth, I considered, and I continue to consider, that my father and my brother were amongst the rare doctors who did not betray the Hippocratic oath. And since I have always lived with it, since for me it is extremely grave, since I saw my father die from it, the story was overdetermined and overinvested for me. The bad doctor and the good doctor are characters that have accompanied me throughout my entire existence, and still today, of course.

But the big question was how to transpose a story that was in the newspaper headlines for a year, and a tragedy from which the victims were *in the process of dying*? How could one take tragedies that were not yet finished and turn them into theatre, make them visible? Tragedies that were before our eyes, under our nose, that did not take place in Asia? And while I was writing *The Perjured City* I thought to myself that in the audience there would be haemophiliacs who were dying. The consciousness of the immediacy and the proximity of this tragedy did not leave me for a second. In every domain: the patients, the victims, the mothers, the children, the men, the women, the doctors, a universe I know very well. And I thought: This cannot be put on stage without the help of all the gods in the world. Which is to say without being transposed, without it becoming something that has been torn away from the newspaper page, and which protects all those who are presently suffering. This is where *The Eumenides* came to my aid. I immediately saw the transposition by way of *The Eumenides*. I thought: This can only take place in a mythical universe where there will be Aeschylus, the Eumenides. Something that is poeticized in such a strong way that the suffering will find expression in extremely poetic words.

Tragedies Before Our Eyes

This is where we see what theatre is: you do not have a vision as in fiction. It is that the subject commands the form. The subject commands the search for a certain form without which this subject cannot be materialized on the stage. This is what happened with the Resistance. The subject commanded a form which we did not find. But for *The Perjured City* it was already there.

PRENOWITZ *The Perjured City* was both different from the Partition of India or the unravelling of Cambodia as events implicated in the entire history of the twentieth century, *and* a story that was much closer to us.

CIXOUS Yes. There was not the least distance. All the distance we had for example as we wandered through Asia was gone. So we had to recover these distances which constitute theatre, and we could only recover them through an adequate transfiguration. It could not take place in Paris. It could only take place in eternity. Even if, in inventing this poetic super-temporality, in mixing the dead with the living, in having characters of all eras enter on stage, I could also have today's doctors enter. But "today" was carried off in a collection of entirely different times and figures. As soon as I realized that *The Eumenides* would carry this I had no more problems. Instead of going to "India," I went to "medicine," to "hospital." I began to talk with the haemophiliacs, with the doctors, as I had talked with the Indians. And I always thought that if I had not been the daughter of a doctor and the sister of a doctor and the daughter of a midwife, and if I had not always lived in that world, I am not sure I would have been able to hear those languages and those secrets. I was already initiated.

PRENOWITZ And what about Asia?

CIXOUS Indeed, it is a very important question. What I must absolutely say is that Asia is not Asia. It is theatre-Asia. I am always talking about another world, a second world: it is not a realistic continent, it is a reservoir, a gigantic cavern of images. I also have to say that since "Asia" is a global word, there are many Asias in Asia. There is India which is itself full of worlds, full of universes, Cambodia which is something else altogether even though it is also related, Japan . . . it is endless. Why Asia? Initially because with a sort of intuition or instinct, Ariane went to Asia at the age of 20 when she decided she was going to do theatre, as if Asia were a cradle and she sensed that she had to go there. And for a year she went from country to country without any theory: it was an initiatory voyage, as in Hesse. But it stayed with her as her book of images. And this is the book she held out to me when she asked me to come to the Théâtre du Soleil. Because my book was not Asia. It was Shakespeare and Aeschylus, but not Asia. It was only then that I went to Asia.

Theatre-Asia

Let me add that the Asias have conserved something that we have not. For example Noh is a relatively recent art, younger than the Indian arts, only about ten centuries old, if you will, but when you go to Japan there are Noh performances every day. In France there is not any Noh. You have to go to Japan. In Asia the traditions have remained alive and present, not past. They have a present, the past has a present in Asia. And the country that has kept the most and the most ancient traditions is India. When you go to India tradition is in the street every day, you go on a sort of voyage across the millennia, and even while being in the twentieth century one is also three thousand years earlier. Now since all theatre is structured in this manner, which is to say that its temporality is age-old, forwards and backwards: three thousand years before and three thousand years after, it is perfectly clear that Asia is the theatre of the theatre. It is the Khora of the theatre. So Asia is not realistic. It is the temple. It is the caves of the theatre.

PRENOWITZ And the present which as you said is the time of the theatre is a present that contains all times.

CIXOUS All times. The present of the theatre – we should always say the-present-of-the-theatre – is a present where all the pasts can present themselves as present.

PRENOWITZ And why is Asia like that? Or why is the West not like that? Why does it seem as if our present were simply the present?

CIXOUS This is a very important question. It is related to industrial, mechanical development, etc. The "proof" is the United States, the country that is the most modern because it is the youngest; the youngest and the most modern. And here we see implacable laws: India, with its three thousand years, must lift three thousand years in order to take one step. And so it is slow, even if we know very well that a part of the Indian population belongs to the twenty-first century, aligned with the United States. Industry and capitalism are all-powerful motors which have pushed the West very hard and have therefore distanced it from its past – I am not speaking of the United

States, which has no past. But at the same time there are also the religions, although this is very complicated. But perhaps it has to do with a certain type of religion, religions such as those we see in India: polytheisms that are so everyday that in a certain sense they also slow the acceleration towards modernity. Because it is difficult to combine belief in the gods, which you see everywhere in India at every second, with a formidable technological advance, since technology and the gods are different gods. But if there is still theatre in France, I would say it is because what nourishes the theatre – and which is this sort of presence under the stage of the gods in which we no longer believe, but which we still believe in – has been maintained in France by the non-interruption, the continuity of the creative literary archive: France is a country of memory, and without being comparable to Asia, it is an old country that can go back with its cultural creations a thousand years. France has a thousand years at its doorstep. When you study the history of France you begin with the Roman empire. When I say a thousand years it is perhaps fifteen hundred years. And all of this is archived. And continues to be, for a certain type of person, because clearly there is also a population in France that does not have fifteen hundred years behind it.

A Thousand Years at the Doorstep

PRENOWITZ If *The Perjured City* came very "close to home," what is the significance of this new departure for Asia-theatre, with *Drums on the Dam*? On the one hand, it seems to me, there is this new marionette form, and on the other, the fact that it's a fiction, a pure fiction as you said. But there must also be an evolution: what you said about the form of the language you found in Aeschylus greatly resembles what one would be tempted to say about the marionette language that resurfaces with *Drums*.

CIXOUS The heart of the subject – with *The Perjured City* we had defined it exactly – is the sickness of the kingdom: what is it that is hurting us at this moment? And what is hurting us in a new way? Because in the end human beings are great inventors of evil, of sickness, of catastrophes. You know, the sentence that is always being pronounced in France, "Plus jamais ça," i.e. "Never again," or "That will never happen again," is a sentence I have always found at once interesting and touchingly naïve, because it is never "that," it is always "that will never happen again." There is never the same catastrophe twice. Evil is always in action and it invents new forms. There will never be "that," of course, because "that" has already happened. There are phenomena of repetition, but it is simply that the forces of evil, everything in man that is bad, cruel and inhuman, is permanent and repetitive. But it can only repeat itself in so far as it can find new masks, which is to say foil the mass of people who say "that will never happen again": they are there, at a place where a catastrophe has happened, saying "that will never return." But of course that will never return there; it will return here, and differently.

New Masks of Evil

With Ariane we look for signs of a new catastrophe, that is, an extremely ancient catastrophe whose mask or figure was unexpected: "that," this particular "that," had never before been seen. Once again we shiver with horror before the inhuman things man has invented. And this is not easy, because we can be mistaken: one can have the ephemeral feeling that something old, something we have already seen a thousand times, is entirely new, but it falls away very soon, it does not hold up.

While we were searching, there were enormous, catastrophic floods in China. The newspapers said there are similar floods all the time. It has been going on repeatedly in China for three thousand years. And so it will go on being repeated for another three thousand years. But why and how is it that there continue to be such horrifying natural catastrophes? Although we suspect, of course, that they are not natural. It is too easy to say that it's nature: there is an element of nature, but of course an element of culture. And at this point we ask the question: What is it that makes states, and governments, be their own destroyers? The enemy does not come from outside; the enemy is inside. So it is not a punishment by the gods; it is a fabrication of men against themselves. It is one of the greatest mysteries of the ethical and political world.

For example, here I have been observing the great debates about the question of nuclear energy. People began saying that if a bomb were dropped on the storage site at The Hague, France would be dead. Now it exists in the open air, and any airplane *à la* Bin Laden could crash into it and France is dead. So one thinks: This can't be possible! But yes, it is possible. It is a gamble, an insane gamble, on the non-catastrophe. But why should there not be a catastrophe? The whole question of nuclear energy is there, and not only in France, everywhere. Chernobyl is everywhere; it is a decisive, terrifying question.

There is nothing that is at once more familiar and more non-familiar than a calamity such as a terrible flood. For example what just happened in Algeria, or what happened in the valley of the Somme last year. There is something awful about floods because it is human beings that create them, and human beings are carried off by what they themselves have unleashed. The theme was very simple. It was then necessary to give it life, a story, characters. And for the first time, and to my great joy, we gave up all reference to current events: we did not need to go to China and to singularize something that is so universal that at one point or another it happens again in one country or another. But in each country the pain is singular, the revolt is singular. We immediately turned to fiction. For the first time in our twenty-year history we agreed that it should be a fiction. But for it to be fiction, and theatrical, we returned to the cradle of fictions, which is to say to Asia. But taking a precaution: it would really be fiction. We would not go to see a flood in China or a flood in Bangladesh. That is indeed the universe we worked on, where there are effectively cyclones, tornadoes, floods, but it was not localized. I would not make reference to one country anecdotally. It had to be the Earth, let us say, and this particular calamity. And as regards the date, it had to be the same thing. In order for it to be embodied theatrically, it had to be a period situated historically, but not precisely: it could be the ninth, the tenth, the eleventh century.

The Cradle of Fictions

Although, since the Earth and the theatre make a couple, a plateau, we had thought of having a figure in the figure, an intrigue in the intrigue, such that the story, which would be a sort of universal poetic fable, would have a metaphorical face like a mask, which would be that the theatre would itself be a character taken up in the turmoil. And for this, we turned to the historical beginnings of the theatre in those countries. Historically, the genesis or gestation of the theatrical arts is rather complex, but we can say that they were born around the ninth and the tenth centuries, in particular in Japan. And to begin with, we thought that the play would interweave a political story, the story of a king, a duke or a lord and his country, with a second intrigue that would act as a mirror for that story: a little kingdom in the big kingdom, and which would be a little theatre-kingdom. That is, the story of a theatre family, etc. I began to write one story inside the other with a theatre-family as a hostage of the political story. The Noh took precedence right away, and all the history of Japanese theatre. We had discovered something that neither of us had known, which was that the first Japanese theatrical arts were propagated by women. In particular by a very famous woman, Okuni, of whom we know nothing, except her name and that she existed. She was a great woman of theatre. I worked at length on this character we know nothing about, and in my first versions of the play you could see the country come apart and the theatre come together simultaneously. At the same time that the theatre was being invented, this theatre was doomed to sink because the country was sinking. So it was an extremely complex plot which finally dissolved because it was too much, it became so immense, whereas for once we had decided to do a play that would not be too immense. To do a double plot we would need two parts. "This time I want a single part, for economic, technical reasons," Ariane said. The theatre in the theatre, the plot in the plot, the whole theatre-family fell away very quickly. I worked on some very famous theatre families, for example the Kanzé family, which still exists in Japan today. These families were dependant on the political sphere, they were protected, a bit in the way the classical French theatre was protected, therefore censured, by the Court. Molière, Racine and the others were simultaneously maintained and encircled, in economic and theatrical terms, by the Court. It was the same thing in Japan, where the theatre companies were at once extraordinarily inventive, but dependant on the authorities. Protected by a Shogun, or else, on the contrary . . . But we dropped all of this.

The Theatre in the Theatre

PRENOWITZ   So there was an organic link between the little kingdom of the theatre and the big kingdom.

CIXOUS   They were completely interwoven. And to give the last trace of it, Okuni, who was the head of a theatre troupe, was the sister of the Chancellor. But it was a sister with whom he had lost contact. He had left the family farm and did not know that his sister had followed a theatre troupe and had invented a new theatrical form. There were many subplots and it became so immense that little by little we were approaching an impasse: it was immense, but we were going towards the marionette form, and the marionette form will not tolerate the immense.

How is it that we went in the direction of the marionette form? It is another story: in writing all of this, and with the double plot at the beginning, I was in the library while the troupe was in Asia – because for two months they were exploring all the countries of Asia in order to steep themselves in forms, colours, etc. I was in Chicago at that point, where I had access to an immense collection of Japanese, Chinese and Korean plays in translation. I read these texts and I used them from the point of view of the projection of images, a bit like Eisenstein, who had studied Noh. I also had a freedom I had gained through a game Ariane and I had played like children: in order to be able to enter into the mythical domain and to shed all reference to reality, one day Ariane called me up and said "What if it were the old and famous Chinese author Xi-Xou who was writing the play?" And I thought: That's brilliant! I am free. I am detached from myself. Xi-Xou is the one who is writing the play, not Hélène Cixous. So I can do as I wish. And in the two days that followed, I dreamed the first scene. Which is to say that Xi-Xou dreamed, and it was the Soothsayer. I called Ariane and I sent her the first scene.

PRENOWITZ   You had to detach yourself from yourself in order to see.

CIXOUS   Yes, of course. I was no longer needed, it was the old Xi-Xou. It gave me complete freedom. There's another border-crosser, by the way, the Soothsayer.

It was during the summer, I had already written a certain number of scenes. In Chicago I was working so intensely on these documents that I was in danger, every night I dreamed and more characters arrived. There were more and more of them. From the moment you are no longer held back by anything, when you are in total fiction, it is like what happens in dreams: there are hundreds of characters. I thought: A hundred is too much . . .

PRENOWITZ You no longer needed to bring the characters over five by five. You had too many characters.

CIXOUS Yes, absolutely. But very quickly the theatre plot fell away. Because of the limits we had set and because it was not vital to the functioning of the killing machine. It was additional victims.

The mental structures, and so forth, came to me from the world of Noh and Kabuki, but I had said nothing about this to Ariane. I never say what I use for nourishment when I write my plays. I never say I am in the process of reading this or that philosophical or poetic text, because I am nourishing myself. Ariane nourishes herself with a certain universe of images, I nourish myself with a certain textual universe. And when Ariane began to rehearse with the material I had given her, once everyone had returned, within a week she said to me "You know how we are rehearsing? As if we were marionettes." I had never said that I had been entirely supported by that theatre, and I thought: The subterranean work happens all by itself. After which everything had to be marionetted in a much more imperative manner. Once we had decided to go with the marionettes, even if marionette shadows were already there for me, I had to marionette everything. Which is to say that everything had to obey the laws of the marionette, whereas at the start this had not been planned. But in the first week of rehearsals this is what happened, and so everything changed: Ariane's job, the actors' job and my job, everything was oriented towards the economy of the marionette, which we had yet to discover.

The Laws of the Marionette

PRENOWITZ So in a certain sense the Japanese Noh, Kabuki and Bunraku are all marionette forms, even if Noh and Kabuki properly speaking do not involve marionettes, at least in appearance.

CIXOUS Exactly. But we were faithful to the principle that it would not have a particular reference, which is to say that there was total freedom. And so for months and months Ariane set aside all Japanese references: the costumes were Korean, the drums were Korean, there were many elements that came from elsewhere, up until the point where . . . something caught up with us.

PRENOWITZ Yes, but it retains the indetermination. I understand entirely that in so far as it was a pure fiction, it was necessary to avoid any precise reference, be it temporal, geographic or cultural.

CIXOUS Yes, of course, but it remained a certain universe. Just as the theatrical forms of China, Japan and Korea communicate, but they are not identical.

PRENOWITZ So you had to completely redo the play, and write differently.

CIXOUS I had to reach the marionette level of writing, just as it was necessary to reach the marionette in the actors and ultimately in the voices. Little by little the law of the marionette established itself everywhere, but it happened gradually. When we began we did not know exactly what this new type of marionette was, since they were not marionettes but actors. We didn't know what these marionettes we had never seen before needed, what they could not endure, and what they required. We felt our way along. Little by little the text had to find its own marionette form. But not any known marionettes, with strings or otherwise: it was these marionettes, the marionettes of *Drums on the Dam*, which is to say marionette-actors. An entirely new form.

12 and 25 November 2001

Enter the Theatre

TRANSLATED BY BRIAN J. MALLET

Everything began in 1940 and up to 1948 in my very early childhood before consciousness, thought, with a play without an author, which was history itself, *res gestae*, the theatre of which was the centre of my native city Oran. The *core* of Oran had by chance the shape of the Theatre, I only realized it fifty years later.

The scene was the Place d'Armes – to the right the Municipal Theatre, to the left the Military Club and the pharmacy. On the corner Les Deux Mondes, my aunt Deborah's tobacconist's which was Ali Baba's Cave and the first version of the chorus. I myself was in the upper circle of Philippe Street and I could see the history of the entire world played out before me. This history was structured by a twofold plot. One world was trying to annihilate one world. In the first plot Nazism plus Vichyism and the fascisms were trying to destroy the wavering democracies, the champions of eternal moral values. In the second plot these same forces of good were divided and half evil, colonialist, misogynistic, repressive. From the upper circle where I climbed on to the rails, flanked by the hen, I wondered how in this entanglement of violent evil good forces, and where it was impossible to separate a pure good from any kind of morbid or diabolical attack, anything other than a tragic ending could be expected. I could not see any possibility of this on the stage. I was three and a half, four years old and searching with all my strength for a beyond. My German family was in the concentration camps, my grandmother had just managed to escape. She had come to us in Algeria where we were witnesses and hostages to many major and secondary persecutions.

From everywhere there loomed the forms of exclusion, exile or massacre. I also saw Fortinbras de Gaulle and the Allies enter the Placedarme. We were liberated but the Algerians were more enslaved than ever.

Democracy showed itself to be a dream, a word. There was no justice, no equality, no respect. Almost no courage. I was on the verge of despair. The world is tragic. If I did not give up hope, it was because my family was without sin and my father was a young doctor, true-spirited and incorruptible. But then he died at thirty-nine. What are the gods doing meanwhile? And we who are small and threatened, what can we do?

"If there is a somewhere else," I would say to myself, "which can escape the infernal practice of repetition, then it is there that new worlds are written, dreamed, invented."

Such was my obsession and my need. Is there a somewhere else? Where? It has to be invented. This is the mission of poets. Assuming that there are any. And that they are not cast into the triturator of history before they have even created.

Decades later I am attending the performance of my plays, and what do I see? That they had begun before I wrote, in Oran, Algeria.

In the meantime I have not stopped asking myself with growing astonishment what evil is, experiencing it in increasingly stupefying and painful ways, trying to understand its structure, machine, ineluctability. And feeling myself cast as the keeper of after-lives (I do not say lives – *after-lives*) or Night Watchwoman. The mission entrusted to me by my father I would define as follows: I must do everything to ensure that I and the people around me are not swept away by oblivion, indifference, I must keep alive the *qui vive* and preserve the dead, the murdered, the captive, the excluded, from the jaws of death. This is my mission. I do not claim to fulfil it: there would no longer be any problem. I live the tragic, I live myself tragically, I am totally occupied by the question of the tragic. Which in no way excludes happiness and the comic, on the contrary. But I live and breathe the sense of threat, imminence and betrayal within the very midst of happiness and the love of peace.

When I use the word *tragic*, I determine the word in a trivial and ordinary way, that is to say that on the one hand there is tragic theatre, with the goat, the rather Greek fatality of making the wrong choice. On the other, and rather freer from etymology and the Greek context, I see it as linked to the need of the double bind, that is, to the fatal rending of what I call the soul or the heart, to situations of divided loyalty, a quartering of the self. It is the irreconcilable as ineluctable: the situation in which I must accept the unacceptable, or renounce what is most dear and most necessary to me because there is no right answer or happy ending, you cannot expect any consolation or justice, I have looked for it, I have wanted justice, I have crossed generations and frontiers, I have spent my life doing this to the point of finding myself almost outside of myself – in vain, because consolation and justice do not exist. But even so it was the right thing to do: because it is in this search and this pursuit that the share of justice and consolation reserved for us is to be found. As I ran, searched, struggled, committed myself to action, something calm was being hollowed out in me, calm in opposition to dramatic, something with which there is no negotiation: since the tragic is, and since it is *implacable*, there is no decision that wins the day, it is unquestionable (questioning is Job – Job is the theatre, is movement, protest, despair (that is, wounded hope), anger).

No, I would have discovered in the end that *there isn't* and *that's the way it is*, *the irreconcilable is the tragic*. That's the way it is. That's why, because it is unquestionable, there is a certain "serenity," a stasis, an immobility. This conviction of *that's the way it is* is often conveyed in my plays by characters who are no doubt fairly close to the secret of my heart, for example Aeschylus in *The Perjured City*. These are people who have lived a lot, thousands of years and of adventures.

The most incontestable example of the tragic, in my view, is *solitude*, the inescapable, un-acceptable part of solitude, and which we experience to a minimal or major degree in all our human relationships, in family ties, and even in love: we do not understand one another *at the same time*. We are the subjects of misunderstanding. Even in the most successful love solitude is not overcome. You say to me: "Do you understand what I am saying to you?" And I say to you: "Yes, yes – of course." And it is only the next day that I understand that when I thought I understood you I did not understand you at all. The lateness, the too late, the lag, the untimely arrival of the message, are our most common and our most painful experience. And it is that which, transposed, transfigured into a theatrical mainspring causes havoc in tragedies: we call it the *untimely letter*; it is sent too soon, too late, and someone is killed. Cordelia is not saved. This solitude (this deafness, this disjunction of our rhythms) exists only if there is someone to make it appear. You have to imagine the conjunction of two conscious solitudes. One can be two in oneself (see Kafka), it is the incurable, the unsaveable or the unsolveable. Or the impossible. We are impossible. And *contretemps*. The Theatre is acted upon, that is to say undermined by *contretemps*.

The tragic is the insurmountable anachrony: the missed appointment. Even when it is not missed. *Sero te amavi*: Beauty, I have loved you too late, said St. Augustine to God. And Jacques Derrida repeats it at the beginning of his tragic text "Un ver à soie": *Sero* . . . How can one *love too late*? It is TooLate who is the demon of the Theatre.

But there is always an unpredictable element. Hazard, chance, a grain of sand in the works: the possibility that the tragic programming will break down, the grace of a totally unforeseen development. *That's the way it is*, it is necessary but at the same time, there is contingency.

But perhaps what is tragic, I fear and suspect, is the fact that it is only *from without*, by leaving society (*The Perjured City*) and even life (*The Perjured City, The Story*) that we can transgress, interrupt the practice of repetition. It is perhaps only the "dead" – or poets – those whom Artaud calls "the suicides of society" – who manage to conceive of a something beyond vengeance, or resentment or reprisal. But that requires passing *through death*, or through something equivalent: the consent of the I to renunciation. To expect nothing. To attain the state of *unexpectancy*. Another innocence. Is it possible?

"Original sin, that old injustice committed by man, consists of the reproach which man makes and to which he does not renounce namely that an act of injustice has been committed against him, that he has been the victim of original sin," Kafka says. Can someone renounce reproach? Who? In what circumstances? This is the question which I can ask only within the space of the Theatre.

The play of which it is my mission to be the author – let us say a story – begins badly. It begins with a storm, a blow, the worst: in full flight, a fall, a mourning in the midst of celebration. See those characters who were the epitome of life itself, how they are being driven to their doom. I run after the story and after the characters who are its hosts its masters its hostages.

Where can it go? The horses have bolted. The play moves along faster and faster. How will it end? No one has any idea. I would like it not to end fatally for those I love. But so many contrary wills and desires are woven into it.

But initially everything began for the unquiet author that I am with a proposal, or rather a temptation, from Ariane Mnouchkine in 1981: Do you want to can you write a play for the Théâtre du Soleil. I was immediately delighted and terrified. I wanted to, but to be able to . . .

The Théâtre du Soleil is not only enormous in everything, in art, in ambition, in ethical commitment, but first and foremost in scale and number. There is an economy of the Soleil, a company made up of sixty permanent staff that imposes obligations on the author; I have to give play to my pen for twenty or thirty fervent and famished actors, and therefore ensure the existence of fifty characters. For my part it is almost superhuman. Every time I commit myself to it, I tremble, I know that it will be very difficult. But thrilling. So I go ahead. I get on board.

The adventure has its conventions: first a long talk with Ariane. Because the subject of the play is searched for and decided in agreement between the two of us. It is always located at the intersection of contemporary events (let us say the *res gestae*) and the Theatre, in its pure reflexiveness. It will not be a question of performance but of thinking through the necessity of the Theatre, its powers – but also its limits, as a party to world events. We dream of *telling* in such a way that something will *move* in reality. If not change – which would be enormously presumptuous – then at least be *recalled*, ressuscitated, delivered from silence. Our job is first of all a *recollection* of what is happening, an illumination of the present itself.

It is this primordial ethical direction or orientation which is the first cause of our theatrical alliance.

I met Ariane in 1972 in overdetermining and prophetic circumstances: I went to see her and took along my friend Michel Foucault to get her involved in the work of the Groupe Information Prison which Michel Foucault had founded. The first "play" which brought us together lasted four minutes and was supposed to be performed outside prisons. But I never saw it: no sooner had we unloaded the boards than the police were at us with their truncheons. Between 1972 and 1981 we called each other and went to all the political demonstrations into which we put body and soul:

I called her towards women, she towards artists and the outcasts and the prisoners of the universe, and we each moved towards the other's side until the day she opened up the doors of her "Globe" to me. It was a real *coup de théâtre*.

In retrospect I see the logic of this turn of events. We have the same political and aesthetic – politicoaesthetic – conception of the Art of the Theatre.

Let me add – for I had already written a few small plays – that in its structure, in its laws, in its modes of functioning, in the acting which is Ariane's achievement, the Soleil is in all ways the place, the magical forge, the workshop of the Theatre itself, the ancient and modern cave where the mysteries of the Theatre are constantly analysed and reactivated. I myself am always an apprentice there. Ariane too, for the Théâtre du Soleil is a world which reflects on itself, sounds itself out, reworks itself from play to play. It is itself its school and its laboratory, and the workshop of all the despairs which accompany theatrical creation.

So we set out in search of the Subject. The directions are always the same: look for the scene, the event, the facts which, taking place "at these times" on the planet come to afflict us cruelly, having taken us (we the public, the citizens) by surprise or treachery, leave us wounded, powerless, appalled. Come or *are going* to afflict us. The poisoned needle which is plunged into our veins. The morbid episode which by attacking a society, a country, whether foreign or not, injures and wrongs the roots of humanity. A symptom, perhaps, the harbinger of an evil which promises to propagate. If no one begins to cry for help.

Crimes dramas scandals are legion. But the choice? It's a long business. We spend months, sometimes years, looking for what will make the Fable irreplaceable. And sometimes we err. More than once I have started out on the wrong track: we had been led astray. Whereupon, sometimes very quickly, sometimes after months of work, I realize that I cannot find the transposition. What then? You give up.

Often the "right" subject, the one that is transfigurable, the subject with roots which plunge deep into the unconscious and into the treasure-house of myths, and with foliage that brushes against the clouds, was just next to the "wrong" one around which we had gone, which has neither depth nor height. This was the case with *The Indiad*.

Once the Fable has been glimpsed in the distance – and we see first of all only the coastline – I set off on my way, and Ariane on hers. While I write, she constructs: the entire Theatre is pulled down and rebuilt as the receptacle of the new arrival.

And now a few secrets about what happens to the "author." Let us say for argument's sake that dozens and dozens of characters are going to arrive from "there," and that I write dozens of scenes.

To begin with there is: *the Place*. The place! The place is magical. It is a marvel to discover. It is from *the vision of a place* that all Ariane's work will be born. And for me from the moment *that the place takes its place*, all that remains is to wait. What place? I believe that the place of *The Perjured City* is the most *fertile* of places theatrically speaking, because it fuses with the structural localization of the Theatre itself: our stage, the cosmos, measures 300m^2 but it also has an address and a driving form: yes the place, however apparently immobile it might seem, must provide the momentum and the passage: Hamlet's ramparts, King Lear's cliff. The place is a great sacred actor. In *The Perjured City* everything *began* with a cemetery which was a city in itself – an enormous cemetery (Ariane thought about the City of the Dead in Cairo where 150,000 "homeless" people live among the tombs) populated with the dead and the living and which stretches outside the city walls. You can do everything with an immense cemetery, the hostile twin of the hostile city, reverse city on the wrong side right side out.

For me the Theatre is by definition the stage where the living meet and confront the dead, the forgotten and the forgetters, the buried and the ghosts, the present, the passing, the present past and the passed past. There is nothing more Theatre than a great City of the Dead. It is a stage through which all the characters of a story make their appearance, from the most ancient, the most distant in the centuries down to the most contemporary, from the imaginary, the invented, the lost found again down to the real familiars. The dead are not always as dead as we think nor the living as living as they think.

A Theatre, a real one, is always a kind of external territory, whose externality is more or less included in or bordering on the City, an inside separated from the Dominant Inside, it is located at the gate, and because it is subversive, gated at the gates of the City, outlawed.

Here is the Place: the Cemetery. This will be the only indication or stage direction in my text. And here is the place of my new play, entitled *Drums on the Dam, In the Form of an Ancient Puppet Play, Performed by Actors: The Dam.*

Now the hour of the characters has come.

Enter – almost always and at least up until now – the character who, I will realize, is going to help me bring this creation into the world.

For the author that I am it is the apparition of this primordial Apparition which will open for me the invisible door of the Theatre. Here, no curtain, no veiling-unveiling. But, before any other, enter, coming from always, the "ferryman." I call him that since I first discovered his existence. Who? Aeschylus, the guardian of the cemetery in *The Perjured City*, Snorri Sturlusson the poet author of the Eddas in *The Story*, Sihanouk's dead father, Haridasi the nomadic Baul in *The Indiad*, the Soothsayer in *Drums on the Dam*. The being who acts as lookout and liaison. The one who is (neither) inside (nor) outside. "Who are you?" the shady lawyers ask him. "Aeschylus the guardian." "Aeschylus as in Aeschylus?" Yes, it was indeed Aeschylus-as-Aeschylus who came to me when I took up my waiting post.

The name was in my mind, because I had just translated his brilliant play *The Eumenides* for the Soleil, and I was thinking a lot about him the author of so many plays which have disappeared and never come back. Unless what we write are the ghosts of his plays, without our knowing it?

But he was not the only one to arrive and did not come back alone. Two years earlier I had just written *The Story*, where I had met Snorri Sturlusson. Now afterwards, fortunately, I had forgotten him. Snorri Sturlusson, a Homer for Northern Europe, a statesman, poet, historian, diplomat, the one who gathered together the immense Scandinavian oral tradition and cast it in a poetic form which he invented, "the author," that is, the ferryman and mediator of Nordic myths and legends and so the adoptive father of the gods and heroes. I felt a singular joy in making of this man from the Middle Ages the ancestor and the contemporary of fabulous characters of whom he was the guardian and the redeemer. Snorri by his presence in my play disconnects the linear order of time, he is himself *the witness* to events which took place "centuries" or thousands of years before, with him before begins again *today*. The creator is himself one of his creatures. But since he is informed of the ancient version of the facts which he has undertaken to report, a violent, cruel version doomed to annihilation, he sets himself the poetic task of dismantling, halting the ancient account and doing everything to ensure that the agents of calamity take a less fatal path. "What if a tiny little poet," he says to himself, "changed the course of history, if he inflected it?" Germanic mythology is a history in which a certain concept of the poet as *Dichter* is possible, after all. He might manage it. If he did then the story of History and of all the concepts of History would be thrown into disarray. And so this Germanic Snorri entered the play with the intention of re-writing it differently.

Aeschylus (mine) does not have this desire and this dream. He is truly, even in 1999, the hero of Graeco-philosophical-mythological thought and of its conception of tragic fatality, and that does not occur to him. And yet – as a poet he overflows his definition and his initial culture. He belongs to the community and the kingdom of dreamer inventors always capable of taking the one step beyond, at least in imagination. And so my Aeschylus is haunted by his doubles or his others; from his mouth come words which surprise him a little and charm him himself, and those among the spectators who have not forgotten will recognize or think they recognize echoes of Shakespeare or Freud or Montaigne or François Villon. Because a poet is always haunted. His word is memory and prophecy. What can a poet do, awake, alone, in the tumult of History? That is my question. Where Snorri tries to forewarn and rewrite by encouraging the actors not to obey what was in the programme, Aeschylus is a tragically modern poet in his confessed powerlessness and his inability to foresee what is going to happen. He knows that he doesn't know. He is the vain watchman of those who sleep. He is the memory which cannot predict whence the misfortune will come. Historical time and poetical time cut across and pass each other in his word and his conscience. But he is the one who is pointlessly "in the know." What purpose will he have served? Accompanying and noting the inevitable. The role of the witness, but of the witness of whom Celan speaks, the witness who asks (whom?) who will bear witness to the witness once the witness has disappeared? Yes, who will bear witness? If "all are dead," "when all are dead," who will be the witness?

A cruel, paradoxical, ludic, fateful question, abyss and wall into which my plays plunge in their slightly crazy course, since they present the tragic in a *performative manner* by asking questions about the tragic, calling into question the tragic, trying to interrupt the end, the teleological, trying to write History in which "there is still some blank space" – still some indetermination. And this whiteness in *The Story* is a "real" white, a Snow which covers everything with a page on which a poet yet to come could write what has just happened in another version.

And in *The Perjured City* it is a Night, a celestial starry fabric.

In each case, I try to engage the possibility of a theatrical writing which overflows tragedy – is it possible? – to write understanding the tragedy and at the same time overflowing it and asking in the play itself the question about the overflowing of tragedy? That is what I hope to do. And that is why my plays have such strange and such unfinal endings. But I will come back, at the end, to my kinds of endings.

For the moment let us return to the beginnings, and to the appearance of the characters. So here I am in the company of Aeschylus or Snorri. And now I await the others. I wait. Let them come. "Creation" of characters for me means: allowing to come, allowing to form; persons either "known" or mythical or not yet encountered, but all of them, however famous or anonymous they may be, equally unknown, mysterious, enigmatic, brand new. No one has yet ever seen them even if they are called Brunhild or Erinyes, or Joan of Arc. As an author I am in the state of receptivity, a concave and hypersensitive state. My "work" consists of being impressionable matter. My state can be compared to a kind of waking dream, very passive, patient, hallucinatory. I am the empty stage. This may last a long time until I hear footsteps. I see nothing. Enter Voices. Characters. I do not move. It is an empty time, an animal time, vigilant, I am submerged, under the earth and under time. I listen. Perhaps the waiting is a form of prayer. By dint of praying them to come, they end up by coming. Enter – A character alone. Sometimes two or four. And there they are making a scene. This scene is of an extreme strength and *naked* because he or she or they are alone. The character enters, naked, the heart naked, he scratches his heart, he looks at his heart, bleeding, he is amazed, he opens himself up without understanding himself, as the characters of Shakespeare open themselves up when they are alone. And yet not alone. Because there is the audience. They confide in a witness who is both absent and present – moreover that is where its strength lies, the characters who confide or confess, Iago, my Hagen, Kriemhild, the Mother in *The Perjured City*, address themselves to an audience (and at the beginning the audience is me, H.C., the author) which is both there and not there, which does not say a word, but whose silence is golden, which listens does not intervene, does not judge, and the character shows himself as he would to anyone or to the devil, to anyone who, in any case, would not prevent him from revealing himself as twisted divided tormented tempted hesitant deconstituted – for you need an interlocutor to show yourself and an interlocutor without an opinion and without a voice. That's me. My characters do that with me the author, they know that I am not there but that I listen to them, they speak to *each other*, question *each other*, sound *each other* out, explain themselves to *each other* and this *Each other* is the dummy, that is to say the author. I however am all ears, dozens of ears sprout on me, I record as quickly as possible, I take note at full speed, I hear their thoughts pass, they are going very fast, I have just the time to note the ultra-rapid beginning, the thread, the end of a passionate confidence. It is not writing. It is a crossing, an arrow, a logic. And suddenly I hear, I understand, the beating heart of a character. In a sense, when I hear a heart beat violently in the grip of such emotion, it is the sign that a character is born. The beating is expressed in a few words, in a brief phrase, which will be the key to that creature. As soon as they are born, they go into battle. I am them and I follow. I know them a little, I recognize the music of the heart of the one whom I call the King, or Nehru, or Siegfried or Immonde or Charles VII, I know who is called like that and who goes off to battle.

I say *battle*: sometimes it is a real battle in a real war. Sometimes a scene, a confrontation, and a scene is always a battle. The entire play wages war and seeks the moment of a peace. Each scene is a duel, or charge, there are invisible or real swords, traps set or defused. Every play is a war or its double: the war with words, the court, the trial. And each character is a king, the king of a kingdom fallen prey to an internal war: I struggle against myself, I attack myself, I accuse myself, I defend myself. The smallest of characters, the porter, the valet, the maid, is king or queen. The smallest is great. Most will experience the fate of human beings in a grandiose or modest way: dethronement, deposition, betrayal, banishment. Eternal themes but each time embodied for the first time. Joyce said in *Ulysses* that the note of banishment echoes throughout the work of Shakespeare. It is true. But it could also be said of Chekhov: the country squires in *The Cherry Orchard* are banished kings. We recognize them but we do not know them. To each his own pain and punishment. And Firs, the too old, forgotten, remaindered, is the most banished of the banished.

The reason why there are 150 different battles in Shakespeare is because one time it is Macbeth who is fighting, another time it is Richard II. What is the heart like, what colour, what heat, what pain, the heart which goes off to that battle, what does it risk, what will happen to it, and what does it hope for, what does it foresee, and what will not happen to it, etc. That can happen only when the characters are born. What for me is an eternal source of surprise is that there is a moment when the character has become so precise, so *itself* that it is totally detached from me, that it is really autonomous in the proper sense of the word, it obeys its own rules, and I have only to follow its instructions. The scenes are going to unfold, the characters are going to meet or provoke such and such a fate and I am merely the scribe in the matter. But before reaching this period of separation, where I am relieved of the anguish of the wait, a lot of time passes. Sometimes a very long time. It depends on the external and internal circumstances of the writing, the effectiveness of a prayer. Sometimes, I may not see what the characters have become for months, I may be in a prehistoric phase of preparation, hesitation, which may last for months. But as soon as the characters are born, things move quickly. Because at that moment there is Action, and action like everything in the theatre is extremely rapid. After having been lost and gone astray in wait in anxiety for six months or a year, *the action of writing* will take me two months. So that if I am asked "How long do you take to write a play?" I say two months, but it is not true. How long it takes me to reach the hour of writing, one year, two years, and then it goes quickly.

But the hour of writing is, for the author, *the final hour*. What I call writing, the textuality, the textility, the fabric, the style, and which, in fiction, is the beginning and the whole, is, in this case, the *final hand*. It will come to give flesh and vision to psychic and dramatic constructions. It is the final wheel of a coach with a hundred wheels. But without it the coach will not move.

Now it is time for the soul of the characters in action to be painted in their words. For each, the author seeks the style of a singular soul, its treasure-house of metaphors, its inexchangeable word. Knowing that the inner world of each "self" is always much richer, refined, nuanced, variegated than we think. They have emotions, I supply the words.

In this respect incredible events may sometimes happen: a character may take wing in a way in which the author would never have imagined: there is for example the story of a scene which happened despite myself and of which I disapprove but in vain.

I was in my office, in the state of an author docile to the passions of the characters. I could see Barout, the rabbi, who is one of the three contrary "narrators" in *The Story*, looking through a Bible in a corner. Enter Snorri Sturlusson, the poet. He is agitated, overexcited, he can no longer find the manuscript of the play, it has been stolen from him, and suddenly he sees the rabbi with the manuscript in his hands, the rabbi, his friend, his pal! It's too much! In Snorri is awakened Sturla Sturlusson the Scandinavian father, the one-eyed and brutal Odin, he throws himself on Barout and with a stab of a knife . . . Wham! End of the friendship, of the history of trust between peoples and poets. Barout crumbles, I want to cry: he is innocent, but I have no voice: I am not in the play. Moreover Snorri realizes but too late his madness, the cruel unconscious blow. The irreparable has been committed. The irreparable? Ah, no. It's not going to happen like that! I get up, my legs trembling. Such a scene by me, in me? Never. I take the pages – because everything had just happened under My pen, by my hand – and with horror, I tear them up and throw them in the waste-paper basket. Then I go down for a coffee and tell my daughter about the terrible scene: "Snorri has just killed Barout," I murmured. I could not get over it. I stopped everything. I did not sleep. The next day I questioned myself about my reaction: "You have thrown out this scene?" "Am I not the author?" "But in the name of who and what are you condemning this scene? Do you want to save Snorri's reputation? Do you want to lay down the law on the characters?" "No, no." "You want to make morality prevail. No blood, no crime?" "No, no," I said, embarrassed. I rewrote the scene. After all, it had taken place. And now, I said to myself, what is going to happen? But that was the business of the assassin and the assassinated. It was up to Snorri to act. And the rabbi too. Both in the state in which they were. Killing each other. Between them they raised and embodied all the questions of homicide, injustice, the laws of blood, Germanic mythology and Judaeo-Christian mythology. The movement of creation does its work beyond the desires habits and laws of the author and takes him beyond himself.

The Theatre is no doubt a propitious place for the taking of action, the carrying out of all those things which in civilian life we repress and hold back. Thoughts, fantasies, virtualities, most of them murderous, take advantage of the exceptional temporality of the theatrical account to fulfil themselves "in reality." But it is precisely for this reason, because it is a magic mirror, that the Theatre is experienced as a necessity by all those who enter under its roof. You come to see yourself do what you swear you would never do: all the excesses. Good or evil.

I would like to speak at length of the language of bodies in the Theatre, but I do not have the time. So just a couple of words: we see, in the Theatre (therefore one sees *oneself*) thanks to acting, all the figures of our blindness, incarnate, visible in a way in which we do not see them in reality: in a real conversation the convention requires that the conversation unfold face to face. Furthermore most of the time we use the front, just one side, of the body in everyday life. But in the Theatre, the word goes, comes, strikes, sees, from all sides of the body. We speak *in the back* of the characters, in the back of the blind that we are, we strike, we see, the back of the characters, all the figures of misunderstanding, deafness, blindness, proximity, separation are present before our eyes, we see ourselves seeing seen from close up, from far away, foresee, foretoken see nothing making mistakes, yes, we see ourselves from the back, we see ourselves believing we are alone while the entire world – or conscience is there. This makes it possible for the author to create an extraordinarily mobile, versatile and manifold discourse. A potential such as we can possess only in dreams. In the Theatre I let people see all the things I do not see and all *those* (beings) we do not see, we have never seen and whose presence around us is so strong and effective that the Greeks gave these presences proper names and the states of divine entities. In the Theatre I see the Night, the Dead, the Furies, the ghosts. This is the quasi-divine function of the theatrical word. One day I was writing a scene in which the guardian Aeschylus told the dishonest lawyers that he was going to have to close the gates of his cemetery. "Sirs," he said, to make them leave "the Night!"

The Night? I the author hear Aeschylus say: Here is the Night!

Whereupon *Night* in person entered. And became one of the most important characters in the play. The Theatre needs the economy of magic. It takes place in the world of the all-powerfulness of thoughts. Magic is necessary. The problem of the author is that I write at a time when magic has been repressed and denied. However, our unconsciouses which are our clandestine masters are magicians. So how can magic be reintroduced? It is the poetical function of language which holds the key: it makes an appeal to the ancient memory which lies dormant in the spectator, it revives images and visions. But this can happen only in the Theatre. He who goes to the Theatre consents. He who goes to the Theatre grants himself the ephemeral right to hear those who are deprived of speech in the city speak: children, poets, the dead, animals, thoughts at the back of our mind, outcasts, the homeless. In that, in this giving of speech, the poetic Theatre is political.

You will note that authors, in speaking of the Theatre, say: "the theatre is . . ."

Conjuration, conjuration of that which is only: convoked. By convocation. Or conjuration. I.e. the Theatre.

And for it to take place, all that is required is a magical object always small in size. For example, at the Théâtre du Soleil, a small rug is placed on the floor. And the theatre is.

The end of my time of speech is drawing nigh. And I have promised to speak of the end. It is difficult, because for me, there is no final end. The spectators end up by observing, and I too, that often my plays do not have any conclusive end. But the play has to end, it will soon be time for the last metro, and this I don't forget because the audience is an essential character in any play: it is there, everything is addressed to it, *and it is the watch* and it calls the tune.

Now from the beginning, the play has been seeking its end.

At the beginning we were already wondering, Ariane and myself how will it end? But this question conceals a concern. Deep down we probably wanted it to "end well," that is, not too badly. With all our strength the characters and myself try to break out of the mortal trap, the circle of blood, the ineluctable repetition. If we knew how to, there would be no play.

On our side, we want the end. Who would not want the end of a tragedy? It will be tragic but it will at least put an end to the agony. Everyone will be dead. Then Fortinbras will arrive and our mourning can begin. In a secret way even a bad end is always at the same time the beginning of a consolation.

One wants to see the end. I too. But as I have said to myself since the age of four in Oran, it is the sign itself of tragedy that *we shall not see the end*, it will come but we will no longer be there to greet it and for it to greet us. There will be no greeting and no salvation. The war will necessarily finish, but my grandfather the soldier died on the front without seeing the end. Hitler died without six million Jews knowing it, at least during their lifetime. I know Khmers who, although saved from the Khmer Rouge camps and living among us, were unable to resume their lives because, since Pol Pot was alive, they had not seen the end of their torture.

It will end nevertheless. But, before the end, I do not know how. At the Théâtre du Soleil, there is a tradition, it is not commented upon, it comes from the well of time: it is understood that I will not write the last scene until the last days of the rehearsal. And it is right. Thus we all experience uncertainty. The players are unable to plan, to cheat. They are in the present.

"How is it going to end?" the characters, the prophetic humiliated souls of the cemetery ask their friend Aeschylus, the guardian.

"Very quickly, very violently. The hour is not far off. The end is coming. I can already hear the axe breathing. Can you hear it?" replies he-who-knows-that-he-does-not-know.

It will be a surprise. It will happen where and when it is not expected. It is like that up until the last minute.

Now I must write it. I have just seen its face at the window of time: it has come. Not chosen. It is the result of so many so-called "intradiegetic" and "extradiegetic" events.

It must be admitted. It enters. Undeniable. It could not end otherwise, despite our efforts. When a world is rotten to the core, it is condemned to the flood. It has been so since the first play in the Theatre: God recognizes that this entire world is evil, all that remains is to wipe it out. For us, it's the same.

The mathematically elegant solution: you wipe everything out. After, we shall see. But it is terrible, cry the spectators. It is unbearable. Then God provides the spectators with an ark. But I am not God, and I was not able to save anyone. When everyone was dead, at the end of *The Perjured City*, and when for the first time the members of company discovered the last scene, they were paralysed with terror and grief. It was worse than *The Eumenides*. At the end of *The Eumenides*, everything is unbearable, the mother does not obtain justice, the matricidal son recovers his assets, and the old goddesses that called for vengeance let themselves be buried like old lambs under the earth. You come out of the theatre with a pang of anguish. But even so the old disappeared goddesses are immortal. Whereas we are mortal. At the sorrow caused by this ending, I, the author, allowed myself to add another scene. Because I, H.C., do not believe that the end ends and closes. Furthermore neither do the players and the people at the Theatre believe in an end which encloses: they are by definition on the side of resurrection.

So we were all agreed that, after the end, there should be a continuation. Objectively, it happens *elsewhere* and *after* death. All our dead character friends reappear. From where they are, they have an extraordinary point of view over the Theatre of the Earth which they have just left. From this distance the Earth resembles an orange of soft light. They see, they see us. How small, agitated, threatened we are.

I must finish my account here now.

This continuation beyond the end had a very interesting fate: the public was split in two. Those who, like us, relished the suspension and the impossible. Those who did not tolerate this fantasy, this childishness. The latter came to see me and asked to cut and condemn to the waste-paper basket this moment of transgression, a caprice, an unreality. The Theatre, they said, must obey, it must not overflow. Once it's finished, it's finished. Remove this filth, this obscenity. It is outrageous. An insult to political borders.

And so the play overflowed into the hall and continued, the battle raged between those who had a conception of tragedy which obeyed the Graeco-philosophical prescription programme, for whom history is an uninterrupted net, and those who like me can breathe only through its interruptions, going over the edge between the threads. For me the Theatre is itself the Proof of the real transgressive force of the Dream, it is a meteor from the other world. The magical place of a story and a history which we will never know, which awaits us and promises always to exceed – all that we have ever feared desired. It is the temple of our fortune. That is why "at the end" of the play-without-end the players return for the final bow, salute and salvation. Ours.

PORTRAIT OF DORA

TRANSLATED BY ANN LIDDLE[1]

Characters (in order of appearance)

VOICE OF THE PLAY   MR K.

DORA   MRS K.

FREUD   MR B., Dora's father

VOICE OF THE PLAY "*. . . These events declare themselves, like shadows, in dreams, they often become so clear that we feel we can reach out and grasp them, but, in spite of this, they elude any final clarification, and if we proceed without skill or particular caution, we find ourselves unable to determine whether or not such a scene ever really took place.*"

DORA [*in a voice that shatters a silence – with a tone between a request and a threat*] If you dare to kiss me, I'll slap you! [*With a cajoling inflection*]

DORA [*suddenly in his ear*] Just dare to kiss me, I'll slap you!

FREUD Yes, you will tell me about it. In every detail.

DORA [*in a faraway voice*] "If you like." [*In an awakened voice*] If you wish. And then?

FREUD You will tell me about the scene by the lake, in every detail.

DORA Why did I keep silent for the first few days after the scene by the lake?

FREUD To whom do you think you should address that question?

DORA And then why did I suddenly tell my parents about it?

FREUD Why do you think?

DORA [*doesn't reply but relates in a dreamy voice*] When Papa was getting ready to leave, I said that I wouldn't stay there without him. Why did I tell my mother about the scene so that she would repeat it to my father?

MR B. Mr K. has always been very kind to my daughter, ever since our two families became such close friends several years ago. When he was there, Mr K. would go for walks with her. With an almost paternal affection. Although she was only a child. He gave her little presents and looked after her with an almost paternal affection. And Dora, for her part, took marvellous care of my friend's two little children. She was like a mother to them. Two years ago, my daughter and I joined the K.'s who were vacationing at one of our mountain lakes. Dora was to stay with them for several weeks.

DORA I'm not staying, I'm leaving with my father.

MR B. But the lake and mountain air would be so good for your nerves. I'm sure that in a few days.

DORA I'm leaving with you. [*Then abruptly threatening*] I'll never forgive you!

MR B. I don't understand you!

DORA You understand me, but you're not sincere. You have a strain of falseness in your character. You only think of your own satisfaction. You don't understand. I'm not sincere. I reproach myself for being unfair to you. Give me a bracelet. 30

[*A pause*

My father is very generous. He enjoys doing things to please poor Mrs K. At the same time, he is generous with his wife and his daughter. My father never buys a piece of jewellery for me without buying one for my mother and one for Mrs K.

MR B. Dora is still a child and Mr K. treats her like a child. He sent her flowers, he gave her little presents. She was like a mother to the children, she gave them lessons, took them for walks. Gave them the same tender care that their own mother would have shown them.

DORA I have never loved Mr K. I was never mad about him. I could have loved him, but ever since the scene by the lake, it's altogether impossible. There had been talk of divorce between Mr and Mrs K. I took care of the children. When my father visited Mrs K. I knew that the children would not be at home, I liked to turn my steps in a direction where I would be sure to meet them and then I would go for a walk with them. 40

MR K. Dora is no longer a child.

MRS K. Dora *is* a child, who is only interested in sexual matters. When she was staying at our house on the lake, she used to slip off and read *The Psychology of Love* by Montegazza and other such books, which excited her. She adores me. She trusts me. She is a child who arouses mixed feelings; you can't give credence to all that she says, this reading material goes to her head.

MR B. She probably "imagined" the entire scene by the lake.

DORA Do you hear him?

FREUD Yes. 50

DORA There's a door in Vienna through which everyone may pass except me. I often dream that I arrive in front of this door, it opens, I could go in. Young men and women are streaming through it, I could slip in among them, but I don't, yet I can't walk away from this door forever, I go past it, I linger but I don't do it, I am unable to, I am full of recollections and despair, what is strange is that I could go through but I am held back, I fear, I am beyond all fear, but I don't go in, if I don't go in I die, if I went in, if I wanted to see Mr K. but if Papa saw me, but I don't want to see him, but if Papa saw me see him he would kill me, I could see him just once. It would be the last time. Then

MRS K. [*in a laughing, mocking voice*] I've always said that the key is in the lake! . . .

DORA Then . . . nothing. Nothing to be done.

As soon as I understood Mr K.'s intention I cut him off, I slapped him and I ran away. I ran away I slapped him, I cut short his intent. I understood his words. 60

VOICE OF THE PLAY "*This initial account may be compared to an unnavigable stream, a stream whose bed is sometimes obstructed by rocks, sometimes divided by sandbanks.*"

FREUD I happen to know Mr K. He is still a young man, with a pleasing appearance. The father, Mr B., was a man of means, mild-mannered, an affectionate father and a patient husband. I never knew Dora's mother.

The father was very attached to his daughter. Every time he was questioned about her health, tears came to his eyes.

DORA My mother means nothing to him.

MR B. You must have imagined it! A man like Mr K. is incapable of such intentions! 70

DORA [*beside herself*] I must have "imagined" it! He said: "You know that my wife means nothing to me." As soon as I understood his intention, I slapped him and ran away.

[*On the side stage*

As soon as Mrs K. understood Papa's intention, she cut him off, slapped him and ran away. She slapped him. And you, *you* say that I "imagined" it! Now "choose"! *Choose!* [*Shouts*]

MR B. *Don't shout!*

DORA Her or me!

MR K. I never made the slightest move that could have been open to such an interpretation. I sent her flowers for a whole year, I treated her like my own daughter. Mr B., who is known for his delicacy with the ladies, is aware of how disinterested my attentions were. 80

DORA Answer. Well, answer!

DORA It wasn't exactly at the edge of the lake. It was in the forest. I had understood Mr K.'s intention long before. During the walk, he rolled a cigarette.

[*A silence, during which, in another time (*DORA *at age fourteen) the scene by the door near the staircase is performed*

Every morning when I wake up, I smell smoke. It's always the same. I don't open my eyes. I sniff, and it's him.

DORA When I entered the store, there was a faint smell of smoke. Mr K. was alone. Mrs K. and my mother were late. The time for the procession was drawing near. 90

FREUD Where there's smoke, there's fire.

DORA Mr K. and my father were like you, passionate smokers. I myself smoked at the edge of the lake. He had rolled me a cigarette. He smelled of smoke. I loathe the smell of smoke.

I remember that the door that led from the store to the apartment was open, and I noticed the smell of smoke, Mrs K.'s perfume, mixed together. When the time for the procession drew near, he asked me to wait for him . . . to wait for him. 100

FREUD Go on. Go on. Go on.

DORA He asked me . . .

To wait for him, when the time drew near.

[*Silence*

FREUD Yes. And then?

DORA There is a door. Which opens onto the staircase, leading to the upper storey; there. While he lowered the blinds. I waited for him. There was a smell . . . that was . . . familiar.

FREUD And then?

DORA

He came back and next and then, instead of going out through the open door, he clasped me to him, he held me tightly against him, and he kissed me on the mouth. I felt such intense disgust then, I hated him with all my soul, I was disgusted, I tore myself free from him violently, 110

I can still feel it today, at this moment, I feel it, so intensely.

I can still feel that kiss, and the pressure of that embrace; his lips were very wet. Here, on my chest, and right through to my back. I ran past him, past that man.

I tore myself free, I hurried away, I gave him a look, I hurried to the staircase, past that man (I thought: I'm going past "that man") to the staircase, and, from there, to the street door.

FREUD And then?

DORA And then . . . Nothing. Only that. The door.

DORA I loathe tête-à-têtes.

MR B. She has suffered from a respiratory disturbance ever since the age of eight. My daughter has always been very nervous, very fragile. At one time her health caused me a good deal of concern.

FREUD And her mother?

MR B. The relations between my wife and my daughter are not very affectionate. My wife doesn't mean much to me. Unfortunately. She is not a very well-educated woman. She has no understanding of her children's aspirations. Dora naturally favoured me. I myself was seriously ill: I have no doubt that her tenderness was heightened by what I went through.

DORA During his illness, Mrs K. apparently saved him. She has an eternal right to his gratitude. When I was ten years old, my father had to go through a course of treatment in a darkened room on account of a detached retina. I liked to keep him company in the dark. He would take me in his arms and kiss me.

I myself saw to it that the blinds were always lowered.

MR B. The migraines and the attacks of nervous coughing appeared when she was about twelve. (I remember, because it was at that time that my friend K. persuaded me to consult you.) The coughing fits sometimes last for three or four weeks. But what worries me most are these spells of aphonia.

DORA But the relationship didn't become intimate until Mrs K. took over as sick nurse.

My mother kept away from the room, because she doesn't love my father. She is a stupid woman.

MR B. I am bound to Mrs K. by ties of sincere friendship. Dora, who is very close to me, felt a kind of adoration for her.

DORA Adoration.

I had never seen such a beautiful, elegant woman. How I loved to look at her! I drank in her every movement. I thought that she knew how to do everything that women should know how to do. I loved to bring flowers into her bedroom. When she and my father changed rooms and they both moved into the end rooms, I understood everything. [Shout directed at MR B.] Everything. Do you hear me?

MR B. [very aggressively, defending himself] An extremely nervous woman herself, Mrs K. has in me her only friend. With my state of health and her fragile nature, I don't need to tell you that we are united by nothing more than an exchange of friendly sympathy. Dora's animosity is unjust. Her irritability, her thoughts of suicide! All of this obviously comes from her mother.

DORA Why haven't I ever confessed this story to anyone?

FREUD Except me.

[DORA exits. Footsteps on the staircase, running footsteps, she stops on the staircase

DORA It's dark here . . .

MR K. [*whispering*] Wait for me, I'll lower the blinds and then I'm all yours.

DORA [*whispers, all in a rush. What is unsaid, lost, in the body, between the bodies*] *No need to open it. It's always open.* I can open up. Not open up. *That man had beautiful teeth, like the pearls of a bracelet. I can open a little. And why shouldn't you open up?* What is open might not be open. What has happened might not have happened.

MR K. Nothing is irremediable. Why not?

DORA [*whispering*] I can still feel it. *I can hardly breathe. I've already felt someone behind the door. Pushing with his whole body. It was a new sensation* . . . But, what about what didn't happen?   170

[*Abrupt return to her normal voice*

FREUD How did you know that it was a man? Since he was behind the door.

DORA [*whispering*] *Pressing against the door with all of his weight. I felt his member stiffen.* Who told you that?

[*Pause*

It was Mrs K. who told me.

She used to read me books that no one has ever read before, when I was doing her hair.

[*Silence*

DORA [*she performs this on a side stage, in a voice that is at once clear and lethargic*] *It would have been pointless to wait for him.* One could wait, if one liked. *I had seen him in a dream.* He was a gentle, prepossessing man, who never took his eyes off of me. *But it wasn't him. Is that him, now, behind the door? One never knows.* I open up a crack. There's a man in the shadows. I can't see his face. He stoops down. I understand his intention. I push *it back.* I have no doubt that he intends to force the door open. And he presses against it. *I feel his erection. He leans forward. Too late. He's going to force the door open.* His decision is already forcing it open and keeping me from closing it. The door weighs heavily and I weigh heavily against the door. I squeeze myself behind it, on the left. I smell smoke. *How simple and deadly everything is! It's Him or Me.* In the obscurity I am obscure. The fictional flesh that fills the door disgusts me. *There will have to be a killing. It's a law.* It's a key. One has to kill the other who kills the one who wants to kill who wants to be killed? *I want to kill him. He knows it. He wants to kill me. I know it.*

A little while later I would like him to kill me. Who will kill me? The one who kills me is the one I want. That's what I want. One can go on for a long time without making a move, then one has to. *Kill me! Kill me! Kill me! It's taking so long. That man* who's behind the door, *I can't see him. He's a tall man. He's still young. Because I*   180   190   200   210

want him like that. He has a familiar look about him: a lady's man. *There's something false in his expression.* His eyes are a little murky, they don't go at all with his mouth. *And now for the throat.* This action requires the utmost concentration of energy. It may kill me, but I put all of my strength into it. *I clasp him, I take him in my arms, I lean forward.* His face seen up close isn't familiar; it isn't terrifying, as if I knew it well. The thing is that we know and there where our   220
knowledge intersects we touch secret places which escape neither him nor me. I'm anxious to get on with it. I'm not sure of success, despite the division and the multiplication of my strength. While I clasp him in front, *I turn him over* halfway and hold his head from behind, my arm encircles his forehead and his skull weighs on my chest, *I hold him tightly and I slit his throat.* The knife has become one with my hand. *How hard it is to cut his throat.* I don't make a big   230
stab because I'm holding him tightly, I cut all the way across his neck, but not through it. Long afterward I still feel the resistance of the throat. *As though I were still doing it* I feel the specificity of that resistance. I used my left hand, and I drew a straight line from left to right. I was holding his head with my right arm. *It takes a lot of pressure, it's like opening a tin can. His pain makes me sick. I had a very sore throat. It's hard for me to speak.*   240

FREUD Mr K. travelled a good deal, no doubt?

DORA I don't know. I'm not interested in what Mr K. does.

FREUD Do you like to write? Yes.

DORA No.

FREUD You sent me a very pretty postcard. Do you like receiving postcards?

DORA I don't much care. Mr K. spent part of the year travelling. Like Papa. Journeys have their uses. Whenever my father feels his health failing, he leaves for Berg.

FREUD Does he stay long in Berg?

DORA [*following up immediately in a very low but abrupt tone of voice, with violent outbursts on the words in quotes*] I'll write a letter. It will be hesitant. It will start with these words: "You have killed me." And I'll write: 250
"You, dear, have killed me." Then I'll write another letter on paper as fine as onion skin, that will start with these words: "That's what you wanted . . ." I'll leave it ambiguous, for him to complete "himself." Because I don't know what he wanted. Yet "it's me" who is dead. My body is buried. In the forest. It's dark there. I am voiceless.

FREUD Tell me about the letter.

DORA [*almost inaudible*] What letter?

MR B. I found a letter on the desk. It was inside her desk. She said that she could no longer endure life. "This is what you all wanted," she said, she was bidding us farewell. I didn't think she was really determined to commit suicide, but I was shaken; a few days later, after an insignificant argument, she had a fainting spell, for the first time. That really did frighten me. 260

DORA How did they find that letter? It was locked up in my desk.

FREUD Is your desk locked?

DORA I don't know. Does anyone else have the keys?

FREUD Who has the keys?

MR B. On her desk. It was a first draft. I worried about it especially when she had her fainting spell.

DORA [*in a painful, staccato voice*] You don't love me!

You think I don't see the two of you? You're abandoning me!

You love her more than me! I don't want anything, do you hear? *Nothing*.

You disgust me!

You think you can buy me? You think you can sell me? 270

[*She is yelling,* MR B. *is frightened, and tries to make her be quiet*

MR B. [*in a hurried voice*] Dora, Dora, Dora, my darling, my little one, my little child . . .

Come, come now.

DORA You can't imagine how I detest that woman! When she is dead, I will marry you.

FREUD What were you arguing about?

MR B. I don't remember anymore. I had just returned from a journey. She looked tired. I remember I had given her a pearl bracelet.

DORA I used to be very fond of jewellery, but I don't wear it anymore. When I was living at the K.'s she used to like to show me her jewels. She would loan them to me. She told me the pearls would be even more becoming to me than to her. 280

FREUD What was your attitude toward Mrs K. before the incident?

DORA I don't know. Normal.

I'm sure that the jewellery my father gave me was chosen by her. I recognize her taste. My father used to give me jewellery, especially pearls. Like the ones I had seen at Mrs K's.

[*A pause*

She used to tell me . . . when I was doing her hair. Me. Standing behind her. The whiteness . . . of her body.

[*The characters change places, as in a ballet*

MR K. [*voice on telephone*] I am prepared to come and meet with you, to clear up all of these misunderstandings. Dora is a mere child to me. You know what respect I have for you and your daughter. Didn't she live in our house? And on the most intimate terms with my wife? 290

MRS K. You haven't the right to criticize your father's behaviour, my little darling; he's a generous man. You know how much your father cares for you. He can't even speak to me about you without tears coming into his eyes.

MR B. . . . every reason in the world, rather, to be grateful to Mrs K.

MR K. . . . always absolute confidence in her.

MR B. A man like Mr K. could not have presented any threat to her.

MRS K. He's a man with coarse appetites; he doesn't know what a real woman is. Men are often like that: they only think of their own satisfaction. Not your poor papa . . . He was so unhappy at that time that he wanted to commit suicide. I was seized with a premonition, without a moment's hesitation, I headed toward the forest, I found him. I pleaded with him and managed to persuade him to go back on this terrible decision. To preserve his life for the sake of his family. 300

DORA Always in white. Milky white veils. Crêpe de chine. I saw HER.

The whiteness of her body, especially her back. A very soft lustre; pearly.

MR K. I am prepared to come and meet with you immediately to clear up this misunderstanding. No girl who reads such books should have any title to a man's respect. When she was staying with us, my wife went so far as to let Dora share her room. And I kept my distance quite willingly, because we thought Dora was in need of affection. My wife was astonished at such curiosity in a young girl.

MRS K. You know that you can tell me everything and ask me anything. There is nothing I need to hide from you. The brutality of certain practices has totally alienated me from men.   310

DORA You are absolutely everything. And I am nothing, nothing. No one.

Listen! I love you as if you were God. Someone.

For whom I do not exist.

For whom I live. For no one.

> [*In adoration, before* MRS K. *who, seated in front of her mirror, looks at her without turning around, with a long, serene, terribly calm and uninterpretable smile*

MR B. There had often been talk of divorce between Mr and Mrs K. It never took place, because Mr K. who was an affectionate father, would not give up either of the two children.

MR K. Neither of my two children!

DORA I went to Dresden. My cousin wanted to take me around the gallery. I refused. I ran to the door. I   320
went out. I wandered about in the strange town. I went to the gallery alone. There is a painting, that I cannot look at – without . . . I stood for a long time. In front of that painting. It was the "Sistine Madonna," I stood there, alone, immersed. In that painting. For two hours. In the aura. A very gentle smile. You couldn't see the teeth. But a pearly glimmer, between the lips.

FREUD What was it about this painting that held you there?

DORA The . . . Her . . .

[*Suddenly, something obvious, which may go unnoticed by everyone: the infant Jesus held by the Madonna is none other than a little* DORA.	[*Filmed sequence, in three scenes. The Sistine Madonna, substitution of the Madonna, and* MRS K. DORA *behind the Madonna, seen in a mirror. The audience won't know who is speaking, Mary or* MRS K. 330

MRS K. [*with infinite tenderness*] You, too, must live.

DORA [*to* FREUD] I shared her room, I was her confidante and even her counsellor. She told me about all the difficulties of married life. There was nothing we couldn't talk about . . .

MRS K. [*laughing gently*] *I* call a spade a spade.

There is more than one way. A body has many resources.

You'll see.

DORA Let me kiss you!

> [MRS K. *smiling, more and more gentle, more and more distant, ephemeral, infinite, very near, inaccessible, says no with her gestures, with her body, resists* DORA's *embrace. Calmly.*

DORA Let me take you in my arms! Just once!   340

DORA [*to* FREUD] I don't know. That's just it. She showed herself to me. Her smile. As if she were smiling to herself . . .

FREUD Two hours? What was it that touched you?

DORA [*after a long silence*] Her.

DORA [*to* MRS K.] I am standing here! Before you. I'm waiting. If only! If only you would tell me!

MRS K. But I have nothing to tell you.

DORA Everything you know. Everything I don't know. Let me give you this love.

Her body, its ravishing whiteness. Her tiny breasts, the smooth skin of her belly.

MRS K. [*her hand over* DORA's *mouth*] Oh! Impossible, impossible, my mad little child.

DORA I ache, I never stop aching, put your hands on my head, hold me.   350

MRS K. My God. What am I going to do with you?

DORA Look at me. I wish I could step into your eyes. I wish you would close your eyes.

DORA Her way of looking at herself. Of loving herself. Of not suffering. Of not looking at me. Of looking at me, so calmly. With that smile.

DORA I owe her everything. I cherished her.

FREUD How could you be attracted to the man about whom your cherished friend had so many bad things to say?

DORA [*replies off to one side to* MRS K.] She is an intelligent woman, superior to the men who surround her, and adorably beautiful! . . . how white your back is! like your skin! How I love you!

[*Murmuring, and the very faint sound of a kiss*   360

May I? . . . and here too, just above.

You cannot imagine how much I love you: if I were a man, I would marry you, I would carry you off and marry you, I would know how to please you.

MRS K. Dora!

DORA [*to* FREUD] They were not made for each other.

MR B. I'm waiting for an explanation.

MR K. No girl who is interested in such things should have any title to a man's respect. She has read Montegazza. She knows more than you know. My wife was so surprised that she had a word with me about it.

DORA Tell me more, tell me everything, everything.   370

[*With, against* MRS K.

All the things that women know how to do: make jam, make love, make up their faces, make pastry, adopt little babies, cook meat, dress fowl. I watched my grandmothers do those things when I was small. But me, do I know how to do them? I should find out. When she told me that if she had to choose between coming back to earth as a man or a woman, she had given a lot of thought to it, she wouldn't hesitate, it's definitely women who run things, I told myself that I wouldn't know, I've given a lot of thought to it, but I don't know. Which side. But if I were a man I'd know. But I would be a quick-tempered man. But what else? I'd be too gentle, I might be brutal, I'd be restless, I'd be shifty.

MRS K. Patience, patience! It takes a lot of work. Patience, my darling, it comes with time. With a bit of   380
cunning as well. Our sex has to learn its lesson. Draw the curtains.

[*Sound of curtains being drawn; then murmuring,* DORA*'s voice fades away*

DORA It's like a cave. Where are you? It's like a cave; it's me! Me inside of myself, in the shadows. Inside of you.

[DORA*'s faraway voice*] Sometimes full, sometimes empty, and always dark. One might understand everything. Then one might change the world. This time opens and closes like hesitant eyes. Don't tell anyone what I know. Swear you won't tell.

MRS K. It's a promise.

DORA [*sharply, hissing*] You have killed me! You have betrayed me! You have deceived me!

"Who" is abandoning me   390

Didn't I write you innumerable letters?

Didn't I worship the ground you walked on?

Didn't I open my doors?

Didn't I break down my heart for you?

There's nothing I didn't do to please you. I followed you.

I stroked, I polished; I put my right hand at your service. I spoke to you when you listened to me, and when you didn't listen to me, I told you, I surrendered, I smashed myself up against your law, I made your bed, I turned the shadow away from your bed, who are you, who is abandoning me?

And now, to whom shall I address this letter?

To whom shall I address my silence? My suicide? 400

And you? Who are you jealous of, how, why "are" you jealous. Tell me? Well, answer! Do you want me to tell you? Draw the curtains! Draw the curtains! I'm going to show you everything you want. That's the way *you* are, too.

FREUD No, if that's how it is, then leave . . .

DORA Is that all?

[Door. Opened. Closed. Footsteps

MR K.'s VOICE But what did she want after all?

DORA Nothing, now. Nothing ever again.

[A still shot, on film, of the Madonna. Before which, in a sad voice

DORA I beg of you, give me something. Do something for me. Tell me the words that give birth. Nourish 410
me. I am dead, dead! I am even unable to want anymore. Make something happen to me!

MR K. Don't be afraid. You know me. Can't you trust me a little?

DORA Yesterday you called me – "darling."

MR K. Come, dear, don't be afraid.

DORA He said to me: "Come. I'll tell you your real name." I wanted so much for him to tell me.

MR K. Come now, come, take my hand – What's stopping you?

DORA He was calling me. I had trouble moving. As if the world were going to open up. He had to pull me.
I wanted him to carry me away.

MR K. You know me. Don't close yourself up. Trust me.
Don't you know you can trust me? 420

DORA I would like to. I don't understand myself. I was so heavy. I want so much to believe you, Mr K.

MR K. Yesterday you called me by my first name. You know we don't have much time . . . Dora. That doesn't
mean that nothing is possible. I'm a man of my word.

DORA Don't say a word. Whatever you do, don't say a word. There's something in your voice . . .

MR K. What should I do? What haven't I done?

DORA You talk too much. It's in your silences that I'd like to touch you.

FREUD And you thought: "I know who the other is"?

DORA I don't know.

MR K.'s VOICE As if she feared the best. As if she arranged to be alone, because she didn't want to be alone.
On the contrary. 430

DORA [*to Freud*] I dreamed that he was rejecting me and that I was seeing him for the last time. He was
saying to me: "I don't hold anything against you. I don't take back anything that I said; I'm a man of
my word, didn't I keep my word, yes." And he was saying: "I hold nothing against you, you know me
a little" – and it's true – yes – I know him better than anyone – and: "I've made everything as bright as
day, and I'm making my decision as clear to you as I always have, and this is the way it is." And the
tears were rolling down my cheeks, but I was saying yes, yes, it's true, then he said these words: "I'm
taking back my pearls!" And it was indeed he who said that, and also: "I gave you the key to the box;
I'm taking it back." What was the use of crying? In the midst of all those strange words? And I was
saying: yes, yes – as if I wanted to die. But what key?

MR K. What key? 440

FREUD What box?

DORA Some time before, Mr K. had given me a very precious little jewellery box. For my birthday.

FREUD Fine. And the key?

MR K.'s VOICE And if I had asked her to wait for me?

DORA In the afternoon following the excursion to the lake, from which Mr K. and I had returned home separately, I lay down on the lounge chair in the bedroom, to sleep for a while. Suddenly, I woke up.

[*Sudden noise*

What are you doing here!

MR K. This is my room, no one is going to keep me from coming in when I like. Besides, I came in here to get something! 450

DORA [*breathless and painful recital*] I got up in a hurry to run away. I was running away. Then *I dreamed that I was running away. I saw myself running away on a beach. The sand was so hard that it wore my foot raw. I was accompanied by a woman who was bigger and stronger than me and who was my opposite in every way. I called her dear Mrs K. She made me feel ashamed of myself. She was what I might have been, in every way. I didn't have to explain to her. She was sublimely indifferent to my failures. On the way down, I felt that I was moving away from myself. I, too, was abandoning myself.*

FREUD'S VOICE As if she were running away from herself. In order to keep from getting there. In order to keep from dying, too.

DORA That's when I saw him again. There! It was Him! So far way! Yet just a few metres away from me. But too far away. So far away. I knew very well that one day. 460

FREUD'S VOICE Searching for Him everywhere, from the beginning of time. As if He existed. As if He were waiting only for her. For her arrival, to disappear.

DORA There was no reason to hope. Everything separates us. He said to me: "Thus, nothing changes." And I couldn't reach him. Because where I am, nothing is living. I was in the past.

FREUD'S VOICE Everything that happened to her, only happened to her in the past. She lived on memories. A prey to the past. Without any hope of ever reaching anything like the present.

DORA She urged me to live. Unaware of the enormity of my suffering. Which doesn't even reach me. I couldn't even cry out.

FREUD Completely lost, between love and desire.

DORA In the afternoon, when I wanted to lock myself in to take a rest, the key was gone! I am sure that Mr K. had removed it. 470

FREUD The question whether a girl is "open" or "shut" can naturally not be a matter of indifference. It is well known what sort of key effects the opening in such a case.

DORA I was "sure" you would say that!

FREUD Didn't you ever feel like giving Mr K. a present in return? That wouldn't have been out of place.

DORA Absolutely not. I never thought of it. I was on my guard. I was afraid that he would come into my room while I was dressing.

FREUD Into "his" room?

DORA Mrs K. always went out very early to take a walk with him. But he didn't bother me any more.

FREUD You regretted it perhaps? 480

DORA Absolutely not. It was then that I made up my mind not to stay at the K's without Papa. Because Papa was living at the hotel and he always went out early. I used to dress myself quickly to run and meet him!

MR K. This is my house. You don't belong here.

DORA There is some mistake.

MR K. There is no mistake. You are in my house.

DORA I'm taking my pearls, and I'm throwing them away.

[*Sound of pearls rolling across the floor*

MR K. [*a cry of anger*] I'm taking back my key. Give me back my keys.

DORA [*childishly*] No. 490

[*from far away*] Where are we going. Where are we going? Where are we going! And if something goes wrong, it will be Papa's fault, Mr K. gave me a jewellery box. So. I give Mr K. my jewellery box. Or rather, no.

FREUD Let's go on.

[DORA *is looking about*

FREUD If it's your little purse you're looking for, it's there on your knees. You haven't stopped fingering it for the past hour. It's very pretty, by the way.

DORA [*suspiciously*] This is the first time you've noticed it?

FREUD This is the first time I've seen you with it. Here, in any case.

DORA I always have my little purse with me wherever I go. 500

[*anxiously*] It gets stuck, you see, I was fingering it because I couldn't get it open. Here: see for yourself how hard it is. It just won't open.

FREUD Don't you think that your words might apply to another meaning for that little purse?

DORA [*scornfully*] Yes, if you like. That's what men think.

FREUD He whose lips are silent chatters with his fingertips.

In the train of associations, equivocal words are like switch-points.

DORA Cross stitch, railway stitch, needle point, petit point. That's women's work.

DORA I have a dream.

FREUD Go on.

DORA I know how to . . . 510

FREUD What do you know how to do?

DORA How to make dreams rise, puff them up, bake them, roll them, put them into my mouth.[1] I sit down at the table next to my grandmothers. They're joyfully eating little cakes. The sounds in the distance announce the arrival of the matrimonial procession. I am shocked by it; sad and ashamed; I realize that there aren't enough cakes left. I myself have eaten several of them, I've gorged myself out of nervousness, violent embarrassment at the thought that I've eaten the others' portions, enter Mr and Mrs K. holding hands, then my father and his wife, holding hands. I don't know what they're thinking. They are all beautiful, and gracious and familiar. As this is the first time I've seen them all together, I don't know whom to serve first. I go to ask my three grandmothers how to divide the cakes equally. They nearly choke laughing, their mouths are full, they've gobbled up everything. 520

Mr K. turns to me and says quite naturally: "Can you, no matter when, at a moment's notice, be ready to set aside two hours of your time?" Shaken by the simplicity of another time, bewildered. What does Papa think about this?

I can't bring myself to answer. For what? Ready for what? I put it off, I apologize for not answering. I ask them if they want to play cards, which I don't know how to play, but maybe checkhers . . . There are five of them for with against me.

And if one of them killed me, ah, if one of them killed me right before my very eyes what revenge. My body in pieces on the table to replace the cake.[2]

DORA I smell smoke.

FREUD Tell me about the smoke. 530

DORA The smell of smoke, came to me, in the last dream. And in the other dreams.

FREUD Yes? And?

DORA There was always the smell of smoke. Like a sudden blow. I would wake up with a start. And I had this dream three times: my father is standing beside my bed and wakes me up. I'm asleep, but I see him. There must be a fire in the house. I dress myself quickly. Mama wants to save her jewellery box, but Papa says: "I refuse to let my two children and myself be burned for the sake of your jewellery box." We hurry downstairs and as soon as I'm outside, I wake up.

FREUD Did you have the dream during your first nights at Linz or during your last ones before your departure?

DORA I don't know. I think it was afterward.   540

FREUD How long did you stay on at Linz after the scene?

DORA Four more days.

The afternoon following the excursion to the lake, I lay down, as usual, on the lounge chair in his bedroom to sleep for awhile. I woke up with a start and saw Mr K. standing beside me . . .

FREUD Was it Mr K.? Are you sure?

DORA What's the matter?

MR B. Quick, get dressed, quick, go downstairs.

[MR B. *cries out violently*

I refuse to let my two children be burned because of you!

DORA As soon as I am outside, I wake up. I wonder why Mama is in this dream? She wasn't with us at Linz.   550

FREUD'S VOICE But it was to her, or to another, that her father brought back jewellery. And Mr K. gave her a jewellery box.

DORA [*to whom? To Papa? To* MR K.*?*] I am ready. I would have given you what your wife refuses you. It will be her fault.

FREUD The secret lies with your mama. What role does your mother play here? She was once your rival for your father's affections.

DORA I "knew" that "you" were going to say that!

FREUD So you know who replaces whom.

DORA [*wearily*] Know. Know. But *no one knows* anything. What does it mean: to know? Do I know what I know, how do I know? Nothing means anything. If there were a god . . .   560

FREUD Who stood beside your bed when you were small?

DORA I don't know. My father . . .?

FREUD I don't know. Someone stood beside you and woke you up. Why?

DORA Tell me what you know.

FREUD I don't "know" anything.

DORA What's the point of this? What are you trying to make me say?

FREUD . . . To make you see.

DORA I forgot. Yes, I don't see.

FREUD Where there's smoke, there's fire.

DORA [*ironically*] And where there's fire, there's water?   570

FREUD Exactly. [*He smiles*] Fire is the opposite of water: in the dream where there is fire, there is water. You surely "needed to go out" because of the fire. But also in order that some little mishap might not occur . . . On the other hand, fire enflames, it can directly represent love. So that from fire, one set of rails leads . . .

DORA I see you coming!

FREUD You don't know how well chosen your words are. You see me coming. To where another came before, a long time ago, a very long time ago.

DORA Don't you think you're interpreting all of this a little too personally?

FREUD That's possible. However, all I'm doing is pointing out to you what the dreams are saying.
I see that the contrast between fire and water has been extremely useful to you in the dream. What does   580
one do to prevent children from wetting their beds? One awakens them. Your father awakens you in
the dream. Mr K. awakens you.

DORA Tell me, Doctor, why exactly did this disease strike me, why me in particular?
FREUD What disease? You're not . . .
DORA [*cutting him off*] It comes from my father. He had already been ill before his marriage. It's a poison
that gets passed on. He fell ill because of his dissolute life. He passed his disease on to Mama. And I
have the disease as well.
FREUD What disease?
DORA Like Mama, when we had to go to Franzensbad for her cure. She had abdominal pains and a discharge.
FREUD Do you think you have a venereal disease? Since when?   590

[*Silence*

Since when?

[*Silence*

Do you know why you cough?
DORA My father coughs too.
FREUD You see, the "disease" comes from your father, but it is displaced from above downwards or from
below upwards, depending on whether it's you or your mama. With the symptom of the cough, you are
proclaiming your father's responsibility for what you call "your disease."
DORA But I really do cough!
FREUD Yes.   600
DORA I was getting dressed quickly. I was afraid he would surprise me while I was dressing. So I was getting
dressed very quickly.
[*murmuring*] I get dressed quickly.
[*panting*] As soon as I'm outside I wake up, I'm wet with perspiration. The smell of smoke wakes
me up.
FREUD You get dressed quickly: to keep the secret.
DORA But I never said anything of the kind.
FREUD He whose lips are silent . . .
DORA Yes, yes, I know. And he whose fingertips chatter? Why do you turn your pen over in your hands
seven times before speaking to me? Why?   610
FREUD We must respect the rules!
DORA [*she mimics him*] "We must respect the rules."

[*She paces back and forth across the room*

Where are your cigarettes?
FREUD [*sound of a lighter*] All right. That's it. See you on Tuesday, right?
DORA Right?

[*She bursts out laughing*

VOICE OF THE PLAY Doctor Freud might have had this dream, at the end of December, 1899. Dora is by
then a blossoming girl, of eighteen or nineteen. There is something contradictory and strange about
her, which makes her quite charming. Ripe-looking flesh but a hard mouth, the forehead of a girl, a   620
fixed icy stare. She resembles hidden, vindictive, dangerous loves. Doctor Freud cannot take his eyes
off of her. Dora, who is holding him by the hand with the firm and irritated grip of a governess, has
led him to the shores of the mountain lake which she points out to him. She does not throw him into
the water; but she insists that he go and pick her a bouquet of those shimmering white flowers that grow

on the other side of the lake, and whose perfume he can smell in spite of the distance. Although his hesitation is natural, Freud is anxious, for he senses that this is some sort of test or maybe a trap. He wonders why they didn't get off the train at the previous station which was precisely on the other side of the lake. But not for long, for Dora suddenly looks him up and down, throws him a glance full of scorn and then turns her back on him with a movement of her neck that stuns him: unrestrained, superb and implacable. Then, without a moment's hesitation, she lifts her dress in a wilfully seductive way, allowing her ankles to show a bit, and she crosses the lake, walking over hundreds of bones. Something keeps Freud from doing the same. 630

[*Then a canon of voices:* MR B., MR K., MRS K., FREUD *and* DORA, *successively*

MR B. The girl insisted that he go and pick her a bouquet of those white flowers that grow on the other side of the lake.

MR K. She loathed those white flowers that grew on the other side of the lake: the perfume they gave off was surely too bitter.

MRS K. She agrees with him that it would be better not to touch them.

MR B. With an awkward white hand she fingered the pearls around her neck. Without thinking about it. Her eyes were elsewhere. 640

FREUD Irritated, Freud suddenly gives her a slap to stop her.

DORA Sometimes she wondered if she herself were not Mr K. In his place, how she would have loved her!

FREUD She said that she would have liked to sleep on the grass of his chest.

DORA Whose? You know that you mean everything to me. To whom? Do I mean nothing to you?

FREUD The worst of it was that he felt like a fool when deep down inside the greatest dream was just beginning.

MR B. Then my fear was perfectly natural.

FREUD Naturally.

MR B. That can't be right! One can have the need to go out at night. 650

FREUD And if someone awakened her?

DORA Papa came over to my bed. He awoke me with a kiss; he protected me. How beautiful everything was when he loved no one more than me and when he would awaken me!

FREUD Go on.

DORA And now . . .

Mr K. smokes. I smoke. Passionately. Papa too is a passionate smoker.

FREUD Given that I too am a smoker.

DORA I have to go. I have to run away. I can't stay any longer.

FREUD But who takes whose place in this story?

DORA Yes. Everyone. Except me. 660

[*sudden outburst*] How I adored him! My God! How he loved me, then.

FREUD Yes, who takes whose place? At one time, he stood beside your bed. He used to wake you up with a kiss. And what if it were your father who was standing beside your bed? Instead of Mr K.

DORA And now, what am I to him?

FREUD And Mr K.?

DORA [*looking at* MRS K.] I feel absolutely nothing for that man.

Papa takes advantage of the opportunities that Mr K. allows him. Mr K. takes advantage of the opportunities that Papa allows him. Everyone knows how to manage.

FREUD And Dora?

DORA He didn't want to look too closely into Mr K.'s behaviour, that would have disturbed him in his   670
relations with her.

FREUD And you?

DORA I never went to see her when Papa was there. It was only natural. I was glad that he had found a woman
that he could get attached to. What my father does is none of my business.

FREUD And what Dora does?

DORA I don't blame anyone. How could I blame him? My reproaches were unfair. He sacrificed me to
that woman. She took him away from me. But how could I blame her?

FREUD Who is to blame then?

DORA Who betrays whom in this story? No one. There are no reproaches? . . . Give me my coat. I'm leaving.

[As she leaves FREUD, *she is repeating all her departures, she is already gone, she doesn't*   680
look at him: she sees herself, moving away again, being abandoned

DORA Alone again. Everyone else stays behind. You let me go. I was the first to hang up my coat on the
coat rack. And you all hung your coats on top of mine. That was a way of saying: You're not wanted
here.

DORA [*in a slow, sleepy voice*] I'm taking back this coat. Too beautiful for me. It was a coat that wasn't familiar
to me, the skin of an animal that I don't know, extraordinarily fine and supple, light-coloured, with an
orangey tint to it.

Is it mine? I went through the pockets to make sure. He had warned me so many times. I might have
left something in the pockets: some letters?

MR K.'s VOICE What carelessness! I warned you a thousand times!   690

DORA It didn't matter any more.

[Sound of paper being slipped into a pocket

FREUD What are you crumpling up in your pocket?

DORA Nothing. Good-bye.

[She exits noisily

FREUD'S VOICE In a dazzling silence, she walks back along the burning streets of Linz, moving slowly,
stiffened with deadly mourning. She says nothing. She feels minuscule. A convulsed speck of dust. She
knows the horror of regret, far more powerful than desire.

DORA Nearly dead from exhaustion. All that might have been. Exhausts me.

MR K.'s VOICE Where are you going?   700

DORA To a place where I, too, may sleep.

As far as going ahead is concerned, I am ready to give that up.

FREUD She felt used. Ridiculed.

DORA I could have said Yes. Just once! His mouth would have smelled of smoke. You haven't understood
anything! You've never understood anything then?

FREUD If only she had been able to speak . . .

DORA It isn't my fault. When one can no longer speak, one is dead. If I wrote him a superhuman letter, with
my blood, if I explained to him who I could have been if I could have if he looked at me if I showed him,
my hands in my pockets, the letters rolled up in my hands, if I proved to him my strength my life my
worth right here where I'm burning if I caught his eye just long enough to set the sea on fire, and cast   710
the sun into a cage, if I stung him with this regret if I excited him. And then if I brought him down, if
I crushed him . . .

[silence

FREUD It remains to be seen why you felt so offended by Mr K.'s advances?

DORA [*in a voice that descends upon* FREUD *from far above from far away*] Good-bye.

[*Blackout*

[*then she murmurs*

[*chanting*] *One never knows who the killer is, dying can kill. Who wants to kill who wants to die who wants to make someone die I don't know who any more*, did I know it before, I know that I did, I knew it before I wanted to, but as soon as I wanted to, what? What's holding me back, if I am held back but I'm not, is the other. But is it, and the other if it is the other is it him or her or? One can kill by putting oneself to death.

MR K. I'm taking the keys and I'm going to shoot.

[*A pistol shot*

And I'm taking back my keys.

DORA How can I forgive you?

MR. K. You know me. I would have given everything.

What I have given I'm taking back.

DORA Give me back the keys. Such tiny little keys.

MR K. I'm taking them back.

DORA This isn't the first time. Is this all that it's come to?

FREUD On the threshold.

DORA Aren't I on time? Why are you looking at me that way? So insistently?

FREUD I'm not looking at you insistently.

DORA Why not?

FREUD No, no. None of that. You know very well that I'm an institution.

DORA Do you mind if I take off my shoe?

[FREUD *is silent. He sighs*

My foot hurts. Does my foot bother you? Is it deformed in some way?

[*she laughs*] All right, tell me something, and I'll do it, just to please you.

FREUD Put your shoe back on and tell me a dream.

DORA Who was that?

FREUD Who?

DORA You know very well. That woman. This isn't the first time I've seen her leaving here. I see everything. You, too, like playing secrets.

FREUD No, she's a former patient; she kept up relations with my family after her recovery.

DORA Relations with my fa-mi-ly.

FREUD Come now, don't act like a child. Believe me. And tell me your dream.

DORA Don't act like a child.

MRS K. Come here. Tell me what's new with you.

DORA I have nothing to tell. There's never anything new.

MRS K. Tell me a little about yourself.

DORA Can't you love me a little? Just a little bit?

MRS K. Why yes, I can love you a little. But what does that mean? To love?

DORA You don't love me at all then? I don't appeal to you at all?

MRS K. Why I don't even think about it! You *are* lovable.

Someone will love you. I love everything about you.

DORA There's nothing I can give you? Is it out of the question that you might need me?

MRS K. I need nothing, no one. That doesn't mean that you are nothing.

DORA Will you see me again?

MRS K. Why not?

720

730

740

750

760

DORA One day, I would like to be lying against you. Not sitting – Lying against you. I close my eyes, and I see. There would be blood all over. I would have blood on my face.

MRS K. How gory! Me, I see you standing up, very much alive, getting ready for a journey . . .

DORA And me, I see you dead. I would like to see you dead. So that no one could touch you. Or see you.

MR K. That's what one thinks when one's ten years old.

DORA When one has too much love.

MRS K. The most desirable the most dreadful.

[*Silence*

DORA I had a dream. 770

FREUD Tell me your dream.

DORA I dreamed about you . . .

[*she stops short*

FREUD Tell me your dream.

DORA What will you give me?

FREUD [*smiling*] Not a jewellery box. But all of my attention.

DORA It's curious, I see myself climbing *the stairs that lead to your apartment. I ring the bell. Your former patient opens the door and says to me: "You may come in, he's already dead"*. I look at her face. Although she's at least ten years older than me, her skin is fresh, her features are full-blown and natural-looking. I don't realize until later that she is abnormally tall. *After she tells me this, I don't feel the least bit sad. I notice that there* 780 *are a lot of women waiting in a parlour; to become household employees.*

Just then I hear a dance melody. The young woman comes over and asks me to dance. She puts her arm around my waist. A little surprised as I was expecting a male partner instead, I accept. Who am I? Who am I following? *I don't know how to dance*; but I let myself be led. I feel awkward. I propose, or she proposes, a third person, a man or a woman, I don't know which.

[DORA *murmurs*] *I wonder who I am to her. We dance our way downstairs; I dance badly.*

Then I realize that I feel awkward too because my knickers have fallen down to my knees.

[*She leans her head on her partner's shoulder and sighs*

I lift my dress and pull them up right in front of my partners. I realize that all three of us have been your patients and I wonder if you had a preference. *What do you think about it*? 790

FREUD And you?

DORA I didn't feel the least bit sad. I felt an unspeakable tenderness for my companion, but my awkwardness kept me from feeling it. It was only when I woke up that I felt overwhelmed with sorrow, as if I had really loved her, and then lost her.

FREUD Didn't it ever occur to you that something stood in the way of your wish to have your father rescue you from some danger: the thought that it was your father himself who had exposed you to this danger?

DORA What does that have to do with anything? Is that all that you can come up with?

FREUD That thought doesn't appeal to you.

DORA [*exasperated*] What's the connection? Good God! What's the connection?

During the dance, I felt very awkward, but very mellow, as if I were overflowing with tenderness. At 800 one point it's strange, she tells me that she has to carry this heavy bag around with her, every day. I offer to replace her, to relieve her for a while. But instead of carrying it by the handle as she was doing, I sling it over my shoulder bandoleer-style, and I tell her that my arms are too weak and limp, but that my shoulders are strong. In fact, this bag was so extraordinarily heavy that, staggering under the weight of it, I had to go and crouch down at the edge of space, at the edge of the road so as not to be carried away by my own burden. Impossible to go a step further.

FREUD And the dead man?

DORA I knew that you were dead. That was understood between us. I wasn't coming to see you in fact, because that's just it, we had this understanding between us. So I was coming to hear or to share the news. 810

FREUD Do you know why you wanted to kill me?

DORA No, do you?

FREUD And with the young woman, you didn't feel threatened?

DORA No, not really. It was more a feeling of awkwardness. As though I were backward, mentally. In one sense, I was flattered that she had confidence in me, but I realized that I was disappointing her: I was dancing badly, I was caught up in my knickers. I no longer thought about your being dead. It was as if you always had been. Or as if it were normal for you to have always been dead.

FREUD That's not untrue. But perhaps I'm not. For you.

DORA Perhaps. Yes. It doesn't matter.

FREUD We'll speak about this again. See you on Tuesday? 820

DORA Perhaps.

FREUD You'll let me know . . . I'll accompany you.

DORA No.

DORA [*sharp outbursts in a staccato voice*] This-treatment-is-taking-too-long. How much longer?

FREUD I told you: one year. So there are still six more months to go.

DORA One year, why? Why not two years? or two days?

FREUD You still need some help for a few more months.

DORA I don't need a governess.

FREUD Did you ever have a governess?[3]

DORA Oh, yes! She was an unmarried woman, no longer young, who was well read and very liberal-minded. 830

FREUD Was she pretty? Seductive?

DORA No. She was flabby.

MR B. That woman is constantly trying to turn my daughter against Mrs K.

DORA I got on rather well with her.
      She didn't like Mrs K. She explained to my mother that it was incompatible with her dignity, to tolerate such an intimacy between her husband and another woman.

FREUD Did she have any influence on you?

DORA She was in love with Papa. But I didn't hold it against her. For that matter, my father never paid any attention to her.

MR B. She quarrelled with her all of a sudden and insisted upon her dismissal. 840

FREUD And what ever became of her?

DORA She was dismissed. And two hours later, she was gone, without saying a word.

DORA How would they be able to walk, were I not there to fall?

MR B. You are stronger than all of us put together.

VOICE OF THE PLAY They all pick up their guns. They spray Dora with thousands of pearls to prove that she is stronger than all of them put together. They prove it, in a cloud of smoke.
      When the smoke clears, one sees Dora's ghost, stronger than all of them, gathering thousands of these little pearls into the lap of her apron, and then releasing the corners of the apron over an open attaché case. This is in case they should run out of ammunition.[4]

DORA There was also a governess who did that at the K.'s.

FREUD Really! You have never told me about her before.

DORA She behaved in the strangest way to Mr K. She never greeted him, never answered him, never passed him anything at the table; in short, she treated him as if he didn't exist. For that matter, he was hardly any politer to her. A day or two before the scene by the lake, she told me that Mr K. had begged her not to refuse him anything; he had told her that his wife meant nothing to him, etc. . . .

FREUD Why, those are the words . . .

DORA Yes. She gave in. Afterward, he stopped caring for her; from that time on, she hated him.

FREUD And what became of this girl?

DORA I only know that she went away. 860

FREUD If he had persisted anyway, if he had continued to woo her with a passion capable of winning her over, perhaps love would have triumphed over all of the difficulties? Incidentally, this scheme would by no means have been so impracticable. Mrs K. would consent to a divorce, and, as for your father, you can get whatever you want out of him.

DORA What I wanted? And you, what do you want?

DORA Mr K. was serious when he spoke to me I think.

FREUD Yes.

DORA But I didn't let him finish.

FREUD What were his actual words?

DORA I don't remember anymore. He said to me: you know that my wife means nothing to me. And I cut 870
him off immediately.

MR K. You know that my wife means nothing to me.

DORA In order to avoid meeting him again, I decided to get back to Linz on foot, by walking around the lake, and I asked a passer-by how long it would take me. He said: two and a half hours. I remember another detail: in my dream I saw the "inside" of the forest, as though I could penetrate it with my vision. From far away, I saw flowers . . . Beds of flowers. They were white. Suddenly, a young-looking woman appeared.

MRS K. What are you looking for?

DORA I saw a big bed of white flowers in the distance. Are they forbidden? No.

MRS K. Those plants grow naturally, and abundantly. 880

DORA How long does it take?

MRS K. They're quite far away. The flower-bed must be about two kilometres from here overland.

DORA That's too far. I give up.

I went back to the boat after all. Mr K. was on board.

MR K. And I beg you to forgive me, and to say nothing about what happened.

DORA And what if I told your wife?

You offer me a cigarette. And I agree to postpone my departure for twenty-four hours because you assure me that you will help me tomorrow. Out of weariness, I agree to spend the night with you. You smoke two cigarettes. You have one in your mouth and one in your hand. You never stop talking. 890

This can't go on any longer. Besides, the cigarette is burning out.

FREUD [*insinuating voice*] Just one more puff!

DORA Well, let's hurry up and get it over with then!

FREUD [*insinuating voice*] And what if we went on a journey somewhere?

DORA I don't have the strength to start all over again. I accepted the cigarette out of weariness. But it's impossible for me to desire. I can no longer smoke or travel. Adieu, adieu! Where is the station?

FREUD Were those lilies-of-the-valley that were growing in big white patches next to the forest, just a kilometre or two away from your hand?

DORA And if the white flowers had been blue, would I have given up?

[Imitating her mother's voice] I am told: Shame on you! Dora, what are you doing? That's poison. It 900
makes people stupid.

DORA Where! is! the! station! [She shouts]

VOICE OF THE PLAY What lilies-of-the-valley say in a dream

Mr K. said with a jewellery box.

What one says with flowers

Papa said with pearls

What Dora did not say

The Doctor said with smoke.

DORA At last, at last, I arrive at the station.

MR K. There's no train. The rails have been cut. 910

Are you annoyed at seeing me?

DORA Frankly – Yes.

MR K. Is this the last time I'll see you?

DORA [a furtive silence – that's like a look]

MR K. Such silence! You, who were usually so talkative.

FREUD [in a normal voice] You knew there would be no train? No flowers for the forest; no train for the station. This is no accident. There is something you don't want to touch or catch.

DORA I arrive at the station. I am alone. You had insisted that I come.

FREUD This journey to Vienna would last six months, perhaps. Or rather nine.

MR K. Dora, my little darling. You know how much I care for you. 920

DORA You treated me like a servant. I'm abandoning you. No one will accompany me. I am alone in a strange city. I am looking at a painting of the Madonna. No one touches me. I will never marry.

MRS K. You are a virgin, my little pal!

FREUD And you spent hours gazing at this portrait?

DORA Her whiteness was so soothing.

FREUD That's what you thought about Mrs K.

DORA No, it's me!

[A dance melody

MRS K. Why don't you dance?

DORA She was a mature woman by then. But age had not touched her. She spent most of her life in bed, 930
for that matter.

MRS K. Wouldn't you like to have children? You have such a motherly way with my children! Why don't you dance? There, that's what I like. One must be gay, active, live life to the fullest. You, you're always so serious.

DORA That's true. No. Yes.

MRS K. You're so serious! You're too serious, my little pal.

DORA She lectured me gaily. It's true that I was serious and reserved. She said to me: you're always so serious, my little pal. My little pal! It's strange, isn't it? I asked her questions about being pregnant and giving birth. And she liked to satisfy my curiosity. To talk to me about virginity and childbirth, things of that sort. 940

MRS K. You're always so serious, my little pal: too serious. Be careful. One must know where to draw the line. Do you know where to draw the line? You can't be a Madonna. You are too handsome, my little pal.

DORA Too handsome! That's strange.

MRS K. It's so easy to make a false step. Listen.

[*Whispering*] You don't know how to live.

It is rather sweet, though. I could be your mother. Listen . . .

DORA What if I pounced on her? Pushed her around? Gave her a spanking? She doesn't love me. If she could see herself. I'm too headstrong to let my head be turned by her. I could take my revenge.

FREUD Yet how do you explain the fact that you've always so generously spared Mrs K., your slanderer, while you persecute the others with an almost sly vindictiveness . . .?   950

DORA She had slow and gentle movements, which I loved. One day, a long time ago, I had twisted my right foot slipping on the stairs. My foot swelled up. She had to bandage it for me. I had to lie up for several weeks. She kept me company and spoke to me as if I were her girlfriend. She confided in me. She told me that her husband didn't want a divorce because of the children.

FREUD Didn't you think a divorce would have been the best thing for everyone?

DORA I had the strangest dream. I was running. I had a bad pain in my right foot. I had to sit down. My ankle had swollen up. I couldn't move anymore. I wanted to talk to Dr K. At the same time, I knew that he wasn't a real doctor. I wanted to ask his advice. I ask for him on the 'phone. Finally I get him. And it isn't him, it's his wife. I feel her presence over the 'phone, obscure, white, insinuating.

MRS K. [*on the 'phone*] Who is calling?   960

DORA She says to me.

It's Mrs K. . . . I say.

MRS K. [*on the 'phone*] You don't say!

DORA Strange situation!

MRS K. [*on the 'phone*] What nerve!

DORA [*in a hushed voice, without any embarrassment*] I know. Put him on.

MRS K. [*on the 'phone*] Very well.

DORA She puts him on. He tells me that there isn't much he can do: that I'll have to wait until next year. I laugh. He says: "You know that . . ." But I don't let him finish. I cut him off.

FREUD Exactly, you don't let things finish. Your ankle swells up. You give birth. Nine months after the   970 scene by the lake. So, in spite of everything, you manage to have a "child" by Mr K. Something happened during the scene by the lake.

DORA Nothing happened!

FREUD Precisely. That's where you made that false step whose consequences, even today, are still affecting you. You regretted it. You still regret the outcome of that scene. It's not the Madonna that you wanted to be. Your love for Mr K. doesn't end there.

[DORA *is silent*

FREUD Why did you keep him from going on?

DORA Is that all?

FREUD I'm not dissatisfied with the results.   980

DORA You're giving birth to a mouse.

DORA Do you know, Doctor, that I am here for the last time?

FREUD Is that so!

DORA Yes, I told myself that I'd try to be patient, but I don't want to wait any longer to be "cured."

FREUD You know that you are free to stop the treatment at any time. When did you come to this decision?

DORA Two weeks ago, I think.

FREUD Two weeks? That's the notice a governess gives before leaving.

DORA Are you alone? Where is your wife?

[*The tempo in this last part should be extremely violent*

FREUD'S VOICE Did he or did he not want to cure her, in his own time, or did he want to only on that 1st   990
of January 1900, he will never know and neither will I and neither will she.

DORA If only I simply knew where I am now, in what country. I could begin to believe.

FREUD You didn't give me a chance to finish expressing myself!

Your tendency toward self-injury profited there. Never before have I felt such violence.

DORA I am here for the last time today.

FREUD [*doesn't conceal his panic*] You're taking your revenge on me as you would have liked to take your
revenge on Mr K. And you are abandoning me as he abandoned you.

DORA You don't understand anything. That won't prevent you from existing! Here is my revenge: I'll go
on "alone." I'll get well "alone." And I've decided to abandon you on a day determined by me. It will
be the 1st of January 1900.   1000

FREUD Listen . . . Your decision . . . We had decided . . .

DORA No.

FREUD You know . . .

I admit . . .

I am stupefied. But I was expecting it. I'd never really thought about it. I could have sworn it. How
well I understand her! Too well!

MR K. I found her beautiful. She seemed taller to me, too.

DORA This desire still this desire. Yes.

FREUD This is a murder that you're committing here. Of someone else whom I rep . . .

[DORA'*s calm smile cuts him off*   1010

Why didn't you tell me sooner?

[*She listens to him in a deafening silence*

DORA Should I have chosen another day? Yes . . . You could have gotten your wife to stay here?

FREUD [*bitterly*] You are trying to hurt someone else through me . . .

DORA Dear Doctor, you are an institution. So, respect the will and the point of view of a patient who wishes
you well.

MR B. *I assure you, Doctor, that my daughter will come back again.*

FREUD *She will not come back again.*

DORA Act as if I had never come. As if I were dead.

Do you deny having kissed me?   1020

MR K. No.

DORA [*to* MRS K.] I know that you're having an affair with Papa.

FREUD Maybe you know too much? Or, in a way, not enough?

DORA [*mockingly*] And what if that were true? What if I did know too much. Always too much? A little bit
more than all of you?

FREUD No. Rather not enough.

DORA Or maybe you love yourself a little too much?

FREUD Stop and think. Don't hurt yourself.

DORA You could make me laugh. But I don't want to hurt you. Because you, Doctor, I would never have
loved.   1030

FREUD I could have succeeded. What stops me short, is the date, the 1st of January, there's still this
one drop of time that resists, that holds my breath in my chest. I would need another lifetime. I
could . . .

DORA [*cutting in and lashing out*] You could – push me, knock me down the stairs? Propose one last session.

Well thought out? Look relieved that I'm leaving, while at the same time letting me see that you're hiding your satisfaction?

Tell me that you're delighted with my decision. That you were hoping for it? Counting on it? That you'd foreseen it. That I'm thus fulfilling your fondest desire?

You could – you couldn't – give me a beating. I wouldn't defend myself. If you could slap me. We would both take a certain pleasure in it.   1040

FREUD I would have taught you what I have learned from you. [*With effort*] I would really have liked to do something for you.

DORA No one can do anything.

FREUD Do let me hear from me [*he makes a slip of the tongue in such a way that it might go unnoticed*]. Write to me.

DORA Write? . . . That's not my affair.

VOICE OF THE PLAY In May of 1900. In Vienna, at a crossroads where there was a great deal of traffic, Dora saw Mr K. get knocked down by a carriage. She saw him fall. It was the most horrible day of her life. It was the happiest day of her life. She walked across the avenue dry-shod, lifting her elegant dress with her fingertips, barely allowing her ankles to show. It was only a minor accident. The inside of   1050 Mr K. was in hell, his outward appearance was still prepossessing. He had seen Dora pass. There is no greater sorrow than the memory of love.

And that, Freud knew.

THE END

Notes to *Portrait of Dora*

1 [Translator's note] This translation is based on the 1976 edition which differs slightly from the 1986 edition.
2 The above sequence was not retained when the play was first performed.
3 The following sequence was not performed.
4 The above sequence was not performed.

BLACK SAIL WHITE SAIL

TRANSLATED BY DONALD WATSON

Characters (in order of appearance)

ANNA ANDREYEVNA AKHMATOVA

NADEZHDA YAKOVLEVNA MANDELSTAM,
a friend

LYDIA KORNEYEVNA CHUKOVSKAYA, a
friend

PAULINE, called Polonius, the neighbour

NINA RADLOVA, Secretary of the Leningrad
Writers' Union

A BABOUSHKA at the Moscow railway station

Present though absent

Osip Mandelstam, died in exile in 1938

Lev Goumilev (Liova), arrested and interned
in 1937

Nikolai Goumilev, Liova's father,
Akhmatova's first husband, killed by firing
squad in 1921

Absent though present

Boris Pasternak

Between Leningrad and Moscow and near these two cities: forests, rivers and country residences.
Between 1953 and 1960. Stalin died on 5 March 1953.

They use countless little Russian nicknames in addressing one another: Nadia, Nadinka, Lida,
Lidinka, Anouchka, etc. The actresses can use these whenever they feel the need.

The landscapes are vast, stretching far, high and wide. Rather than a set, a space with nothing
more than what's indispensable to the actresses.

AKHMATOVA'S ROOM is a whole world in a chaotic nutshell. A chair with only three legs has had
its fourth replaced by any handy object. She mislays everything, hunts for everything. The things
she wears were once elegant, now out of fashion, threadbare and – due to her majestic indifference
rather than the exigences of her day – sometimes in tatters. She neither sews nor mends. Her
silk dressing-gown is in need of repair. She drapes herself in her celebrated shawls when the
occasion offers. Her dress sense is appropriate for grandeur or decadence.

AKHMATOVA'S HANDBAG is her safe, her secretary's desk, her attic, her pharmacy, her boudoir,
her nomad's tent.

NADEZHDA'S SPECTACLES: Akhmatova is constantly borrowing them.

Scene 1

A winter forest on the outskirts of Leningrad.

Enter AKHMATOVA *and* NADEZHDA MANDELSTAM

AKHMATOVA Is there much further to go?

NADEZHDA Hang on to me, Anna Andreyevna, I'm sure we'll see the Neva the other side of that clump of birch trees. There's only this pond to cross.

AKHMATOVA Then I stop here. Don't go on about it. I can't cross that.

NADEZHDA I won't.

AKHMATOVA If you do, I'll fall. Fall and break my right leg here and now.

And on our very last day in Leningrad. On top of skin cancer, I've already got TB, rheumatism all over and a heart condition. As if that's not enough, am I to break my bones in the middle of a forest in order to follow Nadezhda Mandelstam one more time beyond the limits of human endurance?

NADEZHDA Human endurance! One frozen pond.   10

AKHMATOVA For thirty years I've been telling the whole world that I refuse to crawl like a bitch on all fours or wriggle along like a worm. A short walk, you said. We'll gather some wood and then go home. I've done my bit. Now I want to go home.

NADEZHDA Oh, please . . . We're so close to the Neva. We'll take it easy and cling on to each other.

AKHMATOVA Staggering on, you and I, all our lives. Poetry on crutches. Forging onward, slipping, losing our balance, risking death, picking ourselves up again. All simply to survive. Don't push me, Nadinka. It's like my translating. Having to translate and not write. To earn her daily bread Akhmatova is killing herself translating foreign poets.

NADEZHDA Now let's move on.

AKHMATOVA Give me a minute. I don't even know how to translate. You remember how Mandelstam used   20
to moan about his publishers. A pack of hounds at his heels, barking "Translate! Translate! Forget about Mandelstam! Give us some Verlaine!" It drove him mad.

NADEZHDA You're right. Osip felt that translating was serving up Mandelstam's brain as mere fodder.

AKHMATOVA The same for me. It's like crossing this pond. It may mean death. And a pointless one too.

NADEZHDA One more little effort and then we'll see the glint of the river in its casket of ice. Won't we?

AKHMATOVA No more little efforts. The story of my life is one enormous effort to survive. I can get by without a river. Not without a body. *Right here* I'll survive. You go on without me.

NADEZHDA You don't mind?

AKHMATOVA I'll wait for you. It's what I'm best at. No limits there. You go. I'll still be here when you get   30
back. Akhmatova, in the sunshine, a frozen human stone among my sisters, the terrestrial stones. Go.

[*Exit* NADEZHDA

[AKHMATOVA *settles down on a tree-trunk or a rock*

AKHMATOVA [*to the audience, to the clouds, to the world*] You stones and wintry conifers, you clouds, spirits of the living and the dead, riding astride our dismal Russian winds, you find I have changed this year, don't you? I do too, you know. When I comb my hair in the morning, I can see two Akhmatovas: the one in the mirror, a peasant woman, stubborn and centuries old – and just beside her on the wall that other face of a famous beauty captured by Modigliani, Queen of all the Russians, who launched hundreds of poems into our mother tongue. She was once me. This century has cruelly clothed our youthfulness in the vestments of old age. Only our young murdered husbands retain their youth. Look   40
at my hands. The delicate hands of a child, from which so many images took wing, now bloated with anguish and sterility. Osip and I were barely thirty-five, when the establishment said we were too old.

They tried to drive us out. Quick, away with you, poets, you are obsolete. But I'm still here. Sitting on a tree stump in 1953. I look down on a century that we've imprisoned in ice. Year after year the same scene being played out in the square. With the same characters, bodies in funereal raincoats, hats with no faces, dragging Russia off for interrogation. Fashions never change. Yet in one morning sorrow can age us thirty years. I know there's a rumour abroad that the Georgian with the smarmy verminous moustache – as Mandelstam used to say – ended his monstrous existence a few weeks ago. Do you believe it? I don't. Doesn't my son Liova lie in Leviathan's dungeon?

Yet the distant landscape is still as beautiful. It's the loveliest land in the world. The snow smells of apples and the schoolyard. Can you imagine a vista more luminous, more appealing? No, it's too beautiful! It's almost a crime to be here!   50

At this very moment the birch trees conspire, their branches lovely as women's arms, to fill me with joy, so for one whole minute I forget my son in his labour camp and my lovers who have all been shot. To be widowed four or five times and yet still feel the song of the earth pulsating through my whole body. This is my crime, but the forest is to blame. We must go home, Nadezhda.

[*A sound like thunder is heard: it is the melting ice cracking and colliding on the Neva*
Did you hear that? The first thunder of the thaw already! [*She plays with the branches*] I'm pursued by the cross. One for my husband Goumilev, one for my husband Punin, one for Osip, my only friend. A cross for me and a cross for Nadezhda. We don't even know where our dead are laid to rest, whether   60
South or North, as their bodies disintegrate and phosphoresce in the soil.

In sleep and survival our dead are with us. We swallow them with our wine, we inhale them with the pungent air we breathe. With his hand laid lightly on my shoulder the spirit of Mandelstam reads the book of the earth beside me.

I don't know who watches over whom. Our poems, banned from books, wander the streets like minstrels without their lyre. Some give them asylum. Others drive them into exile.

You see how the cross follows me. It signals to me. It remembers dates. Today is the 11th of March, a horrible anniversary. Fifteen years ago at dawn I heard Liova had been arrested. Since then the hollow glow of that dawn keeps the flame of my sorrow burning. That day spelt out my stations of the cross: all those featureless faces in the queue, mine is number 300. Lips blue with cold, parcels suddenly and   70
horribly rejected at those prison windows which were my only hope. Since 1938, one bonded to the other, Akhmatova and Liova have been slowly dying. How many more lifetimes must I kowtow and crawl on my knees?

[*Thunder*

Did you hear that? Spring is in a hurry this year! What innocence!

NADEZHDA [*calling*] Anna Andreyevna! Anna Andreyevna! Did you hear? It's starting!

AKHMATOVA Yes!

NADEZHDA Are you sure you won't come? To see the Neva returning to life?

AKHMATOVA No. How's the sky?

NADEZHDA Mad with birds. The grebes look drunk as they fly. You should come and see them. Against a   80
restless sky spelling out thousands of words. I'll take you there.

AKHMATOVA No, no! I don't need to see them, I can hear. That's enough for me. Come back, Nadinka, you can tell me all about it. How strange! It's as if she herself had become Osip. She lives two lives in one.

NADEZHDA *reappears*

Why should I watch the thaw anyway? It doesn't lie there, my destiny. Shall I ever see for one single hour just one of the faces I long to before I die? Shall I ever see Liova smile at me, when he's released? And my book? *The Poems of Anna Akhmatova*. No: *Anna Akhmatova: Complete Works*. Is that a face I shall ever see? No. What does my friend Esperanza say? What hope is there for me?

NADEZHDA For me it's a duty . . . Yes. A mission. To remain alive in Russia until Mandelstam's poetry rises from the abyss. 90

AKHMATOVA And from where I am, I can see our future as clearly as a bird of prey. Or the dead. And I can tell you tomorrow looks as much like today as two horrid identical twins. Publication is out. Oh, but who can I see over there? . . . It's our Lydia Korneyevna! A white sail or a black one? Well, look, can't you? She's scared of falling too. Can you see her? No, of course you can't. Everyone around me is blind as a bat.

NADEZHDA Can you see someone?

[*To the audience*] Can *you* see anyone?

AKHMATOVA Yet I see everything, before anyone else. Even hawk-eyed Osip. When we took the tram in Leningrad, I was always the first to see if it was an A or a B. I could beat him more than half a mile away. Here she comes now. She's seen us. 100

NADEZHDA Well, what's it to be, Anna Andreyevna? Black sail or white sail?

Enter LYDIA

LYDIA I must love you dearly, Anna Andreyevna . . .! You'll be so happy. They're going to publish your book! It's all settled, I promise you! And I've been accepted at last by the Writers' Union. I've actually seen Fadeyev myself. Trust me. He gave me his word. They will publish.

AKHMATOVA *The Poems of Anna Akhmatova*?

LYDIA *The Poems of Anna Akhmatova*. He promised. You just have to go and see him. He'll receive you straightaway.

AKHMATOVA All of a sudden. After thirty years of being spurned. So what does he want in exchange?

LYDIA Why nothing, I assure you. He admires you, and at last he's had the guts to say so. It will be a real event in Russia. Such a joy! 110

AKHMATOVA And what are they going to exclude? *Requiem*?

LYDIA *Requiem*, I don't know. Of course . . . it's possible the two poems about Mandelstam . . .

AKHMATOVA No, not those. That's impossible. I can't, Lida, no really I can't.

LYDIA You have to start somewhere, Anna Andreyevna. It would be a sin to refuse. It's a long struggle, but we'll win them all back, page by page. Every word, every line must resound. Your voice must come out of the tomb.

AKHMATOVA Nadezhda, how would you have advised Osip?

LYDIA I'd have told him to publish. But I don't know what he'd have done.

AKHMATOVA I'll think it over. I'm going to commune . . . with the birds and with my dead. 120

LYDIA No, that's not right. It's up to us, the living, to be your oracle.

AKHMATOVA Thirty years . . . I'll have to think it over. I'll need you to help me, Lydia Korneyevna. Half my verse exists in your memory. The other half noted down in mine. Perhaps there is some on paper. I must at least see what I've got. Let's go back at once. And then to Moscow. It's all in Moscow . . . Hold me, Nadezhda.

LYDIA So you will publish? You agree?

AKHMATOVA In Moscow, we'll see. First, Lida, pen and paper. I've composed some beautiful lines. I'll recite them to you. You can write them down. Then I'll make up my mind. But what would Osip say? Watch out for my galoshes. I don't want to get too carried away.

[LYDIA *reties the laces* 130

Tell me, Nadezhda, what colour were the waters of the Neva? When she gallops on her own back in full mutation I have seen pink ones riding over grey ones and breaking them up. Tell me about it. You've told me about the sky but you haven't mentioned the river.

NADEZHDA If you give me a chance, I'll tell you.

[*Thunder*

AKHMATOVA Well?

NADEZHDA The mirror was shattered, but the fir trees were still searching for their lost reflection.

AKHMATOVA That Fadeyev has started to melt too. I was sure winter would never end. So what now?

NADEZHDA To think Osip used to call you a dark angel hovering over the snow!

AKHMATOVA He loved to invent me. But the real me loves the sea and swimming in it. Let's move on. 140
No, we are not three widows bowed down by fate. Anyone who could see us now scurrying for
Leningrad would see three sails scudding along to eternity.

[*They go out. Thunder*

LYDIA Break, winter! Let the rivers sing out again! When Akhmatova's work is published, you'll see, her
poems will fall like burning tears on your frozen breasts and melt your wintry thoughts. We'll start to
love and laugh again. Ah, how my dreams overtake reality! How I long to see this spring before I die.
Shall we, I wonder?

Scene 2

AKHMATOVA *and* NADEZHDA *arrive in* AKHMATOVA'*s room in Moscow*

AKHMATOVA My notebook! Someone's touched my poems! Our benefactors have been here! Look! The
hair is missing.

NADEZHDA What hair?

AKHMATOVA I'd slipped it in my notebook, here, at this page. No, it's not here, it's missing. They've been
poking around. I had a premonition.

NADEZHDA No, they can't have been here. I know them. Do you honestly think, if they had, they'd have
left everything exactly as it was?

AKHMATOVA Except for that hair.

NADEZHDA One hair, that's no proof. They'd have left cigarette butts in the ashtray. They leave their mark
when they come, they make a mess of everything. No, it can't be. 10

AKHMATOVA I'm sorry to say it, but *they – have – been – here*. I know what I'm saying. I guessed it at once.
When I had that 'phone call yesterday. Then I knew it.

NADEZHDA What 'phone call?

AKHMATOVA A woman's voice, a mad woman: "Anna Andreyevna I'm so moved to be talking to you. On
behalf of all the women who admire you." "Oh yes," I replied (I'd got the point.) – "Er . . . to read
what you write leaves one speechless." – "Oh yes?" – "I must thank you for all your poems. I'm not
disturbing you, am I?" – "No." – "For one in particular." "For one of them?" I asked. "Which one?"
(I'd cottoned on at once. It was all too obvious.) – "The last one," she said. – "The last one? What last
one?" – "You know. The one about the bees." – "Oh," I said, "You've got the wrong poet, wrong address
for the bees. Boris Pasternak keeps them." And I hung up. They want to know where I am, to keep me 20
on tenterhooks.

NADEZHDA But you do have some bees as well.

AKHMATOVA Yes, but unpublished. Besides, bees are everywhere. In Osip's work too. They're the best
ones. But this time, I tell you, the bees were as phoney as our admirer. Our informer. An attempt to
intimidate and stop me publishing.

NADEZHDA But no, that's impossible.

AKHMATOVA Oh, I know them: the girl students from Bessarabia who come bleating at your door like so
many lost lambs. They cling around you. You expect to find them curled up at night at the foot of
your bed. And in the morning I wake up with aches and pains . . . So I hung right up.

NADEZHDA But an informer . . . why? 30

AKHMATOVA Why? You ask me why? Is there rhyme or reason in their madness? Why on earth did they arrest Osip? For a poem. Because they wanted to arrest him. Are there ever any answers in our country? Look around you at this city. God mocks us with his gardens and his shimmering nights. The loveliest stars in the world up above and stool pigeons swarming below. That's the way things are. Nadezhda, I've started noting down my memories of Osip.

NADEZHDA At last! He will be pleased!

AKHMATOVA Twenty years don't mean much to a dead man! Osip didn't care at all for my verse.

NADEZHDA That's not true.

AKHMATOVA No matter, I worshipped his. He's the greatest of poets. And he had a child's faith in me. He used to come and show me each new love of his, as if they were marbles of agate. Only marbles. 40 He really knew the difference, Nadinka. You were his quartz heart. I'll read you my notes. [*She searches for them*] You were his magic touchstone, the axis on which his world turned. Well, you see what our benefactors have stolen: my notes on Mandelstam. So what about that hair now? And you thought I was mad. Look at the Bible. They've split the back of it.

NADEZHDA My Bible! Cretins! God is infinite. To tear Him apart would take forever!

AKHMATOVA And you want me to believe that Stalin is dead? [*To the audience*] No, he hasn't left us. His poisonous seed will pollute our water and our air for ten generations to come!

NADEZHDA [*pointing to "the curtain" that separates this room from the neighbour's*] The curtain . . . Anna Andreyevna, did you notice the curtain . . . when I said "God"?

AKHMATOVA It's Polonius. [*She opens the curtain*] Come in! Or rather, come out! Madam Pauline, is it 50 you, neighbour, who's been touching my things?

PAULINE What things? I only washed your cups up as a favour. And my name isn't Madam Pauline.

AKHMATOVA Now you listen to me comrade citizen! If you ever do me another "favour" of any kind at all, I'll denounce you to the police.

PAULINE To the police? You?

AKHMATOVA Absolutely. To *my* police. Aha! You think there's only one sort of police, and that's yours. How naive and trusting Russian women are! Only one police force! There are at least ten, comrade neighbour. What am I saying? Always *one more* than you think. Isn't a police force always needed to keep an eye on the police? A whole ladder of them from the cellar right to The Top of the Big House. Do you even know what rung of the ladder you're perched on? I, Akhmatova, will call on my own militia 60 and, believe me, I'll have plenty to tell them.

PAULINE You? You won't! She won't, will she?

AKHMATOVA I will. Let's see now: my neighbour called her filthy hound Iossif Stalin.

PAULINE Who, me? It's not true!

AKHMATOVA I've heard you, I swear it. "Sit, Stalin!" They'll believe me, you take my word. "Kennel, Stalin!"

PAULINE You wouldn't. She wouldn't, would she?

AKHMATOVA Do you think because I was born to breastfeed and wipe the blood off a child's brow, because I love the music of Mozart and Shostakovich, because I hate anti-Semitism, that I wouldn't dare lie like everyone else? Don't kid yourself, comrade. I can do *whatever* I like. Go on, back where you came 70 from, vanish!

[PAULINE *vanishes*

There! At least that's one fly swatted, squashed and flattened!

NADEZHDA I wonder how you could do it.

AKHMATOVA So do I! But I suddenly felt so strong that if Iossif you-know-who had been standing there I think I could have used these fingers to rip out his moustache. Like a Titan uprooting Olympus with one bare hand.

NADEZHDA Poor Pauline. She doesn't even hate us, yet she'd pack us off to hell.

AKHMATOVA "Poor Pauline" will be the death of us all. Scum like her are crawling all over Russia. She's just one of a multitude of Stalins. Nadezhda, if ever I go to the Writers' Union, will you come with me?   80

NADEZHDA Me? Not on your life! To start with, my visitor's permit ends the day after tomorrow. And then, as you well know, I'll never find the courage to face those crim . . . [curtain] cross-eyed creatures staring at me. Being so short-sighted myself. The telephone?

[She puts a cushion on it

AKHMATOVA Just to the corner of the street, Nadinka. Otherwise I'll never get there. Not with all those stairs. And then without you to cross Gorky Boulevard! Russians drive as if the devil were on their tails. And the tram! To die of suffocation in the tram! No. Not without you.

NADEZHDA So you have decided to go?

AKHMATOVA No, not yet I haven't. I'm just trying to imagine how Akhmatova will get there. And I simply can't see it. For my book's sake, you'll say, isn't it worth recanting a little? Would it really be a tragedy   90
to go and croak with the frogs just for once in thirty years?

NADEZHDA No, not a tragedy.

AKHMATOVA What holds me back is Osip. Before he left us he never did recant. And he dared confront Goliath armed with only one poem. I could have stopped him writing that poem. But I didn't.

NADEZHDA Stalin wasn't human. I swear it. The incarnation of a vampire. With lots of hair. Now he's dead, how else can you explain that he still persecutes us?

AKHMATOVA The curtain . . . And what about the capitalist countries?

Enter PAULINE

NADEZHDA They're short of everything. No herring in Paris. No sugar in London. You wait years to have a visitor's permit for the big cities. While I get one every year. And for a whole month.   100

PAULINE At least we're given the essentials.

AKHMATOVA We should offer her tea. Our comrade's working very hard these days.

PAULINE Don't trouble yourself. I just dropped in.

[She exits

NADEZHDA You know, if he'd lived, I think Osip . . . I don't think I'm betraying him when I say he would have published. I'm sure he would.

AKHMATOVA While Akhmatova's poems were suppressed?

NADEZHDA Yes. After a winter thirty winters long who would refuse a rose tree the chance to bloom again? At this moment, when his dust mixes with his much-loved blue sulphurs and his striped feldspars, I am sure he can hear us and dreams like you of an eternity of paper. Don't hesitate.   110

AKHMATOVA If you think that Osip – Then I'll ask Lydia Korneyevna to come with me.

Enter LYDIA

LYDIA Black sail! Fadeyev has killed himself.

NADEZHDA Well, it's no surprise to me! A final act of cowardice.

LYDIA That's hard of you!

AKHMATOVA A suicide! The demon! To escape the courtroom of life and not pay the penalty!

NADEZHDA How I hate these men who grant themselves a death they've denied to others. He could have seen Akhmatova, published her book and then said good-bye!

AKHMATOVA And published the works of Mandelstam. As he was going to die anyway! But no! Ever since Pushkin, we've known poets must get themselves killed! Shame on you, Fadeyev! A fake poet, fake man   120
and fake corpse.

NADEZHDA To the devil with him! And may he live in Hell in Akhmatova Street.

AKHMATOVA An Akhmatova Street in Hell! Heaven forbid!

NADEZHDA Mandelstam Street then! And who's to replace Fadeyev?

LYDIA Surkova. She's a good friend of my father's.

NADEZHDA So all is not lost?

LYDIA It all has to begin again. I'm off.

AKHMATOVA Brave captain!

NADEZHDA Let's hope she'll hold firm, this Surkova.

AKHMATOVA The Russian soul no longer has a right to sweet and gentle death. Death doesn't kill us now.   130
We die of murder and remorse. And no one to bear witness. Even Shakespeare with all his genius, with
all his murderers, his kingly assassins and assassinated kings, his stunning villains, his startling parricides,
could never have portrayed our violent history. He never has foretold us. Our Dante died with Osip.
The one violin that could sing of our new infernos lies broken now beneath an avalanche of ice.

NADEZHDA Now it's your turn, Anna Andreyevna, to garner our petrified tears.

AKHMATOVA One day in 1937, outside Leningrad's prisons, I was in the queue in front of the one . . .

NADEZHDA Curtain! Ssh . . .

AKHMATOVA Polonius is on form today! We need a raft, we'll go and look for a park bench.

[*They prepare to leave*

Once I was queuing at our "department stores." A blue-lipped woman whispers in my ear: "Could you   140
write about this?" I said I could. I was full of myself in those days. But I never did. "Department stores"
were beyond me. I never could curse in verse.

[*They go out*

There'll be no hymns to our glory. History has cut our throats.

[*They are gone.* PAULINE *comes back and starts poking about.*
She drapes herself in AKHMATOVA's *shawl, sniffs the empty perfume bottles, etc*

Scene 3

On a bench in Gorky Park. AKHMATOVA *is seated.* NADEZHDA *and* LYDIA *arrive. Springtime*

AKHMATOVA You're late! I love watching roses opening out, but there are limits!

NADEZHDA We've been looking at the roses too. But you did say the fifth.

AKHMATOVA The *fifth* bench? The *seventh* I said. You know perfectly well I'd never choose the number
5. Not the 5th. And never March. Right. Sit down! Lev Kvitko has been rehabilitated. Liova's friend.
Posthumously. And Meyerhold too. Posthumously of course.

NADEZHDA So there's still some hope for the dead! You hear that down there, Osip? My glorious mole?

AKHMATOVA He hears. And not just for the dead. I've been told the time has come to start campaigning
for Liova again. Dearest Lida, you must send off two letters at once. Let me tell you . . .

LYDIA But why me . . .?

AKHMATOVA You don't expect me to do it?! How could I? Find the right tone, the formal utterances, no,   10
not me. That means you.

NADEZHDA And the punctuation.

AKHMATOVA And the punctuation. So I'll pass you this precious address they gave me . . . of the person
to send it to . . . If anyone holds the key to Liova's fate, it's this man . . . And his name is . . .

[*she hunts through her handbag, dumping everything out onto the laps of*
LYDIA *and* NADEZHDA

No, that's a prescription – a reader – a woman admirer – a poem, etc. – it was a folded piece of paper
. . . Those young lads. Just now, in the bus. It was strange, at my age, they pressed so close to me . . .
They didn't take the money! . . .

NADEZHDA You don't think they just took that one piece of paper?   20

AKHMATOVA Surely not . . . My identity card! They took my identity card!

NADEZHDA Your identity card and not the money? Why do that?

AKHMATOVA Why indeed? To own Akhmatova's identity card? No. They don't know who Akhmatova is. So it's not even for my photo and my autograph. Just vindictiveness.

NADEZHDA You may have left it at home?

AKHMATOVA I'm not that crazy. Now those young hoodlums have taken my identity card, here I am namelessly adrift in the crowd, one of the herd.

LYDIA Now you have no papers, there's no point anyway writing those letters today. The card comes first.

AKHMATOVA Will I have to go to Leningrad, do you think, to get one made up?   30

LYDIA Perhaps. But that's something I can't do for you. First I'll go to the depot and make a complaint.

[*She goes out*

AKHMATOVA I did say the seventh bench, didn't I? Yet you waited for me on the fifth. I'm not superstitious, but I must say . . . You remember my poem: "A Tear"?

NADEZHDA No.

AKHMATOVA "It's as though I were hanging from my own eyelashes, growing larger and heavier . . ." Remember?

NADEZHDA "Playing every part in the play, till they destroy me." I remember that poem very well. But it's not yours. Osip wrote it.

AKHMATOVA Osip? "A Tear"!? No, I'm sorry, I did. Anna Akhmatova, 1934.   40

NADEZHDA Osip Mandelstam, 1934. It's Osip's. I remember him reading it. In Voronezh, Linenaya Street. We had drawn the curtains to make it night.

AKHMATOVA Precisely. I was standing there, leaning slightly against the wall. I had my mauve silk shawl wrapped round my shoulders.

NADEZHDA You stood there transfigured, almost spreading your wings. You were listening to Osip reciting his verses, your head thrown back as though waiting for the breath of genius to reach your own lips. As you usually did. He was inspired . . .

AKHMATOVA By *my* poem. No one read my poems better than I did apart from Osip.

NADEZHDA His poem.

AKHMATOVA I'm sorry, dear Nadezhda, but that poem is *mine*. After Liova was first arrested, it fluttered   50
round my sleepless room for three whole months. As if it was still too weak to make itself heard distinctly. Hard as I listened, it was too far away. It was I who struggled to catch it. You can't know that. You are not its mother. I am its mother, the frightened mother of Liova.

NADEZHDA Its mother is Osip. Or I should say its father. Its mother is me. Yes, I myself. That tear is mine. The one moreover that I never shed. My grief transposed into a moist image. He'd just had those terrible blackouts. I felt sure he was going to die. When I got back, to *my* eyes . . .

AKHMATOVA That's enough now. I've had blackouts too, I can't imagine why you need to rob me of my "Tear." Ever since 1934, from the very first day, I've done everything for you. Given you half my bread, half my life. Why did I go and freeze in Voronezh in 1935? To alleviate the desert-like exile of my friends. Who else came to visit you?   60

NADEZHDA Nobody.

AKHMATOVA When every door in Moscow was closed to you, I waited for you, as one waits for one's own flesh and blood to kill the fatted calf. That was 1937. I was all your friends, your entire city, rolled into one. Did I have one thought that wasn't for you? Even my one and only pair of shoes from Tashkent, didn't I want, didn't I have to give them to you, Nadezhda so you could skip through the winter of '41 in magic slippers? The ones made for me by an admirer who was a cobbler. In 1938, the last February of the Apocalypse, wasn't mine the one last loving look fixed on your faces as you went away? And let

me remind you it was in 1938 on the 18th of February that I recited to Mandelstam the poem I'd
dedicated to him. His last poem.

    And since then for you I've given refuge to Mandelstam's poems, I've made a place for his soul in   70
my memory, I'm an open house for each one of his words.

    And you want to rob me of my "Tear"? I know Osip can no longer murmur new cantos to you,
and I know how you must suffer, because I do a little too. Such an absence weighs heavy on us. So many
dead children. Mandelstam's unwritten poems, how many of them are there? Yet this one is mine.

NADEZHDA I'll let you lash the empty air with your words. Yes, you have given your all like no one else.
    Yes, of all our contemporaries you have been uniquely loyal. But that's no reason why I should allow
    you, even by mistake, to lay claim to one iota of Osip's work. I'd rather die.

AKHMATOVA Will you believe me if I swear on my Liova's head that it was I who invented "Tear," recited
    it and sang it to Osip, who then repeated it to me? I swear that . . .

NADEZHDA No, don't swear it, I beseech you! I'll give it to you. Yes, keep it. But don't swear. It's so stupid   80
    – but if God who doesn't exist really existed. . . . Poor Liova. No. You're driving me mad. Right. It's
    decided. You are the mother. I agree. Let's say no more about it. Forgive me, Osip. And forgive
    Akhmatova. As for the rest of your work, on every fragment of every verse I'll mount guard like a dragon.

AKHMATOVA But I don't want you to . . .

NADEZHDA Say no more! No more *Tears*! Never again. Or else I might suddenly feel . . . Agreed?

AKHMATOVA Agreed. I give in.

NADEZHDA *She* gives in! How we suffer. We're going mad. So mad we steal a child. Kill a child. The dearest
    part of oneself. We're so hungry and so cold, we eat the child. And the memory.

AKHMATOVA Remember Ugolino in *The Inferno* the thirty-third Canto? Are we perhaps about to turn into
    the Ugolini? Walled up alive in towers of silence we're devouring ourselves. I gnaw at myself, I devour   90
    my own hands . . .

NADEZHDA I remember. And you remember, I hope, that it's Osip who told you that story. He had just
    learned Italian to be able to follow Dante from one circle to the next. It turned him into a Florentine.

AKHMATOVA He knew *The Inferno* by heart. Like my verse. One day I was reading him the 33rd Canto of
    the Purgatono. Suddenly I saw that my voice had made him cry.

NADEZHDA Don't start again . . .

AKHMATOVA I'll stop.

NADEZHDA It's a bit much, I must say. Does she never have enough of herself? Enough of her voice of
    her ways and means? Of living creatures? Must she also lay claim to the bones of the dead?

                                                                                              [*A pause*   100

AKHMATOVA Nadezhda . . . do you really believe . . . that "Tear" belonged to Osip? Tell me.

NADEZHDA That's what I said.

AKHMATOVA Yet I remember each line bubbling up through every vein. Could it really not have sprung
    from my heart? Is that possible? Yes? It is possible. Is my memory . . . no longer my own?

NADEZHDA It could be true.

AKHMATOVA Does that mean that I'm mad then? Quite touched? Tell me.

NADEZHDA Not with madness. Perhaps a surfeit of love. Look, here's Lydia Korneyevna.

LYDIA Have you been crying? Well, dry your tears! Your identity card, I found it at the depot. You must
    have dropped it. A young man handed it in to the inspector.

AKHMATOVA *I* did that?   110

NADEZHDA You *did*.

AKHMATOVA Forgive me, friends. And don't ever abandon me! I'm losing myself, my own identity. I
    actually believe I wrote one of Mandelstam's poems. This year is unlivable. I haven't the heart to get
    through it – I feel I'm going to die. Next month. By June at the latest. Tell me you still love me, in
    spite of my faults?

NADEZHDA In spite of and with all your faults.

AKHMATOVA Thanks.

LYDIA As for me, I worship you. You have nurtured me. More than you suspect. I'll always be here, Anna Andreyevna. For whatever you want from me. Let us leave now. At once. It's time those letters were written for Liova.   120

NADEZHDA And then renew our efforts to have *your* poems published.

AKHMATOVA Oh yes! I'll go and see anyone you like. Draped in my loveliest shawl, the one with silver dragons, titivated, perfumed, I'll sweep along the river to the beat of a hundred oars. With Chukovskaya at the helm.

LYDIA I've already talked to Surkova at length on the 'phone.

AKHMATOVA And?

LYDIA She said nothing, but I heard her listening. Very hard.

NADEZHDA They never say a thing. They're afraid they'll be overheard. Crouched behind a stone curtain, they look through the tiniest crack to spy out how human is the face that's approaching.

LYDIA She was listening. I could hear her breathing. And sighing.   130

NADEZHDA Sighing? That's good!

AKHMATOVA Perhaps a real woman still breathes behind that stone curtain. For seventeen years a mother has waited in a lonely house. Then a new year dawns and things are boiling up, full of promise. Oh who could live through a year like that? No, one falls apart. It woke us up, Liova and me, only to torment us with hope. Shall I ever find my child again?

NADEZHDA Anna Andreyevna, to come back to our "Tear" . . . When a poem emerges from trembling lips, who knows through what air, on what tongues it has travelled? Who knows? Perhaps Osip was not far from your side when you gave birth to "Tear." You expressed the same pain in the same accent.

AKHMATOVA You think so? You know it sometimes seems to me that my own *Requiem* was spelt out to me, step by step, by my blue-lipped companions beneath the walls of the Kremlin.   140

NADEZHDA Well, look who's walking over there! It's Pauline? How can that be?

AKHMATOVA She followed us. She gets bored when I'm not there on the other side of our curtain. I have to keep her company, even at a distance.

LYDIA So you knew she was here?

AKHMATOVA Of course. I'm used to it. She was sitting on the sixth bench.

NADEZHDA And you said nothing?

LYDIA All the same, it seems to me she is looking for you.

AKHMATOVA Oh! That's unusual. Hello! Hello there! Come along, Polonius! It makes her nervous to be outdoors.

PAULINE I didn't want to disturb you before. It's my day off today, still I wanted to tell you there's a *zakosnoie*   150
pismo for you.

AKHMATOVA A registered letter?! Then I must go to the post office.

LYDIA I'll go with you, Anna Andreyevna.

AKHMATOVA I'm afraid, Nadezhda, in my life August has always been the cruellest month. Will you recite me one of Osip's poems on the way?

NADEZHDA I'll recite you: "No, let there be no supplication, no lamentation! Ssh! Not one moan . . ."

AKHMATOVA "Despite the darkling terrors . . . " At the post office perhaps this envelope will prove to be a white sail?

[*They go out*

PAULINE All that lot thinks about is words. How do you imagine they keep alive, widows like that?   160

[*She exits*

Scene 4

At AKHMATOVA'*s. Enter* AKHMATOVA *leaning on* NADEZHDA

NADEZHDA If you don't let me call a doctor, I'll pack my bag and go back to the country. She half fainted on the stairs. And now, on top of that, deaf and mute. You'd think she could speak to me!

AKHMATOVA I have. The answer's no. No doctor. No. No publication. I-will-not-publish-any-more.

NADEZHDA Sheer selfishness. Pure pride. Whimsicality. It's quite infernal. Don't publish then. Osip won't forgive you. You refuse?

AKHMATOVA Do you know what misery is? Yes, I know you know.

NADEZHDA And you? Isn't Liova still alive?

AKHMATOVA But you don't know the depths of despair. No, listen. A letter from my son arrives. The first for six months. Is it a joy? A dagger through my heart. The grief I endure since his internment is a mere scratch compared to this latest blow. This letter, here . . .   10

[*she hunts through her large handbag*

. . . it's like flames rising round the cross, it's . . . oh, where is it?

NADEZHDA But what does he say?

AKHMATOVA He says: "Mother, at night I drop dead like a corpse. At dawn, when the whips whistle through the air, I drag myself out of my coffin in tears . . ."

NADEZHDA Poor Liova. Those poor men.

AKHMATOVA It made me cry. But that's nothing. Listen to what he says. "I'm no more than a stone clad in rags. A bleeding earthworm. Speechless. Motherless. Why can't you rescue me?" I do nothing but hurt him, drive him further into the ground. He blames me for writing an arrogant letter to Sholokhov. For refusing in my terrible pride to join the Writers' Union. Me? Did I write to that Sholokhov? Wasn't   20 I expelled from the Writers' Union, spat on, sent packing? You can witness that.

NADEZHDA I can indeed.

AKHMATOVA And he goes on: "Now it seems you're going to publish. Draw attention to yourself again. I'm sick of paying this price for you. You love your poems more than you love your son."

NADEZHDA That's unfair! It's not true!

AKHMATOVA It's true I haven't saved him. And behind that barbed wire he may well believe me to be blindly responsible for the cross he bears.

NADEZHDA And you think it would save him not to publish? Just the opposite. Twenty-five years of silence haven't freed him. Publish we will! *All* your voices must ring out, your victory voice and your prophetic voice, not just the voice that trembles in front of iron gates.   30

AKHMATOVA No. It's over. I stay mum. It's better I play dead. With his dying breath my beloved son lays his curse on me. Mother, don't you see I'm being burnt to death? And I have no idea how to put that fire out. I'll never see the thaw, I tell you, see the torture come to an end. That's my fate. No book.

NADEZHDA Don't publish then and you'll see! You'll be forgotten.

AKHMATOVA Forgotten? Am I surprised to hear that? I've been forgotten a hundred times.

Enter LYDIA

NADEZHDA She won't publish. She's been forgotten. So I'm leaving.

AKHMATOVA Did you hear?

LYDIA Yes.

AKHMATOVA I know I hurt you, Lydia. This book owes everything to you.   40

LYDIA Yesterday, to be frank with you, I'd have been in despair. But today I'm almost relieved.

NADEZHDA What's this? Another suicide?

LYDIA A change of heart.

NADEZHDA Aha! "A change of heart"!

AKHMATOVA Haven't I said all this before? Poets and children get snuffed out like candles. With each shower of rain the Zhdanovs, the verminous moustaches, grow back again like the Hydra's heads. What right have I to this joy in a world that has trampled on Mandelstam and worshipped Iago, and his Iagodas?

NADEZHDA So this joy is something you regret now?!

AKHMATOVA True. Why should I have refused to publish? What a mad fool you are, a dreamer from the   50
past! As if they wouldn't have stopped me one way or another. The butchers chase after me with their axe and I dumbly offer my neck in holy sacrifice. Liova my son, you'd like me to fall on all fours and enter a den of wolves, wagging my tail and barking like a bitch on heat. But it would do no good. They won't forgive me for having once been Akhmatova.

NADEZHDA We must save this book, Lida. Think! Don't you know anyone else . . .?

LYDIA The new secretary of the new Secretary for Leningrad. Radlova was one of my father's students.

NADEZHDA Ask for an immediate interview.

LYDIA A rotten student. But still, I'll try . . . through my father.

[*The telephone rings*

AKHMATOVA Answer it, Nadinka. Say I'm dying.   60

NADEZHDA No, Boris. This is Nadezhda Mandelstam. It's Boris. He goes on and on!

AKHMATOVA Hasn't he asked for news of me? No, he wouldn't. He only 'phones to complain. What's it about this time?

NADEZHDA [*listening and giving a commentary*] His dacha, as usual. Too many visitors. He's afraid he'll get the Nobel Prize. What should he do?

AKHMATOVA Grasp it like a sword, brandish it like the archangel.

NADEZHDA [*on the 'phone*] I'll tell her.

[*She hangs up*

Glory's too heavy a burden for an old wild horse to bear.

LYDIA Perhaps Boris could help us? He couldn't refuse you a letter. What do you say? She's stopped listening   70
to us.

AKHMATOVA Ssh! A poem. Listen: "Forgotten? Am I surprised to hear that? I've been forgotten a hundred times,

A hundred times already I have lain in my tomb,

Perhaps I am still there now . . ."

Perhaps I am still there now. Did you get that, Lida?

LYDIA "Forgotten? Am I surprised to hear that? I've been forgotten a hundred times.

A hundred times already I have lain in my tomb,

Perhaps I am still there now . . ."

NADEZHDA It's very fine! What really is a poet? They extract golden tears from their pain. Where we see   80
nothing but filth, pollution, life wasting away, the poet catches the glint of the tiniest possible grain. When I listen to you I feel sure that Osip, buried as he is beneath the floorboards of time, his teeth crammed with earth, his carcass stripped of its jacket of flesh, is still germinating. Like a magic seed.

AKHMATOVA In my tomb – perhaps I am still there now . . . To be reborn . . . Oh I've lost it. The curtain has driven it away. Curtain?

PAULINE Black Armenian tea, does that suit? It would raise the spirits of the dead.

AKHMATOVA Back to the real world. No, wait, I'll make the tea myself. I stand up. I'm cured. Above all, Lidinka, remember my poems. I'll carry on. [*To the samovar*] Come on, my Karapet, be a good boy and boil. You have to know how to speak to my Armenian samovar. He only works when he wants to. It's the same with everything: the doorbell, Karapet, the WC. As well as poets. We all do as we please.   90

PAULINE [*to* NADEZHDA] So you, you're not going?

NADEZHDA If you don't mind, I'm taking a rest.

PAULINE Yes, that's it, we'll all take a rest.

AKHMATOVA You don't forget a thing, do you, Lida?

LYDIA Not one ounce of sugar! But why not jot down your poems?

AKHMATOVA Entrust my children to paper cradles, so our "benefactors" can come and steal them from me?
No. You are there to mount guard.

LYDIA But what if I were to . . . disappear?

PAULINE That can happen to anyone.

AKHMATOVA Don't count on it. With sugar, tea and our memory, we have all we need to pass through 100
Purgatory. Well, Karapet, are you asleep?

PAULINE You're not the only one. They've pulled my man in too. I've drained my cup to the dregs as well.
And who is there to console me? To blow my nose for me.

AKHMATOVA But who knows what Hell is really like? I don't. Neither do you. We are only in the
antichamber of Hell. This is not really Hell. Travellers say that's to be found in South Africa. [*To
the samovar*] Boil, won't you? I'm berated by my friends, my country tries to ignore me and my
samovar needs persuading. If I could catch a train for the next generation, I'd make a dash for the
station.

PAULINE Here, you'd be better off on my side of the curtain. When life's tough my black Armenian tea
perks you up like a monkey on a stick. [*To* NADEZHDA *and* LYDIA] Just to please you, I invite you both 110
too.

AKHMATOVA Thank you for that. It's something I'll owe you, comrade.

NADEZHDA Where did you find this tea?

PAULINE I'm not telling!

[*They go out*

Scene 5

At AKHMATOVA's. LYDIA *and* AKHMATOVA *prepare for* RADLOVA's *visit*

LYDIA [*by the curtain*] Let me tell you quickly before she arrives. Nina Radlova is also the niece of our beloved
Party Secretary. She comes and goes to the Sultan's Palace as she pleases. And she was willing to put
herself out. What wouldn't we do for the great Akhmatova, as she put it.

[*Doorbell*

Once more into the breach dear friends.

[*She goes to open the door and returns with* RADLOVA. *Greetings*

RADLOVA They tell me you're writing again?

AKHMATOVA Again? I've never stopped writing. For various reasons it may not appear so. I may seem to
have been hibernating. It just looked like that.

RADLOVA And what are you writing about these days? 10

AKHMATOVA About . . . rivers.

RADLOVA Rivers? How's that?

AKHMATOVA How's that? How's that? In verse of course. Classically. About rivers . . . that flow to the
sea. The Black one. About people drowning as well. All in verse of course.

RADLOVA People drowning? Why not about our dams?

AKHMATOVA Our dams? But why . . .

LYDIA Anna Andreyevna has not had occasion to write about dams as yet, but . . .

AKHMATOVA If a dam occurs to me in the silence of the night and if it's followed by whisperings and other audible signals . . .

LYDIA Then why not?　　　　　　　　　　　　　　　　　　　　　　　　　　　　20

RADLOVA It will be an honour, in any case, for the Leningrad Editions to publish a small collection of poems by the great Akhmatova. We don't want to turn our backs on our immediate past, so of course we must select them carefully.

AKHMATOVA You do it, Lida. I'm hopeless at choosing.

LYDIA I'd love to. But regretfully too, they're all so beautiful.

RADLOVA We must lay great importance on the oldest poems. To think you were writing already before the Revolution. That's quite a thought.

AKHMATOVA I'm a rare enough monument! Everyone knows I was alive long ago. It's time they discovered I was equally alive in the fifties.

RADLOVA As for me, I really love your poems of yesteryear. Some of them are extremely charming.　　30

AKHMATOVA You think that?

RADLOVA Most sincerely, yes! There's a lot one could say about them, a great deal.

AKHMATOVA You're an admirer of mine, as I understand it.

LYDIA Obviously. Who isn't? We all rally round, Anna Andreyevna.

AKHMATOVA You do me proud. But you haven't read everything. The one about the bees? . . . No?

RADLOVA No, but I shall, I promise. And you must tell me which are your favourite Soviet poets?

LYDIA Anna Andreyevna is passionately fond of so many poets.

AKHMATOVA And yours?

RADLOVA Well, I would put Sholokhov above the rest.

AKHMATOVA So would I.　　　　　　　　　　　　　　　　　　　　　　　　　　40

RADLOVA Then Demian Bedny.

AKHMATOVA Demian Bedny? So would I. And then Bezymenski, no?

RADLOVA And Bezymenski, yes. And . . .

AKHMATOVA Me too. So there.

LYDIA We agree then? I confess I . . .

AKHMATOVA Agree perfectly. Mandelstam is a case apart. He's not of our time. He's way beyond us. But I can clearly see the stars you favour burning brightly.

RADLOVA I'm delighted to hear it. So I'm sorry to say I can't help you about the flat. There really isn't anything just at the moment.

AKHMATOVA The flat? What flat? Who asked for a flat?　　　　　　　　　　　　　50

CURTAIN You asked for a flat?

AKHMATOVA Down, Polonius! Lydia Korneyevna, is it you?

LYDIA Certainly not!

AKHMATOVA What's this? After fifteen years in a dungeon – and I mean that – I'm favoured with the publication of a small volume of my poetry, which restores to me the free air of all the Russias. And on top of that I should ask for a flat of my own? I wouldn't *for anything in the world* want to deprive anyone at all, least of all another of our writers, of the meanest room, the slightest reasonable comfort or a well-deserved bathroom! Never on your life!

RADLOVA Anna Andreyevna, don't take it this way, I beg you. It's quite common for me to be asked . . .

AKHMATOVA Common! You seem to forget who I am! The whole world is my home! A month by the　　60 Fujiyama and there's nothing more beautiful. Listen to this: "In summer it is clad in nothing but earth and sky." I have spent a year on the borders of Armenia. I can change the floor I live on, my season or my century, as simply as I can change my language. I am fully aware of the enormous effort the Writers' Union must have made to support me. Overcoming whole mountains of silence . . . Isn't a small volume enough for an old woman?

LYDIA Anna Andreyevna, please don't shout! I'm afraid for your heart.

AKHMATOVA [*shouting*] I'm not shouting! I'm explaining myself! Allow me to add that I am unreservedly grateful to you, Nina Radlova, more than I can say. You are forever inscribed in my memoirs.

RADLOVA I shall in any case take a personal interest in your dossier, Anna Andreyevna.

AKHMATOVA I have confidence in you. I trust you entirely.   70

RADLOVA I'll expect you in three months in Leningrad. Then we'll sign your contract.

AKHMATOVA Leningrad in three months! What a day that will be! I'll take my own pen, and with a flourish I'll sign it.

LYDIA I'll see you out.

AKHMATOVA Women like that, if they *are* women, should be forbidden to breed and multply. I meet my enemies and I avoid my longed-for friends. Somewhere there is a land inhabited by everything that makes my heart beat – poems that have never been written, bridges that have never been crossed, books that have never been published and lovers that have never been kissed. That's a country I've never known.

LYDIA *returns, followed by* NADEZHDA   80

Take a good look at me! Do I still have a shadow? Or have I sold it to the Devil? Tell me the truth. Shouldn't I have screamed blue murder?

LYDIA You were regal and devious. And as for screaming, you almost did.

AKHMATOVA I controlled myself. I should have screamed. But today I was playing Ulysses. I passed through customs hidden under a sheep. Baa! Baa! But I should have screamed.

NADEZHDA And the book?

AKHMATOVA It'll be a minuscule volume. A wingless bird without claws. Nothing but the beak. But I should have screamed. Do you know that I was born the same year as Hitler? Don't panic! Chaplin was born that year too. Between the two of us, Charlie and I, we make the globe spin round on our fingertips.   90

But still, tell me, will my voice be recognized? The voice of my sisters, women convicts, widows or the dumbstruck mothers of Liovas?

My room has grown hard and dark as a tomb. We can't stay here, my friends. Let's go and talk together beneath a roof of linden trees. We'll share our sad stories of hatred and exile. I want to give rent freely to my tears.

[*They go out*

PAULINE A volume without claws, without wings? Does such a bird really exist? When that woman takes her voice away, the silence in this room is quite chilling.

Scene 6

AKHMATOVA *and* LYDIA *arrive at* ANNA ANDREYEVNA'*s loaded down and muffled up*

AKHMATOVA A breakdown! Way out in the suburbs! All that mud! Oh! I'm exhausted! First I decided to go to Siberia to try and find Liova. Then I decided not to go. Then you decide I should go to the country with you. To cap it all, you let us break down in the mud, and my heel snaps off ! I'm at the end of my tether!

LYDIA I'm so sorry. I just wanted to please you. "I want to see Zagorsk and its holy mysteries once more before I die." That's what you said, again and again. So for a month I scour Moscow, ringing a hundred doorbells, until finally from the cousin of a one-time friend, a well-placed bureaucrat I renewed contact with on purpose, I managed to obtain a car, so your wish could be fulfilled. And this morning you were overjoyed.

AKHMATOVA And this evening I'm disappointed. I didn't get to Zagorsk and I'm exhausted. The car is almost brand new, she tells me. But just look at my legs now! Don't they shame you? Anyone who knows how hard it is for me to walk should take more care to spare me this unnecessary pain.

LYDIA [to the audience] I'm ashamed, Your Majesty. [To AKHMATOVA] I despair of you. You'll never get in a car that's almost brand new with me again. Never again.

AKHMATOVA Never again. And I'll never see Zagorsk again.

LYDIA And I'll never attempt the impossible again. To waste my time and lose my dignity hunting for one insect in a haystack, it's just not worth it!

AKHMATOVA Let's say no more about it. But what if it had happened in the depths of the country? How would I have come home? Dead. I'd have come back dead.

LYDIA Oh, please stop, Anna Andreyevna! After all, we did break down luckily almost at once and we did get home safely.

AKHMATOVA Oh, wonderful luck! Such imprudence! One can't rely on anyone. No response about Liova. Your letters had no effect. And still no news from Radlova. Three months she told me!

LYDIA I suppose that's my fault too?

AKHMATOVA Oh, come on! Let's stop tormenting each other. Let's forget it.

LYDIA Yes, let's forget!

AKHMATOVA So show me those potatoes. They're for me? Where did you find them? They're all frozen.

LYDIA Frozen! They cost me two hours in a queue. Perhaps they are frozen, but they were the best I could find.

AKHMATOVA It's a swindle, Lydia Korneyevna, and you let them get away with it! You should have made a scene.

LYDIA You should have stood in line in my place. Then I'm sure the potatoes would never have dared to freeze. First the car, then the potatoes, what next?

AKHMATOVA And you found some beetroot too!

LYDIA Beetroots, yes. They're frozen as well.

AKHMATOVA Never mind. You did your best. It's alright.

LYDIA Alright?

AKHMATOVA Here, take this knife. It's not as blunt. Look, the house is empty. That's wonderful, it's so unusual. Our Pauline must be going about her very private affairs. Let's profit by it. I've wanted a quiet day like this for a long time. To be alone with you and my poems. Not a quiver from the curtain.
I'm worried, you see, about my *Requiem* poems. You are their guardian. But what if they should publish them after all? What state are they in? I want to check them. Would you kindly recite them to me?

LYDIA Now? What about the potatoes? Tomorrow, I'll do it tomorrow.

AKHMATOVA Now. To my mind *Requiem* contains my most necessary but my most fragile poems. They're trifles but they carry a punch. They're like heartbeats. If ever they stopped . . . all these memories would fade. Do you think they'll survive?

LYDIA Of course they will.

AKHMATOVA I'd like to hear them, one after the other. Then we'll have dinner. I think I've got some tea. Do this for me. As a special favour. I'm terribly tired. For the last three months I've been translating those Korean poets (who mean nothing to me) and I only take a break to translate Victor Hugo. Then I feel old, bearded and pompous and, what's more, exiled from myself in a rhymeless world I have to trudge through or get trampled underfoot. Recite me my *Requiem*, Lydia Korneyevna, and bring me back to life.

LYDIA I can't. I can't.

AKHMATOVA Yes, you can. Wait. I'll get Karapet launched. Then I'll listen to you. Come on, Karapet, boil, my pet.

[*She lights the samovar*

LYDIA [*to the audience*] And she'll listen. No! She'll listen to herself through me. She won't hear me at all. Poor abigail, poor commoner, inanimate as a tree or a chair. I know I don't write and the thirsty mob   60
can never drink at the fountain of my grieving mouth. But still, in my own small corner, I too need a life of my own. [*To* AKHMATOVA] And I *adore* Victor Hugo!

AKHMATOVA So do I. Sometimes. Well now. Will you please start with "Verdict"? It's drifted away from me lately. As if the mounting silence from Liova was lengthening the distance. "It's a long time . . . "

LYDIA "It's a long time since I was foretelling
    Our last day and our final dwelling."

AKHMATOVA Our final dwelling? Or our lonely dwelling?

LYDIA Your final attempt was "our final dwelling."

AKHMATOVA Our final dwelling? Yes perhaps. Let's go on.

LYDIA Those are the last lines.   70

AKHMATOVA Oh yes, of course. I'm sorry. You see how fragile it all is. So what about the first lines.

LYDIA Anna Andreyevna, I don't know what's happening but the first lines escape me at the moment. Do you remember: "Memory's a host that teases, Gives, withholds and rarely pleases"? Have you forgotten them too?

AKHMATOVA It's such a long time, you see, since you last recited them!

LYDIA They'll come back to me. Let me be quiet for a moment.

AKHMATOVA That's how it is. We're always waiting for them to come back, just waiting. Careful! You haven't gouged the eyes out.

[*She takes* LYDIA'*s potatoes back again*

    I don't suppose you could tell me what those first two lines were about?   80

LYDIA Not just now, please! Let's change the subject. We only need to look the other way and they'll flock back, like the birds.

AKHMATOVA That's reasonable. Reason! Didn't that word come in the second line? No. So can you please recite me: "For seventeen months."

LYDIA "For seventeen years I've been crying, Come back, calling you to come back home."

AKHMATOVA Seventeen *months*. For seventeen months.

LYDIA No, it was seventeen *years*.

AKHMATOVA Are you sure?

LYDIA How do you expect me to recite *your* poems if you stop me at every breath I take to tell me I'm wrong? I am sure it was seventeen *years*.   90

AKHMATOVA Seventeen years? I could have sworn it was seventeen months, but she must be right. When I wrote that, Liova had been taken from me three years before. I must have had a premonition how long my martyrdom would last. Seventeen years! To be pregnant for seventeen years with a phantom son, that's why I'm so fat! And then, God willing, I'll give birth. To an embittered old man, drained and wrinkled, who won't love me anymore.

LYDIA How can you say that?

AKHMATOVA Because it's true. Separation separates. Severed hands never grow back. What would your husband have become, do you think, if instead of disappearing around 1938 he'd gone on suffering, rotting away in that camp at Chita?

LYDIA Stop that! I've warned you before I won't have Mitia referred to. If you must tread that path of   100
poisonous brambles, I shall leave you. Nothing could ever separate us, Mitia and me.

AKHMATOVA Seventeen years and everything's changed. Why so afraid of the truth? The one good thing we have left?

LYDIA Enough, I tell you!

AKHMATOVA They've all gone. No one will come back. And in years to come, like a corpse in water at springtime, when this age re-emerges on the surface of time, no lover will ever recognize his loved one. I wrote that already in 1940. Do you remember that poem?

LYDIA No.

AKHMATOVA No?

LYDIA No. And you? I've supported you and you've tormented me for thirty-five years. You're a genius. 110 Heroic. But you're also an Empress of China and you're a tyrant to your lowly subjects. I am old too and my legs are swollen. My loved one was taken from me too and cast into eternal night. Write your poems, Anna Andreyevna, but please jot them down and so spare me. I don't want to spend my life trembling more for your poems than I do for my own daughter. Or wear my eyes out re-reading your translations when I still haven't finished mine. Allow me my own words to weep for my dead.

[She rises

AKHMATOVA You abandon me, Capitaine? Abandoning old Akhmatova? A woman who's all alone? On account of her poems she's taken for a god, a father-figure, the sun itself. Whereas in fact she's nothing but an old wicker basket with fine fruit inside.

LYDIA I must leave. I'm going. 120

AKHMATOVA I'll always be there, you once told me.

LYDIA I've changed my mind.

AKHMATOVA Who will preserve my poems if you let me down? You were my only protector.

LYDIA Ask Nadezhda Mandelstam.

AKHMATOVA She can't. No visitor's permit. Besides she already has Osip to watch over.

LYDIA Write. And then publish!

[She starts to go out

AKHMATOVA Should I write them on separate sheets? Or in the order I compose them?

LYDIA Separate!

[She leaves 130

AKHMATOVA "I am what I am, may you find someone better." One who makes no call on you, who knows how to cross the Nevsky Prospect all alone, is never cold or hungry and has no tears, no memory. What have I done to them? What ought I to have done? Do I ask you for words to make me cry? Do I complain that you have no music in you?

After all I can't deal with everything myself. Cooking, correspondence and poetry too.

Enter PAULINE

PAULINE What's all this? *You* doing the cooking?

AKHMATOVA No, it's not me with the knife and the potatoes, that's my double, sweating in silence in the long Soviet night. Whereas I am at one with the breezes and the reeds, dreaming of a new year when I am young again. 140

PAULINE What are you on about? Feel all right, do you? Or is that another poem? Get away with you, I'll help you.

AKHMATOVA Thank you, but there's no need.

PAULINE Oh yes there is! Your potatoes are horrible. I'll cook you some real gems . . . I've found out about a new racket. Interested?

AKHMATOVA A new racket?

PAULINE My niece's comrade, her boyfriend, knows someone on the building site. I've been waiting a long time for this. There's nothing we need more than a new racket these days and they're hard to find.

AKHMATOVA That's true. One always needs a helping hand. But what I need most, comrade, is a man's suit. 150
PAULINE What if I could find a pair of trousers to start with? Would you pay me in advance? A hundred roubles?
AKHMATOVA Take a good look at me and ask my double! She might be able to give you a hundred phantom roubles for a pair of phantom trousers.
PAULINE You take some beating, you do!
AKHMATOVA You can always depose an empress, but you can't remove her rusty crown of thorns. Comrade citizen, the house felt heavy and deserted today. I almost missed you. The curtain hung motionless. Like a shroud that hid History.
PAULINE I've got a shirt too. A real shirt for an angel. Come and I'll show you my secret hoard.

[*They go out* 160

Scene 7

At the Moscow to Leningrad station. Smoke and sound effects.

Enter an old peasant woman, BABOUSHKA

BABOUSHKA You see that train over there, the one all alone, gleaming gold like a cathedral. That's the Red Arrow. They say it's all gold inside and smells of perfume. One look at you and they bring you caviar and Butterbrod. No need even to ask. I wish I could see what it's like, but for that you must be a foreigner. Russians not allowed. Or maybe not even Communists. When it leaves our station, I wonder what country the Red Arrow takes you to. And what the foreign station's like.

Enter NADEZHDA *and* AKHMATOVA

AKHMATOVA I'm the one going off all alone to confront the Minotaur, and you're the one that's shaking?
NADEZHDA Forgive me. This station's not just a station to me. It's the noisy, smoke-filled entrance to the hole we fell through on our way to a camp from which Osip never returned. What can I fetch you?
AKHMATOVA Mineral water. A Barjomi please. 10

[*Exit* NADEZHDA

It's true. Our glorious Russian stations now just register our moments of separation.
BABOUSHKA [*to* AKHMATOVA] I say, come over here and sit down. I knew who you were at once.
AKHMATOVA You knew, Baboushka?

[*She sits down*

BABOUSHKA We've really earned our white hair and our sunburnt cheeks, haven't we? We can hardly help looking alike. I was number 217. I'm going too, you know, to Ta-ta-grad. I never say its blessed name out loud. Holes in my shoes! How old do you think we are? Tell me.
AKHMATOVA It's hard to say, Baboushka.
BABOUSHKA You could say eighty for me. That's what I look. Knock about twenty off and you're there. 20
You too. Don't fuss about the train. It's always two hours late when I take it. I once said to my son – I only had one – "You want to be a survivor, my boy? Forget about your mother, the good earth, and the hay. Learn Communism. You'll have all you want. Car, clothes, apartment. Everyone should go in fear of you. Friends? Don't have any. What you really think? Say the opposite. Or rather, say nothing. Don't trust a soul." Wasn't that good advice? Well, he got fifteen years. Can *you* understand that?
AKHMATOVA He must have spoken his mind, Baboushka.
BABOUSHKA Just imagine. And your child?

AKHMATOVA Baboushka, I gave him no advice.

BABOUSHKA Just as well. What difference would it have made? Ten years ago I used to pray that God would act against that other one Up There and pull the rotten tooth out. Now we've got the Old Man. There's no end to the evil for us. White's black and black's white. What do you say? 30

AKHMATOVA I don't know, Baboushka. If only I did. If only I could imagine just one day with my son. Even the last day of my earthly life. Just one day.

BABOUSHKA Bad luck never lets you down. Like a faithful old hound, it hangs on to you. I've brought some sausage for the journey. What about you?

AKHMATOVA Cucumber and Butterbrod.

BABOUSHKA No onion? You can have some of mine.

[A train announcement is heard

Was that for us? What did he say? Are you coming? Now listen here, don't be afraid. Stick close to me.

[They go out 40

LYDIA *arrives and meets* NADEZHDA *coming in with the water*

LYDIA Where is she?

NADEZHDA She must have boarded the train. You've come to see her off after all? She will be pleased.

LYDIA No, no. As you're here, I'd rather not see her. It's another black sail. The editors want to drop the Burnt Notebook cycle. What can I do? All because of the word "burnt." You see why?

NADEZHDA Yes, of course. "Burnt" is a dirty word. It has a nasty smell. They need poems without water or fire, airless and odourless too. Soon they'll be without music and verse. And in the end with no words at all. Down with burnt! Down with God! Down with river! Out, out, out!

LYDIA But what shall I do? I can't cut the word "burnt." "The Notebook Cycle." No sense in that.

NADEZHDA "Burnt" can't be burnt out. Better consult the poet. 50

LYDIA Lord, no! I won't risk causing a second stroke.

NADEZHDA We can't let her go to Leningrad to sign this contract and not warn her.

LYDIA What if we called the cycle "The Eglantine in Flower?" You remember: "Never shall I use words of mine/to repeat those that were missed/when we failed to keep our tryst/But not to forget, I shall plant an eglantine."

NADEZHDA "Failed . . . tryst?" Do you think they'll accept "failed?"

LYDIA Oh, there I'm adamant! I'll fight for it. So about the title? Will *you* tell her?

NADEZHDA No, let's say nothing. Anyway, by the time she's arrived they'll have changed their minds again and shifted the goalposts. Let's try and slip through the net. Even amputated, mutilated, poetry can still bring tears of joy to our eyes. 60

LYDIA I ought to have gone with her. But I swore I wouldn't. I can't take it, you understand? With her it all ends in a quarrel.

NADEZHDA I know. My life with Osip was one row after another. Yet every row was bliss.

LYDIA You two used to quarrel?

NADEZHDA Lots of times. In a wonderful way. Our last argument, I believe it was at this station. Then on the Kalinin Bridge. It was the last time we'd tried to sneak into Moscow, though it was one of a dozen cities out of bounds to us. Anna Andreyevna's window was the only one open to two nervous ghosts like us.

The argument had started in the train. About a hansom cab. Osip wanted to take one and I wouldn't. A cab cost us what we needed to live on for two days. And a cab can cause no end of trouble: hatred, warfare, rejection. 70

LYDIA Life, you mean.

NADEZHDA As we glared at each other, that cab divided us like a magnifying glass, exaggerating every fault.

And did we hurl Russian insults at each other! Go to the Devil! Not without you! There was no cab at the station. The bridge was interminable. I let Osip walk on with bravely faltering steps, feebly nosing our way through the cold air that lashed our faces. I was pitiless. Our quarrel went on in the wind as an exchange of soundless epithets. We cared nothing for the Moskva beneath the bridge. We only had eyes for the field of battle.

What a bridge! A bridge made for playing the hate game, to make one feel the full luxury of fury and the too acrid taste of solitude. All that we permit ourselves when we feel positive that our life is out of   80
harm's way. How happy we were on our last bridge, separated by anger, fatigue and the cold, the bridge and the cab. Everything that divided us brought us closely together. Our misery was simply the other face of joy, for weren't we both still among the living?

LYDIA With Mitia I never knew this other face of joy. Things are never what they seem. And *I* would never have dared.

NADEZHDA I think the train's about to leave. Will you come and see her off? I'm going to hurry or she'll climb into the wrong coach.

[She goes off

LYDIA I can't, no, I just can't. Parting can etch an eternal profile on the window of a train. I'm not watching her leave.   90

[She goes out

Scene 8

Back from the trip, AKHMATOVA *enters with* NADEZHDA *accompanied by* PAULINE. *Suitcase, etc.*

AKHMATOVA Who's stolen the light bulbs on the staircase again?

PAULINE You ask me who? Does a thief leave his address? While you were away, if it interests you, I did find a few screws and nails.

NADEZHDA Later, we'll see to that later.

[Exit PAULINE

Now, tell me! Did you sign!

AKHMATOVA Sign what? My own disfigurement? My deposition? Just listen to this. Their choice. They've removed all the poems that sing of my love of Russia. Not to speak of London or Paris. I have no idea what goes on in Tashkent, still less in Siberia. Who am I? A twin to Narcissus. The world is there behind my back and I don't even turn round to look. And not a single unpublished poem. In 1940 I faint away,   10
vanish into my mirror and disappear. So that was Akhmatova, my readers will say in disgust. That hysterical woman surrounded with adulterous lovers. But why should I worry? The book won't appear. I could see that in their faces. The more they pretend to publish it, the more determined they are not to.

NADEZHDA So nothing has changed. The same machine for lying and pretence that drove my Osip mad. No. They don't even lie anymore. They've put the truth so far behind them, they've lost sight of it now.

AKHMATOVA Then I said: "I'm not worried about this book. I don't even urge you to publish it. On the other hand I do ask for some justice for Nadezhda Mandelstam. A visitor's permit, a lodging and some work. She's the widow of such a great poet. You do remember Mandelstam, I hope?"

NADEZHDA That was risky. But who knows? Perhaps the book will show up all of a sudden, like a prisoner   20
who escapes?

AKHMATOVA Arrested in the pale light of dawn and shot that very evening. That's how they banished from the air of Russia the voice of Gumilev, my first husband. When I entered the Writers' House in Leningrad I heard a woman say: So Akhmatova is still alive!

Do they want me to die?

But I warn you, I won't lose heart again. I will not die. I won't let this country go or the age I live in, even when I am dead. Transformed into poems with flaming wings I shall blaze through the darkness of your dreams, singing of your hopes, your betrayals, your defeats.

NADEZHDA And Leningrad? How was Osip's beloved Leningrad? "Petersburg! I don't want to die yet: you know the 'phone numbers I have had. I still have your addresses, Petersburg." 30

AKHMATOVA "I can call on the houses of the dead, The voices of the dead will answer me." Wherever I called I was answered by Osip. How we laughed and rhymed in that cradle of granite. Petersburg was never so lovely. As if smothered in flowers for my funeral. The Summer Gardens had spent enough for ten years on roses and Oriental poppies. And up the paths behind me stretched out a procession of ghosts. All our dead friends to offer me a regal escort. I'll never go to Petersburg again.

Enter PAULINE *with a telegram*

PAULINE A telegram. You want it?

AKHMATOVA What is it? No, you take it, Nadinka.

PAULINE It's for *you*.

AKHMATOVA I can't read telegrams. 40

NADEZHDA It's Tvardovski! Novy Mir is ready to publish *Poem without a Hero*! Good old Tvardovski. He's a brave man.

AKHMATOVA No! Is that true? Show me. [*To* NADEZHDA] Lend me your glasses.

PAULINE So can we read or can't we?

AKHMATOVA He wants an afterword from Pasternak . . .

NADEZHDA From Pasternak? Very right and proper! Pasternak as escort for Akhmatova. Magnificient!

AKHMATOVA But Boris has never read me!

NADEZHDA Oh, please, Anna Andreyevna, don't start!

AKHMATOVA I mean it. I had sent him a manuscript copy of *Poem without a Hero*, dedicated to the leading poet of the twentieth century. 50

NADEZHDA You told Pasternak he was the leading poet?

AKHMATOVA Let me finish. He telephones to thank me. And do you know what he said? "What I specially like is 'Everlasting Flowers Have a Dry Aroma'"! A poem I wrote in 1910! "And the rest," I said, "Did you read it?"

NADEZHDA Our leading poet . . .

AKHMATOVA And you know what he said?

NADEZHDA No. What's important is that tomorrow he's with you. We must go and see him at his home in the country.

AKHMATOVA You're right. We must go and see Boris at once. Forward march! Tomorrow Peredelkino. Leningrad next year, and my work will spread out over Russia like maternal sunshine. But how do we 60 get to Peredelkino?

NADEZHDA Could we ask Lydia Korneyevna? Her father's dacha is just next door.

AKHMATOVA Lydia, of course! My dear Lydia Korneyevna! She'll be so pleased. I'll call her.

[*She 'phones* LYDIA KORNEYEVNA *at once*

Hello! Akhmatova here. I know we're not getting on just now, Lydia Korneyevna, but would you mind in spite of that popping round straightaway? It's for a very special reason. Let me explain . . . She's coming. She'll wait for us downstairs.

PAULINE You're off again already? Right now?

[AKHMATOVA *and* NADEZHDA *dress to go out again*

AKHMATOVA I'll finish my story. "And the rest? Did you read it?" I asked. Well, my *Poem without a Hero*, 70 he didn't have it anymore. "I don't know what I've done with it," he said. "Someone must have borrowed it." *Someone*! What do you say to that?

NADEZHDA What do I say? Serve you right! So Pasternak's our leading poet this century, is he? No, no excuses! Let's go on down.

[They go out, arguing

AKHMATOVA I don't know what came over me that day. But after all he is a great poet.

NADEZHDA Was, you mean. Very great.

PAULINE [*shouting*] When will you be back?

NADEZHDA [*shouting*] Within the hour.

PAULINE In an hour's time?! Do you take me for a halfwit? An hour! They'll need a whole day to go to   80
Peredelkino. Let's see now. What shall I do next?

[She starts rummaging around

What did she bring back from Leningrad? I hope she didn't find any shoes, because I've just got some. A notebook. Another notebook. You see, you don't eat, you don't drink, you don't dress properly. It's all spent on paper!

[She exits

Scene 9

At Peredelkino, in front of Pasternak's dacha, outside, with the forest all round

AKHMATOVA This may be the forest of Peredelkino, it may be the garden of Pasternak's dacha, but it looks more like a haunted cemetery in a short story by Edgar Allen Poe. A vampire in every birch tree. And in every thicket I spy a policeman disguised as a bush. It scares you too, Lydia Korneyevna.

LYDIA Not a bit. It was just a shiver . . .

AKHMATOVA A shiver of fear. We're all scared, aren't we, all three of us, Nadinka? This empty woodland is overcrowded with raincoats. There's no shame in being scared, Lydia Korneyevna. Even Joan of Arc was afraid. And she wasn't ashamed. They asked her: You see that stake through the window? And the fire that's waiting for you? Well, she was frightened and she recanted! I see all those leaves moving and I'm afraid. I'm ready to . . .

NADEZHDA What shall we do? Shall we leave?   10

LYDIA Boris will turn up. Let's wait a bit. He told me I could come at any time. Perhaps he's gone out to do some shopping.

NADEZHDA Boris goes shopping now!?

AKHMATOVA You should have mentioned a time.

LYDIA Yes, I should.

NADEZHDA We've been here for an hour.

LYDIA Exactly. He can't be away much longer. I'm sure. I know him.

AKHMATOVA We'll wait.

NADEZHDA Last time I came here I was with Osip. A very long time ago. At first Boris invited us to stay for tea. Then there was "a change of heart." His wife was afraid we'd contaminate them. No cake and   20
no tea. We found ourselves all alone again under the stars. And hungry for humanity.

LYDIA It's his wife. Boris is such a nice man.

NADEZHDA Adorable. And the older he gets the more naively he behaves. You know how he dealt with the great Tsvetayeva in his autobiography? He buried her in a chapter called "Three Shadows." Which of the three is the shadow today?

AKHMATOVA Boris never had any understanding of women. His first wife was a tortoise. His second a spluttering dragon. His third a "Madame" out of Marcel Proust. Three times he propositioned me. I gave him his marching orders. I didn't want him to spoil our friendship.

NADEZHDA You said exactly the same thing about Osip, word for word.

AKHMATOVA Men have always propositioned me three times. And I married three of them. I sent all the others packing. Anyway, men don't know how to love us. By the way, last night I dreamt about you, Nadezhda. We were alone, you and I, in the Empress's palace, which I have never been to. All those moonlit rooms should have frightened me. But they didn't. There was an air of great tenderness. You too were heartbreakingly tender. In my arms you were yourself and Osip, inseparably. All three of us together melting into a silken transport of joy. With our eyes closed, we . . .

[*she opens her closed eyes and sees*

Oh, look! Look! There! Over there! Can't you see? At the window? The curtain!

NADEZHDA What curtain? Which window?

LYDIA For God's sake, Anna Andreyevna, what can you see?

AKHMATOVA But it's him! There! The one on the left! He's there! He was a moment ago, I tell you. Watching us through seven veils. Wondering when we're going to break camp.

NADEZHDA You saw him?

AKHMATOVA No. Felt his presence. As if I was in the house myself, all at once I had such a clear vision of his face. Like a startled horse. And a dark tormented soul. He's in anguish, because of us.

NADEZHDA Are you sure?

AKHMATOVA Absolutely. I know, you see, at this very moment that when he looks at me out of his own dark night, what he sees is a dream that he will never realize.

[*She shouts*] All of you who live in great Pasternak's house, tell your master that Akhmatova came in person to greet him.

We'll go now. Follow me.

Poor Boris. So goodbye then. Death will reunite friends that fear has divided.

[*They leave*

Scene 10

AKHMATOVA's *empty room*

Enter PAULINE

PAULINE [*alone, trying to make out a page*] "A dream"?

"The world of my staircase is dark. It misses its 30-watt moon.

I am dead.

When I was alive, think I, waiting was gnawing at my lungs.

Now I'm dead, waiting gnaws at the silence.

My staircase is dark. An inkwell without ink. What if he happened to call and failed to find me?

Light up, I cried! It's a dream. But never-ending."

It means nothing to me. Is that meant to be a dream? Somehow it makes me feel very uneasy.

Enter LYDIA

LYDIA Oh! She's not here then? Has she gone out?

PAULINE Like a mad thing without a hat. You should have seen how she ran. Not like her at all.

LYDIA She didn't leave a word for me? She wasn't ill, I hope?

PAULINE Not to worry. She rushed off because of her son.

LYDIA Her son? She didn't say anything to me.

PAULINE Or to me. She got up, said: Liova! And off she went. She left me standing.

AKHMATOVA *and* NADEZHDA *return*

AKHMATOVA Forgive me! I suddenly just *had* to go to the station to wait for Liova

LYDIA He's . . . he's not . . .?

AKHMATOVA No. I was wrong. He didn't come. I felt it so strongly, a presentiment. I was sitting in the three-legged armchair. Suddenly I *saw* him a long way off, stepping down on the platform. As if coming back from the long distant past, frowning, looking for me, hoping to find me. I just raced off. Do you understand?   20

I get no news any more. All I have are presentiments. And they deceive me, delude me. He won't come back.

LYDIA He will. We're not still living in 1938. And while we wait for him, your book will help us all to cross the gulf.

AKHMATOVA My book's not coming out. I already felt sure of it and I was right. I've just heard. I don't conform to the strict spirit of the Revolution. It's been withdrawn, Lydia Korneyevna, from the Orlov Collection. It's been thrown out of the gates of Leningrad and there's one door in Moscow I shall never get through. They'll send my book on its travels. To Voronezh. Then to Vladivostok. Then they'll   30 try it out on the bears on the ice floes. And there we shall wait for the age we live in to thaw out. No, it won't appear on this earth nor at a time when I am still breathing.

And tomorrow I'll agree to translate Lope de Vega. Then follow on with Anatole France. One has to live, hasn't one? And commit suicide to live.

LYDIA We simply have to go and see Fedin.

AKHMATOVA Out of the question. I've done all I could to save the skin of this book. Acted all the parts in every kind of play. I've played the queen, the beggar, the dead woman and the fool. Not any longer. I'm played out. I've not got the guts to pull faces any more. I went to see Vinogradov: I had a stroke. I went to see Furtseva: bilious attack. I've lost the strength to climb the countless stairs that lead Akhmatova up to a blocked-up doorway. Lost the strength to take off my fur-lined cloak. Lost the   40 strength to pull off my boots.

LYDIA So have I. What's more I'm losing my sight. The day will come when I'm unable to read back to you any more.

AKHMATOVA Then night will have come for me. Is this true, Lida?

PAULINE And for me it means asthma, that's what they said.

AKHMATOVA So if we're all crippled in some way, who will go to market? I'd love to invite you to dinner, but in this house there's nothing, and no one ever comes.

NADEZHDA I'll go, of course, as I've no one to wait for now and I've no fear of dying or not dying.

AKHMATOVA I want to live, you know. All I need is a smile, a little care and a wet-nurse.

NADEZHDA I'll go now.   50

[*Exits*

AKHMATOVA Let me tell you: it's all my fault. They wanted to print my verses. It had all been read, sorted out, chosen and accepted. At which point, instead of agreeing, I don't know why, such a sense of loss overcame me, that I include the poem you can guess, a real scream of fury, to appear as a preface. On top of that I insert a dedication full of tears, the grating of keys and the footsteps of soldiers on wooden cobbles. I just couldn't help it.

LYDIA But you were within your rights. And after all, they'd asked for some new poems.

AKHMATOVA They'd asked for some new old ones. I knew what I was doing! And if I hadn't done it, Liova
would be here now. No good discussing it. I know. I wasn't able to give up my *Requiem*.

At the very moment I was trying to slip into eternity – I had put my head through to the other side.   60
I could already see the poets' heaven over there in a rustling flurry of verse, I was almost there – I felt
a hand, no, it was a well-known shaggy paw, grab me by the sleeve and hold me back. So instead of being
weak-minded, giving in at once, I held firm.

I tell you, my whole story, my work and my terror, it's all Akhmatova's fault. You don't say a word?

LYDIA Novy Mir won't publish you either and you can't be blamed for that.

NADEZHDA returns

NADEZHDA What have I brought you? A bottle of the best Georgian wine!

PAULINE And me? A letter from Siberia!

AKHMATOVA Give me that! A letter from Liova!

PAULINE So he *is* still there? You're lucky. Mine doesn't write to me. Aren't you opening it then?   70

LYDIA Anna Andreyevna, would you like us to go?

AKHMATOVA No, no. Stay. I'd rather you stayed. If it's a good letter . . . we'll drink to Liova! No. Let's
open the bottle first. What is it? A white Gordyeni?

NADEZHDA A Tzinindaly. Osip and I came across it in 1931 in a marvellous village in the mountains. There
was this wine, and then the locals, a race of peasant jumpers.

AKHMATOVA Peasant jumpers?

NADEZHDA A religious sect. Once every generation the gates of Heaven fly open for all those who have the
strength to jump.

AKHMATOVA Any advance notice?

NADEZHDA No. You have to be ready for Heaven. If you're ready on D-Day, it's just feet together, up   80
you go.

AKHMATOVA It would only need those heavenly gates to open, and I'd jump.

NADEZHDA Jump first. That's enough to make the gates open.

PAULINE You think so?

AKHMATOVA Right you are! Whereas for forty years we've been here, with our swollen legs and our burden
of memories – craning our necks in an effort to leap up to Heaven – to the Heaven that never opens.
Yet this century's only Heaven is right here under our feet, around us, between ourselves. Look now.
A few birds about. The wine of friendship. A lean-to sloping up to the sky – that's our ladder. All at
once the wind drops. The howling of the tempest fades from our ears. I look down. It's for me that
the Moskova strives so hard to sparkle. And for you as well. Just for a moment I am cradled in the arms   90
of something approaching joy.

NADEZHDA I can almost share it.

LYDIA Aren't you going to open Liova's letter?

AKHMATOVA In a while. I'll open it, but I'm so afraid I'll collapse. A minute of eternity please. Now let's
be courageous. Nadinka, your glasses.

[Exchange of glasses. She reads and closes the letter again

NADEZHDA Well, Anna Andreyevna? . . . Well?

AKHMATOVA [*to* PAULINE] Now, comrade citizen, I believe you told me about a man's suit that cost 600
roubles.

LYDIA [*to* NADEZHDA] White sail.   100

PAULINE I did? Never! 800 roubles. An almost perfect man's suit. Trousers, jacket, with a shirt as well,
and all to fit the same size.

AKHMATOVA Yes, but what size?

PAULINE That depends. For 800 roubles I'll find the right one. So what size is it?

AKHMATOVA Well, just now, how can one know?

LYDIA After seventeen years, it's not the same.

AKHMATOVA I shall find out, I'll know before long.

PAULINE But if you wait too long, it'll be 900, you know.

AKHMATOVA Oh no, 800 or nothing. Got it?

PAULINE Got it.   110

NADEZHDA Listen! Ssh!

LYDIA What's the matter? A bug?

NADEZHDA The gates of Heaven. It seems to me they've started opening, way over in the Far East. Osip, my sublime mole, can you hear a cracking in the bowels of time?

AKHMATOVA [*to the audience*] All of you, living in the future, have you heard of Osip, and his wife here with me now? Or of Anna Akhmatova? I'd really love to know. One ought to die, skip a century and then return.

NADEZHDA Or receive a telegram from the future: Poems arrived safely. Signed: on the coast of the twenty-first century.

LYDIA *Anna Akhmatova: Complete Works.*   120

AKHMATOVA And tell me, you who live in the future, do you know what Mandelstam was really like? Akhmatova? And Pasternak? Gumilev? Tabidze? Tsvetseva?

Do you know which of us was loyal, who was betrayed and who was the traitor? Who saw the airy gates open? Can you see this in our poems? Has the History of Truth begun?

NADEZHDA When will it begin?

THE END

THE PERJURED CITY

Or, the awakening of the Furies[1]

TRANSLATED BY BERNADETTE FORT[2]

Our Bad Bloods

> Once the blood [. . .] is on the ground,
> It is quite difficult to bring it back up, popoï!
> The quick liquid spilled to the ground runs away. . . .
> *The Eumenides*, 261–3[3]

"Blood" once spilled can never be spilled again. Irreversible is the loss of blood shed by murder. It is this irreversibility that Aeschylus sang and decried.

Not reversible for the victim. Nor erasable for the murderer. No, all the perfumes of Arabia will not sweeten the little hand that killed.[4] Never again will the hands of a Macbeth be purified. Today they still smell of innocent blood.

Leaning over the bank of the red river of terrifying fate, powerless to retain life that flows away, all the poets watched, from century to century, tragic horror run its course. Hear them wail their indignant hymn, Aeschylus, Shakespeare, Balzac, Hugo, horribly fascinated by the carnage wrought by man, and the city. In the streets, one sinks ankle-deep into the red mud.

Blood, how it freezes, boils, curdles, intoxicates, inundates, blackens!

Blood, we take it for the substantial soul, the vital principle that makes the round of our internal domain, that part of us that must remain hidden and that can be taken away.

Blood with religious properties, that which has value, which, poured on the altar according to the rites, has the power to redeem crimes and sins.

Blood that was called pure, that was claimed to be blue and incapable of lying,[5] blood that had to be kept within its borders and not mixed.

Blood today: behold it always discoloured and recoloured and bearer of evil thoughts and evil memories. We say "blood" and to our misfortune, behold the first word of racism.

Poor blood, your image speaks to the worst phantasms of our century. We say "blood" and immediately, the word "contaminated" binds itself to the old word of life. On the one hand, blood contaminates, on the other it is contaminable and contaminated. Through blood our love and hate flow wild. Certain bloods are declared hateful in advance, they might infect the bloods of noble races. What's more, crowning the history of this precious fluid, there comes to us through blood the scourge of AIDS.

One recalls here that a certain Mr So-and-so associated AIDS with Jews. The fear of contamination by AIDS is, we know, an anti-Semitic reflex. It has to do with the myth of blood purity. AIDS, Jews, Blacks . . . Off we go on a crusade against crossings! To each his own blood!! How widespread and insidious is the fear of contamination of blood by blood.

These same frightened people, however, are not much afraid of the contamination of the soul by bad examples and bad company. Against a moral plague one takes few precautions. You see people driven by craving for the poisons they adore – I mean gold and power – rush to the banquets where the dishes that feed their ambitions are served in abundance.

But a sour smell hangs in the curtains of these palaces – do you recognize it? It is the "rottenness of kingdoms." The same that was smelled in the kingdom of Denmark. Such a stench is like a cry. It is this cry that awakens many a character in our play. Some, like the Furies, had been sleeping underground for 5000 years, others for barely a week. A cry of horror, of alarm, of revolt.

We are witnesses to this: millions of human beings can be reduced to dust over decades and decades, and the earth stuffed with the murdered does not tremble. One does not hear millions of cries. Until the day when suddenly *one* cry pierces the heavy layers of silence. The cry of a stricken child, perhaps? Or of a mother overthrown by unheard-of grief? And this is the crack in the wall.

Here is the story: one day, lambs learned in spite of themselves[6] that their shepherds were wolves. Wounded, losing their blood, they lie dying. Can this be? Did those who cared for them kill them? No!? Yes! Who can imagine such a thing? We who see the victims expire one by one, it is with dread and stupefaction that we are forced to admit the worst: cut-throat shepherds.

And how and why such an unthinkable crime? Especially in our proudly advanced countries, where it is fashionable to repeat the word "ethics" all day long?

What if this strange and monstrous crime were born just of our era? Just of the numerous injustices and tangled unjustnesses of our own time? Is it not the symptom of the new sickness of the kingdom?

All the perfumes of Arabia would not sweeten the soiled white hands. But in our kingdoms certain persons may have invented ways to desensitize the nose.

Yet, this is not a fable.

Characters (in order of appearance)

The MOTHER	USHER
AESCHYLUS, caretaker of the Cemetery	MINISTER
BRACKMANN, a lawyer	MAINTENANCE
MARGUERRE, a lawyer	FORZZA
NIGHT	MONSIEUR CAPTAIN
The CHORUS, including THESSALONIKI and	ABEL
JOHN-CHRISTOPHE LAMERD	ELIMINATE
The CHILDREN: DANIEL and BENJAMIN	PROFESSOR HORNUS-MAXIMUS
EZEKIEL	PROFESSOR ANSELM
The FURIES: ALECTO, TISIPHONE and	DR BERTHIER
MEGAERA	DR TWIN
X1	PROFESSOR LION
X2	DR BRULARD
KING	MESSENGER
QUEEN	

The Cemetery

Scene 1

Enter the MOTHER

MOTHER Today I leave you, accursed City,
    I leave this castle crawling with wolf-snakes,
    Never to return.
    I am escaping, but I'm not running away from you, society of the ferocious.
    No! It is I who repudiate you,
    The mother leaves, but she confronts you.
    Listen, child-eater, gravedigger of our trust,
    Impostor, with all my might I hurl my fury against your stony brow.
    I, a woman, will break you!
    I cry out "Shame! Shame!"   10
    To the ears you've carefully plugged shut
    With a thick dribbling mud of gold.[7]
    I will pierce you through! As I go, I cast against your walls
    The last horrified glare of a woman
    Who knew you flesh and bone.
    There is not one place in you,
    Not one vital organ, small or large,
    That is not rotten to the core.
    Your stench will rise to the nostrils of generations yet to come.
    This woman has taken the bit in her teeth.   20
    No, I'm not lacking inspiration.
    Your endless infamy arouses in me
    Cries stronger than myself.
    I have a curse for you too,
    Kingdom haunted by eminent doctors,
    Wolves dressed in white.
    Stay shut up tight within yourself, you Hospital-Capital.
    Keep your jaws clenched on your venomous tongue,
    Erect in the City
    Like a monument of lies.   30
    Swallow your own infected phlegm!
    But what am I saying? This, a kingdom?
    No! You're nothing but a huge slaughterhouse,
    Managed by honourable, oh such honourable devourers,
    An atrocious mob of exceedingly certified MDs.
    I know this now, but it's too late,
    And I didn't save my little ones from your forks.
    Woe to me, who for a long, a cruelly long time,
    Left my lambs in your care.
    Oh, how I used to bring them to you,   40
    Docile, necks innocently bared, with soft curls,
    Their obedient eyes large and round.

Take good care of my young ones, I begged the executioner.
I myself kept the wild beasts supplied,
And I thanked them.
Too late for me, but not too late for you,
Or you, or you.
Beware, you women without hatred, parents without distrust,
Children innocent of any wickedness!
Fear appearances!   50
I am warning you: this country which is your nest
Is full of breeds hard to imagine.
Your friends are your worst enemies.
The empire belongs to the beasts.
Listen, mothers! Mothers of offspring that blind luck
Has not yet taken from you,
Mothers meekly waiting by the bedside,
Do you hear me? No one wants to believe me!
Oh! God, I heard nothing, either!
A mother, stricken two steps away from me,   60
May have cried out, and I didn't believe her.
Why would I have believed her?
Why would anyone believe me? My child was killed!
Dinner is served! The doctor puts the child on his plate,
An old story, they'll say, another old wives' tale.[8]
It's true. It's not true. Who tells the truth?
I blame you, commonplace King,
Bag of dust standing on legs of dust,
All wrapped in a safe net of serenity.
Meanwhile, the rivers flow wide,   70
Bloated with children's corpses,
And in your horned eyes, not the slightest glimmer.
I blame you, dark grey crowned cat,
Erecting your cold dullness
In the midst of shuddering anxious crowds.
I blame you, chill grey King, and this one as well,
And that one, cold King grey;
All equally turned cold and frighteningly calm,
Motionless colleagues,
Banners of indifference.   80
I blame you, sinister law of the cold,
Menace to the planet,
Fearsome storm with numbing claws,
Habit, you who take the burning bitterness from the salt of tears,
Who blunt the ear and dull the sharp cry,
Muting everything! Leveller, unnerver of souls,
Absent voice, bitch, empty throat,
I blame you first,
Demon dripping drops of tepid breath
Into the shrill trumpets of alarm,   90

To silence the shouting angels.
If only I could, outside your walls, become a rebel trumpet
Of sounds intolerable to the ears of wolves!
Well. And now, where shall I live?
Where do unchilded mothers go?

Enter the CARETAKER

CARETAKER So, you're really leaving? And where will you go?
MOTHER I'll go . . . I'll . . . I don't know yet.
    I hear my dead children calling for me, my dead children.
    I want to live close to my ghosts.   100
    I thought of staying in the camp of my loved ones,
    Which lies under your care.
    A lodging in your city of the dead
    Would be logical. What would you say of that, caretaker?
CARETAKER On the one hand, I'd say, be my guest,
    I have a fine vault to offer you.
    A clay apartment, that's fitting
    For a mother who rejects fate.
    But on the other hand, I must tell you:
    Do you know that this cemetery, which yesterday was magnificent,   110
    Peopled as it was with the most venerable of the dead,
    Haunted by the noblest spectres,
    Occupied by a great vanguard of liberty's friends,
    Comrades of death, lovers of the open air, prophetic laggards,
    A whole human glory in rebellion against the lying City,
    Do you know that today it is grievously abandoned?
    Since the rotting dam
    That raises its rotting scaffold
    Above our encampment
    Has started heaving, night and day,   120
    With a frightful creaking in the celestial roof,
    The guests of my ark have become fewer.
    I'd rather warn you now . . . There, do you hear it,
    This grinding of cliffs?
MOTHER Is that the dam? This sobbing in the rock,
    This tremendous wheezing of worms?
CARETAKER That's it all right.
    So you're changing your mind, of course.
MOTHER On the contrary.
    This wailing dam fills me with courage.   130
    Nothing on this earth will ever again frighten
    The mother whose young nest in a grave.
    This dam, death, it's all the same to me.
CARETAKER Be welcome, then, in my harsh city,
    A city with no roads, nor cars, and no violent traffic,
    Where my lambs graze, still starving for the milk of human kindness,[9]

No matter how deep they lie under the earth.

Look around you.

This is the land beyond all lands.

Won't you be afraid to live among the stones?   140

MOTHER No.

I'll hold the hands of those I have lost.

I won't be alone. Here separation ends.

CARETAKER Well then, come in. Make yourself at home.

MOTHER Once again, I can hope! No! City too sure of yourself,

The mother is not crushed by your sweeping victories.

What I will do against you,

I do not yet know in the least. We'll see.

But what I know already is that the dead

Are never as dead as we believe.   150

Some who walk and ride heavily upon the earth

Are deader than those who, standing under the earth,

Passionately dream of an astonishing future.

[Footsteps are heard

CARETAKER Shh! Listen! Ah! Already! On the trail! Hear those footsteps?

It's looking, it's probing, it's sniffing! It's in a hurry! It's hunting!

Go! Go! Hide among the hidden.

I'll find you there later.

MOTHER I will go down.

But no one should expect me to vanish.   160

[Exit the MOTHER

CARETAKER Things are happening fast. The winds are edgy,

Flags are snapping. Already the City's in a rush.

Have no doubt, some who live up there

In lofty apartments,

Have caught in their ear

The maternal war cry.

Scene 2

Enter the lawyers BRACKMANN *and* MARGUERRE

BRACKMANN Sir, do you know where I can find the Ezekiel children?

CARETAKER Some would say they're in heaven, if there is one open.

As for me, I'd say they are spinning

In a garden under the sea,

Or perhaps in a holycopter[10] . . .

BRACKMANN Strange answer! I meant their graves, obviously.

CARETAKER Their graves? Oh that, I don't know. Are you family?

Who are you?

BRACKMANN I'll tell you. But the family, that is to say, the mother, would you happen to have seen her?

I mean, has she been visiting the graves lately?   10

CARETAKER Look no further. I myself am the mother for all those whom death has entrusted to my care.

BRACKMAN Strange mother!

CARETAKER But, even so. The mother, what do you want with her?

MARGUERRE Here it is, counsellor! I found it! The grave's right here! And there are fresh signs of the
mother. Cut flowers.

CARETAKER The flowers, that's me.

MARGUERRE And a box of butter cookies.

CARETAKER That's me, too.

MARGUERRE And a bottle of perfume.

BRACKMANN The perfume, that's you too? Listen, I don't know who you are, Sir . . . but I'm telling   20
you . . .

CARETAKER Aeschylus, the caretaker. And you?

BRACKMANN Aeschylus? As in Aeschylus?

CARETAKER Yes. And you?

MARGUERRE Brackmann, Attorney at Law.

AESCHYLUS Mr Brackmann, counsellor . . .

MARGUERRE No, not me, him.

BRACKMANN My name doesn't mean anything to you?
Yet, for months and months . . .

MARGUERRE The papers have been talking of nothing else but my colleague . . .   30

AESCHYLUS Ah! But here young glory stops, like a stunted giant.

BRACKMANN Enough joking around. I'll be frank. The mother of the children is nearby, I'm sure of it.
Tell her that we came here
In person, Mr Marguerre and myself,
Urged by the wish for a just settlement.
I am a man of experience –
I know the price of mourning
And the price of a good compensation.
We stand ready to comfort very, very, generously
A person we've learned to value . . .   40

AESCHYLUS How much, would you say?

BRACKMANN Everything's negotiable. I am prepared to go quite far.

MARGUERRE But what holds us back is this rumour
That has begun to spread throughout the City
An extravagant rumour . . .

AESCHYLUS What kind of rumour?

BRACKMANN It's being said everywhere, but we don't believe it,
That, driven to madness by the sad death of her two children,
This lady suddenly overstepped the limits of the law
And the boundaries of reason and justice.   50
They say she went underground[11]
There to join some band of nameless people,
A mafia, a sect, a bunch of separatists, a phalanx, a network, an army,
A rabble of vengeful individuals
Whose hideout lies
In the depths of this Cemetery.

AESCHYLUS In truth, that's what they say? The underground?
But against whom?

BRACKMANN My unfortunate client.

AESCHYLUS Is *he* unfortunate, too?   60

BRACKMANN Who would not be? Put yourself in his place:

    A man, a worthy citizen, a doctor,

    A CEO, a director, a deputy, soon to be

    In the cabinet, a man so worthy, and suddenly thoroughly unhappy.

    You know the story.

    Children died, it's awful, I agree.

    They say he is the cause of it, I disagree.

    They were quite sick before. I discount that.

    I confine myself purely to the question of the death.

    We wanted to save them. The opposite happens: 70

    We lose them.

AESCHYLUS *You* lose . . .?

BRACKMANN The children.

MARGUERRE Thereupon, she accuses us of infanticide.

AESCHYLUS The mother accuses? She really believes

    That you killed the children?

BRACKMANN Not me. My client. Absolutely.

    And she won't give up. Her pain makes her crazy,

    But for us, what a blow!

    Injustice takes off and follows its endless course.   80

    There isn't a thing we can do about it. So. Here we are in prison. It's disgraceful.

AESCHYLUS It could be worse.

    Imprisonment has an end.

BRACKMANN That's exactly what I said until yesterday!

    The man is alive! He is in prison, I was saying, but he is alive.

    We accept an unfair, cruel punishment,

    But the man is noble.

    Like Goethe, he loves order above all else.

    "Better an injustice than disorder."[12]

    We consent to pay an unfair bill   90

    To put an end to these upheavals.

    There's nothing more to do than submit and let it pass, I say.

    But tomorrow, when the winds that whip up this affair

    Have subsided,

    History will put its true face back on,

    And we'll write the story for eternity, I say.

    It will be an account stripped of the passions

    Which horribly distort still too recent events.

    I'll put myself to the task.

    That's what I told my client.   100

AESCHYLUS Amen.

MARGUERRE At that very moment, the awful rumour breaks out.

    All the papers print it: this woman wants death.

    Now she talks of dismemberment, throat-slitting, amputation,

    Tearing of flesh, and an intolerable destruction of virility.[13]

    Women are capable of inventing just about anything

    As soon as a death shakes them up.

It's a bit too much, don't you think?

Where is the executioner? Where is the victim?

Where can innocence be found? 110

AESCHYLUS Do you believe her threats?

BRACKMANN Certainly not. And yet, who can say for sure?

Who can tell where the pain of a traumatized woman will stop?

We need to set limits.

Madame Ezekiel could cause herself irreparable harm.

It's for her I plead, first of all.

On our side, there is no obligation,

But we, too, consider ourselves victims

Of a dreadful fate that struck without rhyme or reason.

We all suffer. And have, for too many years. 120

After a cyclone has devastated a region,

Must one also demolish the houses left standing?

That's not my philosophy. Me, I'm for resurrection.

And then, I plead for the country as well.

This rumour is a very contagious disease.

A wind of savage vengeance is blowing,

Frightfully loaded with cruel and irresponsible images.

It whirls through the streets, the squares, the subway stations,

Whipping up the imaginations of young and old alike.

By suggestion, hypnosis, fermentation, and apparition, 130

This ill wind foments all sorts of small insurrections, heralding more serious sedition.

Families are already infested by squabbling.

Tomorrow, civil discord will charge in, with a huge uproar,

Invading the playgrounds of grammar schools and high schools,

Trampling everyone under its stormy hooves.

That's what this rumour does,

For nothing spreads faster than a bad example.

AESCHYLUS For nothing spreads faster than a bad example.

BRACKMANN Such a beautiful and ancient kingdom

Threatened by a mortal infection, and why? 140

Nothing much. A thorn in the foot,

Let's pull it out. Enough whining. I'll be the first to stop.

I offer this woman a very, very sizeable compensation.

Listen to me, do not listen to the sorrow that surpasses the limits of sorrow.

Deceptive are the desires of vengeance

Suggested to the surviving parents

By the children whose ghosts are stirring

In the shadow of our existence.

If moderation prevails, this long, too-long story

That poisons our era will come to an end at eleven o'clock tomorrow morning. 150

I'll await this lady in my office. She'll come. She'll sign. I've seen to every detail.

And the slate is wiped clean.

AESCHYLUS Without a single trace.

MARGUERRE Nothing. A new era begins.[14]

AESCHYLUS At one stroke, the losses in cash, in years,

The pain in thoughts, in children,
    In crime and punishment, everything is incinerated!
MARGUERRE What are you saying?
BRACKMANN At one stroke and on both sides, everyone accepts,
    Everyone forgets, it's the best solution.   160
AESCHYLUS I don't like that, forgetting.
BRACKMANN That's your problem. But, think about it.
    If our conditions are turned down,
    Then we'll know how to extirpate from this country
    The roots of bad blood. I would add . . .
MARGUERRE Don't add. I hear strange creaking sounds up there.
AESCHYLUS It's nothing. It's the rotting dam.
MARGUERRE Let's go. I loathe cemeteries.
BRACKMANN Two more words . . .
AESCHYLUS Night is coming, gentlemen.   170
    I'll have to shut the gates
    Of my humble city.
BRACKMANN Just two more words!
    All of you who are listening to me and whom I don't see,
    Hidden here or there, in the graves, in the thickets,
    Under the cloak and the stone,
    I advise you to linger no more
    In what can no longer be called a cemetery.
    A zone with neither head nor tail, a leprous no-man's-land.
AESCHYLUS Oh, don't listen to him!   180
BRACKMANN A heap of stones taking advantage of the respect due to the dead
    To plot an uprising.
AESCHYLUS Now, gentlemen, I am going to close . . .
MARGUERRE True, I have never seen Night fall so quickly.
BRACKMANN Let me tell you, infernal citizens,
    A nasty case coming from here
    Would be too much for our wise Senators!
    Let's have no provocation!
AESCHYLUS Night, gentlemen!
BRACKMANN We're off. Till later, Madam.   190
    We'll be expecting you. At eleven o'clock without fail.
    And I'll have more to tell you!

[*The two lawyers leave*

Scene 3

Enter NIGHT

AESCHYLUS Here you are at last, Night, my mother,
    You who end the unending.
NIGHT I came as quickly as possible, preceding myself by an hour,
    And without even putting on my stars.[15] Did you notice?

What did they want from you, those rats with two voices,
One honey-coated, the other barking?
I think I know them,
They fall under three principal headings:
Insinuation, masked violence and nefarious speech.
Falsehood for truth, poison mixed with justice, 10
The thistle in the law, the stench in the bouquet.
AESCHYLUS It's them all right! It's their spitting image!
They swooped down on my fragile camp.
A nothing raises its tiny head, and they bombard it.
Even a bedbug prevents them from sleeping.
And now, you saw it, they want to capture the mother.
If they succeed, then . . .
NIGHT Then what?!
AESCHYLUS Then, it's the end of the world.
Here, this mother is all we have left. 20
NIGHT They won't get her.
Let the mother reappear now.

The MOTHER *reappears*

MOTHER Here I am.
AESCHYLUS Did you hear the lawyers?
MOTHER Yes, how I haunt them!
These dogs are thinking of me, I make them gasp for breath,
Bitter joy for the mother!
So they are afraid of this exhausted, shattered woman?
And this story about the "underground"! 30
Do they take me, all by myself, for a whole army?
Me, so small, so tired, stripped of my past powers.
Didn't they see, at the trial, it was I who was losing?
To keep my honour, losing my blood and my youth,
Losing my rank, my position, my beauty,
All the goods of a woman, without exception –
Husband, friend, lover, respect,
And all the rest, as if I had the plague.
That's not done in good company! A woman,
Holding her head high, too high, for too long! 40
I spent everything, burned everything,
To pay the ransom of Truth, and I never saw it appear.
I'm nothing but debt.
AESCHYLUS But today they want, or so they say, to change
The too-brutal course of this story,
And give you back in silver and gold
As much as possible.
MOTHER Give back! No, call it take back!
AESCHYLUS Take back what?
MOTHER The rest of me, the shadow, the breath, I don't know. 50

Far from the City, nearly blotted out, I am still too much there.

She is still alive, they fume, she lives to think of us.

AESCHYLUS Killing you wouldn't be difficult, if they wanted to.

MOTHER They do not want my death. Am I not buried here,

In a land as far away as death,

From which it is just as impossible to return?

No! They want to give me gold, yes, that's it,

To give me a transfusion of their liquid,

How horrible! They want to mix their yellow soul with my boiling metal.

I'm invited to their table.   60

Look! They're serving me: Eat, eat, and forget.

Eat and become what we are!

Such a feast for them if I taste the slops they love.

There I am, a wallowing sow,

Received with pomp by the pigs,

I am growing a snout, already I don't remember anything any more.

How was it yesterday, when I was in a rage,

Eaten up by maternal suffering,

Never resting, I will ask, giggling,

My mouth full of cream,   70

My eyes dazed. If they converted me to their religion,

They could at last sleep in peace!

But I shall not go to their appointment,

I see the lure shining too brightly.

I'm not biting. I will stay here, at the cemetery, and send them

My thoughts to persecute them.

At night, I will enter through these gentlemen's windows

In the guise of a ferocious black ewe, and I will bleat out:

"So, did you feast well on my lambs?

Was it tasty, this stew of children cooked in blood?"[16] Night after night.   80

NIGHT They will soon get used to it.

MOTHER Alas! That's all too true! Well then, the underground!

Yes! A forest of rancour. There, I will plot

And stir up the offended crowds and . . .

What do you think of that?

AESCHYLUS But, after all, why not accept

The lawyer's offer?

Have you weighed everything?

They are offering you the gold you hate.

But they are offering you what they value the most.   90

They reject you: you scream.

They invite you: you spit.

Will this conflict ever end?

MOTHER You're taking their side?

AESCHYLUS Don't you fear that your stubbornness

Will broaden the rift that already splits the City?

I've seen plagues ruin prosperous lands,

Plagues that began with a little scratch.

MOTHER Am I a little scratch?

Am I the cause of the plague?   100

AESCHYLUS You are letting vengeance speak.

But is she your loyal friend,

Or the one who leads you too far,

Up to the limit, one step too far?

There, a red mist shrouds your head,

You stagger, you stumble,

The friend who urged you on does not follow you,

And you fall all alone on the inhuman shore.

Do you follow my reasoning?[17]

MOTHER You believe that I don't know where vengeance leads?   110

I know exactly, and how at the end

The path makes an abrupt twist

And everything is turned into its opposite.

The executioner seizes my place,

I fall into his,

I hear the tyrants proclaim themselves victims,

And guilty Sin, with claws drenched in blood,

Comes to perch on my shoulder.

I know all that.

AESCHYLUS Good. So, you accept their proposal?   120

MOTHER I want neither vengeance nor this foul thing

That you recommend.

I am sad. I am anguished. You look pale.

If you are wisdom, I want to be a violent red

That terrifies people's gaze.

AESCHYLUS Tell me, then, clearly, is it fire or ice

That runs through your veins?

MOTHER What I feel right now

Is anger pacing my entrails.

Striding through like a furious panther, its heart sounds the charge,   130

Its body keeps growing, bigger and longer.

I also have in my soul two blessed, yet unknown words:

Honor and truth.

These are the names of the Gods that Earth chased away.

But I revere them, and so I leave.

Enter CHORUS

AESCHYLUS No, no, stay. I only wanted to sound you out. Forgive me.

I didn't dare believe that you might exist.

Do you believe me? Do you? I am with you!

Ask my myrmidons.   140

Put us to the test. What do you want?

MOTHER I want, I want, I want.

Ah! God, if only there were one God

Or another. Ah! God, if you existed,

Ah! If doctors could heal!
If for the atrocious wounds
That consume the soul and never heal,
We found the cure that never existed.
Ah! The world is without miracles . . .

CHORUS With two coffins at her side 150
She wants something,
Something that doesn't exist.
She wants something to counter hopelessness.
She wants the wondrous thing,
The star hidden behind the stars.
Will her day ever dawn?
No human person has ever seen it,
And yet her pseudonym is engraved
In the memory of all hearts.
We all sigh: "Justice, oh beloved," 160
Dear and radiant image,
Oh, non-existing Divinity,
Like the poet who wanted Beatrice,
It is you she wants, oh Justice,
She wants Justice to love her.

MOTHER Ah, I want, I want, I want!

CHORUS

STROPHE 1

God the father, the Wise Queen, the Silver Knight,
The bride with crystal eyes, 170
The orphan's champion,
I, too, when I was little, believed I saw traces of their footprints
On the fine sand of the sky, it was beautiful,
But it was all my invention.
Today, my nectar is cheap at five francs a bottle.

ANTISTROPHE 1

As for me, if my voice weren't hoarse,
I'd shout at cynical Justice, that deceitful and venal liar,
Shout to pierce her marble eardrums:
"We are all equal before death, 180
This world without ears is not eternal;
I'll wait for you outside
And we'll settle accounts before eternity."
My vocal chords are completely broken
By the cold breaker of thoughts,
But someone besides me can scream!

STROPHE 2

Because we have no money,
No roof, and no right,
It's easily believed we have no words, 190
No letter, no spirit, but that's not true!
We are geniuses excreted by Society.

We are the cigarette butts. And why?
Why are we stripped of all our human traits,
Exiled in dirt and filth?
I'll tell you.
It's not because we are fools,
Although some of us are,
Since there are fools below and above ground.
On the contrary: it's because we are   200
Too much like ourselves and not enough like them.
Too brilliant and too alive and not like everyone else.
Not round, not limp, not willingly battered,
Not good for the yoke and harness, not manageable.
I'm called an outlaw. Yet,
I live here legally, according to the law that says:
All those who are not like everyone else
And are not happy, for them it will be
The closed factory, the cross, or the coffin.
So, I chose the coffin, and I fixed it up.   210
Absolutely. My name is Filth
And I am proud of it!
....

As for me, I've visited all the hells:
The bowels of the subway, the hideouts of the damned, the cardboard shacks.
I've been a phantom in the doorways,
I've spent short nights huddled in public urinals,
I've brushed against the oven of the crematorium.
Step by step, I slipped into exile between immovable walls.
But no regrets, no! No!   220
On the way, I collected a hell of a wisdom,
I stole a horse named Liberty.
The beast led me, galloping triumphantly, to this cemetery.
Here I am happy, I have my sarcophagus.
Death and I, we keep a happy house.
When I think my bold thoughts out loud,
The stars don't draw their guns.
In short, here I am the whole Man, down to the cry,
Whereas the rich in the City
Are only meat devoid of inspiration.   230
I live, and they get fat.
This cemetery is noble misery. I am all tattered and torn,
But even so, in the end,
It's the City that will put a bullet in its own head.
In fact, the bullet is already on its way.
So, I live here, waiting for the hour of Revolution.
....

As you can see, our barrel is full of powder.
All it would take is a spark.
If I wanted, the City would be in ruins   240

But I am waiting for suicide.
Don't repeat my words,
They'd be too happy to accuse me of attempted murder
When I am the murder victim.
I don't know why we accept
Being buried alive on earth.
It may be that one day we'll be fed up
With keeping quiet and burrowing in our burrows.
If that day comes, we'll know it.
It will come carried through darkness   250
On two red eagle wings glued to each side
And a wing on each shoe,
And under its feet, wheels bespangled with prophetic eyes.

....

That's why it will never come.

ANTISTROPHE 2

Poor little one all alone with ghosts for children
Where have your men gone?
Brothers, uncles, cousins, friends, allies?
And there is God too, on whom one must not depend!   260
Poor, unfortunate, discomfited God!
There is a lord who keeps very quiet,
Knowing full well, since he knows everything,
That, in a matter of law, he'd be beaten by a lawyer.

STROPHE 3

So, what is to be done?
It's been so long since I last dreamed.
I have no more ideas.

....

However, one cannot not try   270
At least once, to snatch the lambs from the butcher's knife.
It's never too late for new courage!
Ah! The intoxicating fragrance of heroism!

ANTISTROPHE 3

We'd have to produce a miracle.
That's what worries me,
That's what exhilarates me.
Let's change the world! Let's try!
Let's make the river flow uphill!
Let's break open the doors of hell!   280
Let's unmask false Justice!
That the true one may appear!
Do you not believe that it has come today,
This day whose wheels are studded with sparkling eyes?
Yes, yes, I believe it has.
But, speaking concretely, what's to be done?

....

The dead trial that was held, was bad,

The other one, the true one, did not take place

In their refrigerated chamber. 290

Let's hold it right here.

It's our turn, us the vermin, to be the gods of this cemetery!

What a great stroke it would be!

MOTHER Right here? In the absence of our opponents?

CHORUS What are you saying? Wherever the opponents may be hiding,

In the furthest foreign country or in the shelter of a prison,

Behind false papers,

Or taking refuge in convents,[18]

We could look for them, and we'd find them.

MOTHER But they are protected by armoured doors,[19] 300

By bolts, bars, and bodyguards,

By alarms and double-barrel locks:

CHORUS There are plenty of professionals, you know.

STROPHE 4

I already see myself doing the impossible

And doors fall one by one as I shoot.

I jump from a Chrysler into a Chevrolet.

They burn, they explode, the enemy shoots,

I always get out alive. In the end, we are

In the depths of a gigantic garage, 310

We can't go any further in the universe.

ANTISTROPHE 4

Once the enemy is at bay, I jump on him,

And I say: unjust Justice is not an inescapable fate.

And everything has not been settled long ago,

For ever and ever.

We are going to demonstrate this for you.

He protests: Io! Io! Do you see that?

With all his strength he clings to the pillar,

He even goes so far as to beg *me*, to implore *me*, 320

But we are incorruptible, it's innate in us.

So, I lift him, you hand me a gag

To muffle his shameful cries.

He thinks we're going to slit his throat.

CHORUS But we're not butchers here.

We are dispensers of justice.

AESCHYLUS If you bring the murderers back here,

Despair will flee.

CHORUS

STROPHE 5 330

Ah! Yes! But how can we manage all this?

Because, just think, if we were to fail,

In another version, see what I mean?

ANTISTROPHE 5

Yes, if I don't capture him in the garage,

Due to the black fumes rising from the burning cars –

This garage is an infernal shaft –
I exit half dead, the alarm sounds.
If I come back to hide here,
I'll be hunted.   340
A sinister net will swoop down upon our camp.
Eight dead, about a hundred wounded
And we all perish in the dust, we must consider this.
There was a time when I was invincible.
Ah, if only this whole affair had fallen upon us
Some twenty years ago.
I was stronger then. And so were you,
And so was he.

                                                    [Noises are heard from the dam

CHORUS And this one here didn't exist.   350
AESCHYLUS So, we are at a dead end, aren't we?
CHORUS We are.
NIGHT You won't even try? You give up?
CHORUS The world is without miracles.
    Everything rusts. Except dreams.

    ....

    Excuse me, it's getting late, I'm going to bed.
    It's wiser. Let's be frank,
    If you had seen me thirty years ago,
    I was a lion. Now I am a gnat.   360
NIGHT A gnat, you say?
CHORUS No. Now I am a louse
    And I'll exit like a louse. There.
NIGHT Does not the brilliance of my astral lights
    Give you courage?
CHORUS Not really. I'd like to rush ahead,
    But one must be prudent.

    ....

    That which is already dark, let's not make it darker.
    Victory does not always come from combat.   370
    One can also wait.

                                                                 [Exit the CHORUS

AESCHYLUS You're disappointed. Creatures without roofs, without teeth, not dead, for sure,
    But a bit hazy, others might call them crazy – ants, seashells, nutshells on the Ocean.
    They lack training. It's my fault.
MOTHER I, however, cannot give up
    And if I must die before victory,
    Once dead, I will shake the earth.
    I will be like the ancient Greek vessel
    Resting, heavy with the silt of millennia   380
    In the port of Lakydon until yesterday.
    Three thousand years have damaged neither its soul nor its wood.[20]
    If I lie sunk in oblivion three thousand years deep,
    Under muddy layers of silence,

I'll keep my wreck in a shipshape state of memory.
Have no doubt, the day will come
When my wreck and I
Will bear unheard-of witness.
Ah, if I could sleep a thousand years!

[*She goes to sleep*   390

NIGHT Sleep a few moments.
Meanwhile I will conjure up
My three faithful and fabled daughters.
They need only a signal to arise, panting,
From the tenebrous nest of time.
And you will experience
A wonderful visitation!

[*Exit* NIGHT

Scene 4

Enter DANIEL *and* BENJAMIN EZEKIEL, *the dead children*

DANIEL [*singing*] Get up, little brother,
Stand up on your skeleton legs,
The hour of war has come, I am ready to bolt,
I spit iron, I spit fire,
I sharpen my fangs,
I make pellets of black blood,
I split worms all around
Are you dawdling, or are you still alive?
BENJAMIN [*singing*] I am still alive, I still want,
I want to stay with mama.   10
Her heart is my apartment.
Child of air, child of wind,
I'm afraid of gold, I'm afraid of blood.
I am still living with mama.
DANIEL [*singing*] You're dreaming, little brother,
We have been killed and subtracted.
Benjamin, what are you waiting for?
Get up and sound the charge with your xylophone bones.
The hour has come to start the hunt
For the sons torn away from the mother   20
Prematurely.
BENJAMIN [*singing*] Daniel? Is it you, older brother,
Calling to me in the wind?
I don't recognize your voice,
Your old face has changed.
DANIEL [*singing*] I am Daniel Ezekiel, the elder,
Born 5 March 1980, died 14 July 1990,
Murdered.

They put mildew in my blood and my brother's blood.
Now do you recognize me?   30
BENJAMIN [*singing*] I am Benjamin Ezekiel, your brother,
        Born 20 May 1983, died –
        In an hour, it will be eight whole days.
        I am happy for my brother
        That I am now at the cemetery,
        But I am sad for my mother.
        We are the two sons mama had for naught.
        Had I known, I'd sooner have died in her womb,
        Mama would have been my tomb;
        And I would never have known   40
        The double wrenching pain.
DANIEL [*singing*] I, however, regret nothing.
        I didn't come here to cry and rot.
        While the day lasted, I was rough and happy.
        Such will I also be at night,
        In body clad, or worm-eaten.
        Turn into dust if you want,
        I'll go alone to war.
        My mission is to pursue our murderers
        And to take them, livid with fright   50
        To the altar of atonement.
        Either follow me, or stay with the worms.
BENJAMIN [*singing*] Don't get angry, big brother.
        My crying, that was a joke.
        I'd rather die a hundred times than disobey you.
        Quick, tell me, what do we do from here,
        Shadows of boys that we are?
DANIEL [*singing*] The men who withered our blood
        Can't be saved by their silver and gold.
        We are going to wreck, ruin, taint, haunt, infest   60
        All their appetites, and then . . .
        But first do as I do, Benjamin,
        Put a haughty look on your face,
        Very serious, very appalling,
        Go ahead! Stomp your foot! Chin up!
        Get mad! Higher, more terrible! More serious!
        Very good. As soon as our ghosts appear,
        Everyone must tremble, screaming:
        Popoï ! Here are the Ezekiel brothers!
        Here they are, the two sons newly reunited   70
        For our misfortune. Do you follow me?
BENJAMIN [*singing*] Yes! As soon as we died, this role was assigned to us.
        Those who murdered us,
        We must hunt them down.
DANIEL [*singing*] Then, ringing with all our dead bones,
        Let's rouse up all the divine officials

Who might be willing to help us
If only they heard us!
Hello up there! You starry grown-ups,
Do you hear us? It's the two Ezekiels calling!   80
Is there anybody up there?
BENJAMIN [*singing*] Louder, shout again!
Call them all, gods and goddesses!
DANIEL [*singing*] Oh gods, clouds, powerful lords of the heights,
Oh Night of limitless embrace,
Ezekiel the elder,
In the name of sacred and massacred blood,[21]
Begs you to come. Come!
I'm scared of becoming too dead
Before avenging mama.   90
We were murdered very young.
The men who sacrificed us,
Sticky with our blood,
Will never forgive us,
And for their intolerable crime
They will want to punish mama!
No answer? Io! Io! Io!
BENJAMIN [*singing*] Wait! Listen!
DANIEL [*singing*] Alone in the wind, we are waiting!
Iooo!   100

[*They exit*

Scene 5

Enter the three FURIES, ALECTO, TISIPHONE *and* MEGAERA

FURIES I'm coming! I'm coming!
But I see that nothing has changed!
....
Everything changed in appearance,
But during these last five thousand years, while we were underground,
Nothing has changed, neither for the good nor the better,
In the human tune.
Still the same grinding sounds, intolerable for my teeth.
The tears of mothers are still flowing.[22]
....   10
Hearts still pour out irrefutable complaints
And the courts, needless to say, still judge them inadmissible.
No longer say that I am old,
If today is the same as yesterday.
Time, you spin your wheel for nothing,
You dig and redig the same hole.
I see the same aberrations, over and over again.

Only the costume is new.

....

Let no one tell me that I am worn out.   20
Have I become other than who I was
When, faster than the beast who runs
One hundred miles an hour and whose name is . . .

....

Leopard

....

Leopard, that's it, and faster than a lemur,
I would, in a powerful leap, jump
From the city of Delphi to the city of Athens,[23]
On the furtive heels of my criminals?   30

....

Me too, I'm the same, I still support the mother's right,
Above all contrary rights.
It wasn't for me to change
On the famous day when with Queen Athena I signed
The treaty of civic peace for all time to come.[24]
A radiant sun made its entrance there on the earth.
The new gods were in the olive trees,
Swinging naked from the branches.
I was wearing red . . .   40

AESCHYLUS Black . . . the Furies always wear black. Draped in black robes striped with black . . .

FURIES So? What did we agree upon?

....

On the one hand, I'd go down to live
In rooms under the earth,
And I'd be silent day in and day out,
And people would never even hear me cough – ever.[25]
On the other hand, up there on earth,
Democracy would prosper and grow
In height and breadth under the blue breezes   50
Which blow with a good sun.
And the race of the just would become more and more just.
Go down under the earth, Athena told us,
And don't send diseases or evil destinies upon my citizens.
No, no. Yes, yes. So I said. So she said.
So we went down to live under the earth, as promised.

....

And for tens of hundreds of years
No one saw us!
We remained seated, our mouths full of dirt,   60
In the agreed-upon darkness.
And see what came of this wonderful contract!

....

What's new here,
Except the telephone? I'd like to know.

....
The flowers all around are soaked with blood,
These are the same flowers and this is the same blood,
It always runs in the same way towards the dust
And once spilled, it still can't be unspilled.   70
So, our treaty, what good was it?

....
On our side, for five thousand years
We kept our word.
No deadly evil blows over the trees,
No sterility thievishly enters
The wombs of ewes or any other female creature.[26]

....
None on our part, at least.

....   80
And no dust, having soaked up the black blood of citizens
And thirsting for retaliation,
Exacts from the City
Calamity for murder and a tooth for a tooth.[27]

....
None on our part, at least.

....
The plagues, I'm not the one who spreads them.

....
Nor me either. Not a single plague,   90
Whether it's called plague or otherwise.
But others, I see,
Have let loose a flood of plagues,
Totally invincible, incurable.

....
For the past 5000 years, no more Furies,
And just look at this planet, what a state it's in!

....
Well, I've had enough!
At one time, when we were part of the landscape of crime,
Every murderer clearly knew that he was a murderer   100
And that we would be his unflagging and intolerable companions
To the very ends of the continents.
Venomous lice on the heart,
Paralysis on eyelids
That would never close again –
That's just a little of what we were.

....
But at last, the world without Furies is over.
Since the young Ezekiel died,   110
It's over. We've returned.

....

You're going to say, why the young Ezekiel, why him?
He was so thin, so gay, so wise, so tender,
So quick-tempered, limping a tiny bit, and so transparent,
....

But that's not why. They are all so thin,
So gay. When the end comes, you see their bones through their transparent skin.
And they all limp a little.
....   120

Why him? That's the way it is.
No one ever knows who will be the last drop.
Suddenly, the bottomless bottom of darkness
Is pierced by a minuscule moonbeam.
....

It is thanks to the last drop.
It pierces the drum of rock.
Suddenly, its voice cries "Io-Iooo."
We heard it and right after
Came the dull scent of blood.   130
But blood is no longer the blood that told us everything.
It is no longer as simple, or as frank,
As odouriferous, as decisive.
It's an unusual essence of blood,
A potpourri of red blood and pale blood,
Some bloods are bleached, others are discolored.
This is what misleads us, this aroma of false blood.
Nevertheless, it's the real stuff,
This concentrated, distilled, alchemized vapour of something,
Separated into billions of atoms and then reconstituted,   140
It's blood, nevertheless.[28]
And above this skimmed blood full of unknown perfumes, harsh and striking,
Floats – hm . . . – a strong scent of eau-de-toilette,
That of an elegant man, a bit too strong, a bit too much man,
Applied a little too liberally. There, that's it:
Like a veil of perfume over a stench.
You see who I mean?
No, you don't see.
....

You, who belong to this century   150
And have lived since your birth
In the era of technical reproduction,
Could you help us?
....

In the first place, we're looking for a gentleman,
Who is like this and like that.
....

The name? No, I will not name the name.[29]
Because if by misfortune or inadvertently,
I say the name, immediately, this man will send after us   160

His lawyers, etc.
The police will appear and stop this play here and
For all time to come.
....

I don't want to say the name,
I don't want to sully my teeth with this name here or that name there.
I do not want to make the transparent air of this sacred enclosure cringe
With abominable syllables.
Besides, I have forgotten the names completely.
Like fish, they slipped   170
Through the mesh of my amnesiac memory.
....

We'll have to call them by some name, however,
So they can answer for their abominations.
....

In that case, we will call them: that one there and that one there-there.[30]
Or . . . the other one. . . . It all depends.
....

But neither the thick skirts of a prison,
Nor the walls of a convent,   180
Nor those of a World Bank,[31]
Will be able to protect them from our irresistible raid,
Since today we embrace the mother's cause.
....

We could tear old verdicts into a thousand pieces,
Reduce them to ashes,
Start over all the courtroom scenes,
Begin the Trial at square one.
....

Kidnap the man in question.   190
....

Kidnap this one as well as that one,
And all their kind.
....

And bring them here, the whole pack.
....

Listen, all of you,
You cannot even imagine
How powerful we were!
The Universe trembled at the sound of our voices.   200
....

We didn't need to raise the voice,
Raising an eyebrow was enough!
Am I right?
AESCHYLUS It's the truth, I saw kings bolt before the Furies,
    Just at the idea of them, just at their name.
FURIES Well, do you take us for sisters? Do you?
    She doesn't say a word, therefore, she takes us for sisters.

NIGHT All right. All right. Let's get going.

    Our enemies are still sound asleep.   210

    Go ahead, pounce upon them, take them by surprise,

    Strike them with panic,

    Act in everything as if you were nightmares armed to the teeth.

    They will want to call the police, the army, the cabinet,

    The government, the head of state: smother their calls,

    Prepare the nets and the narcotics,

    Cut the telephone lines,

    Freeze their spirits. And bring them back alive.

ONE FURY It's as good as done.

NIGHT Come on, my daughters, at a gallop and no detours.   220

    Already I hear the Sun stirring in his sleep.

FURIES Come on, let's go, let's strike Europe with astonishment!

    ....

    Let's go. Let's fall on these people.

    The faces they'll make crack me up!

    Oh, the flight! Oh, the fright! Oh, the massacre!

NIGHT Alive, I said!

FURIES Those who believed they had won, have not won.

    Mu . . . Mu . . . Mu . . .

                                             [*they exit*   230

NIGHT And you wise spirits, geniuses,

    And worthy gods from all countries,

    United by the love of the Just,

    Shepherd them safely through

    The obscure and pitiless day.[32]

    From high above I will watch over their course.

    You, meanwhile, go prepare the next act.

                                             [*Exit* NIGHT

MOTHER It may be folly, but I'm for it.

    Everything is going so much faster and stronger than my reason.   240

    They precede me, they lead me on,

    And yet, it's as if they just came out of

    The burning bush which since my children's deaths

    Crackles in my chest.

    I am transported with joy . . .

    But if it is a dream, I implore all humanity,

    Do not wake me before we've won.

AESCHYLUS Who can say where the border lies between "here" and "there"?

    "Such stuff as dreams are made of . . ."

    It seems to me, sometimes, that I am an Other,[33]   250

    But I do not fear him.

                                             [*They exit*

Enter DANIEL *and* BENJAMIN

DANIEL and BENJAMIN [*singing*] And my anger lifted me up into the air and carried me away

And I went, exalted by anger,

And my brow was like a diamond, harder than rock,

My resolute brow against their ormolute brows.

The men who withered our blood

Cannot be saved by their silver and gold.

[*They exit*   260

Scene 6

Enter two CHORUS *members*: THESSALONIKI *and* JEAN-CHRISTOPHE LAMERD

THESSALONIKI So: three old goats arrive, even skinnier than we are, they spew big words, bellowing with
a strange accent,

And presto, you're a believer! Justice! Truth!

Soap bubbles, and you take them for constellations.

Twenty-five years of scorn, of starvation, of passing the hat around,

That didn't teach you anything?

LAMERD I never said: I believe.

I said: I'd like to see.

Is that forbidden? What does it cost to imagine? It comforts me to say:

"The end of iniquity is coming!"   10

It's such a long time since we had any hope for it!

Five thousand years divided by twenty, how many generations does that make? And look, today, here
it is, it gladdens my heart to believe that I see Justice coming: jealous of her glory, she has climbed
into her chariot,

The interminable wars are going to stop cold,

The outcasts will be invited to the feast.

THESSALONIKI Fat chance, you scum! How dare you believe such great news, knucklehead!

A perfectly just Justice never existed except in the dreams of young exiles.

You, a poor lousy rogue, you mount your scraggy donkey backwards, and on to Jerusalem.

And tomorrow Jews and Arabs will fall into each other's arms just because you're going there! Don't   20
you know how dangerous it is to hope?

Go on, you bat, go on hoping and knock yourself senseless against the Wailing Wall!

LAMERD Shut your mouth, you doormat, lie down, you shivering old cur!

Stay, don't follow me. It's not your fault if you are dying of fear. The leash has become second nature
to you.

THESSALONIKI It's because you don't know hope, the heartbreaker.

One day a young girl in a deportation camp,

In Ravensbrück, embraced a rumour

That spread madly through the barracks.

Someone had said that this young beauty   30

Would soon be freed.

It was a tale to give her patience.

She believed what she shouldn't have believed.

Then came the too-heavy day when the razor was held

– No, not to her throat, but to her beautiful hair.

That meant: you will stay here.
Her cries didn't count. Her locks fell.
Do you know what happened?
She wrapped her pretty bare head in a rag
And snap! she died. Snap! Right next to me. 40
So, don't hope.
She will never come, the beauty with long curls,
She will never come, the divine one with straight back
And nostrils flaring in fury-
We used to call her "Dikè"
But she would not answer us.
The ones we wait for never come,
It's always like that.
The Messiah doesn't come,
Justice doesn't come, 50
The beautiful gods do not respond.

LAMERD You Jewish whore, shut up!

THESSALONIKI Greek. Not Jewish. Thessaloniki is a Greek name.

LAMERD Thessaloniki! Who could have given you such an awfully true name?[34]
    It suits you well, you Greek Jewish slut or Jewish Greek slut,
    Always preaching distrust and despair.
    You play into the rich bastards' hands.
    It's easy not to hope,
    You crouch in trash,
    You scratch your scabs with the shards of a Coke bottle, 60
    And you croak.

THESSALONIKI And you, Jean-Christophe Lamerd![35] What a French name!
    Phew! I won't tell you what I think of it!
    With a name like that, one always tries to deny
    That, by definition, the streets of the Universe
    Are for eternity paved with the skulls of niggers.[36]
    You're born either on the black or the white side.
    Heads or tails, the die is cast.
    You'll never change hemispheres.
    And I'll give you another example: 70
    One day, a black man . . . Ouch! . . . Stop! . . . Help! Murder!

LAMERD Stop trying to cut short my hope with your words,
    Or I'll cut your hopeless throat with my knife.
    You're nothing but a walking corpse, so silence!

THESSALONIKI But . . . Listen! Wait! Don't kill me just yet!
    Listen to this, I'm telling you!

LAMERD Quiet! Listen to what?

THESSALONIKI That noise! Don't you hear it? Listen! Listen!
    Lo! I'll never say again
    That hope is dangerous, 80
    Because it's for us alone, the cast-aways of the Earth,
    That the Incredible may happen!

LAMERD This whirring of wings, of wheels, of death-rattles, of mingled flames approaching[37] . . .

Oh! My God! I fear disappointment!
I fear disappointment!

Scene 7

Enter AESCHYLUS, NIGHT, *then* FURIES *and the two kidnapped adversaries,* X1 *and* X2

FURIES Mu! Mu! Catch! Catch! Get him! And hop,
    We caught him,
    Not the slightest contrary god
    Interfered to steal our prey.

    ....
    Their hands are all feeble.
    Their knees are knocking.
    The terror we cause them, we read it in their eyes.

    ....
    Here you are, and you as well, here among the rats   10
    To pay what you owe
    For the pain that gnawed at the flesh of small children,
    And made the dying and the mothers cry.

    ....
    Oh! My back is broken.
    These men, how heavy!
    The bodies we carried
    Were lined with the lead of stupor and rage,
    And filled with hardened organs.
NIGHT Do you see this huge crowd pressing toward you?   20
    All they want is an explanation from you.
    Give it to them and you will behold the human sea
    Parting to let you go
    And walk home with dry feet.
    I advise you:
    Feed them with humble and truthful words.
FURIES But first tell us how many children
    You took away from their parents, how many parents were bereft of the apple of their eyes,
    And how many fathers you stole away from their children,
    Thus robbing them of roof and shield?   30

    ....
    I'm listening. Tell me how many hundreds already
    Have gone under the floor of the world
    And how many more to go in coming years?

    ....
    Say it quickly, before I murder you.
MOTHER What are they doing?
    Caretaker! Aeschylus!
    Wait, Venerable Ones, wait,

You're going so quickly,   40
    This is not what I wanted.
FURIES So quickly? What do you mean?
    It always went like this.
    The man who killed, first we'd chase him
    For ten years or so.
    Then, with a long leopard's leap,
    We'd jump on him
    And make him roll in the waiting dust.
    That was the moment of sacrifice,
    No temporizing. I'm taking you as a witness.   50
AESCHYLUS That is true, that was the way in the old tradition.
    But today, we cannot content ourselves
    With too quick a satisfaction.
    Time is required.
FURIES In the blink of an eye
    We'll slaughter him like a pig.
CHORUS We can also knock him out, if you prefer.
MOTHER Oh! No!
FURIES Then how do you want him to die? Tell us.
MOTHER Well, of shame, maybe. Yes.   60
    With a terrible blow from the inside.
    Do you understand?
FURIES No. Explain yourself.

    ....
    Death from shame? I've never heard of such a thing.
    What about you? And you, Night, our mother?
NIGHT Nor have I. But one could check.
    For none of what is happening just now under my pavilion
    Has ever happened before, has it?
AESCHYLUS All of this is unprecedented. It's a story unheard-of   70
    Until now, voiceless, truthless, endless.
    Countless, nameless victims,
    Some are dying while we speak
    And in ten years, others will go off dying
    Without a just tale to accompany them.
    This is a story peopled with deaf, mute and muzzled people,
    Full of suppressed cries, drained blood,
    And paralysed tongues.
FURIES Exactly. That's why we must make a clean cut.
AESCHYLUS It would be unthinkable to botch a drama   80
    That will haunt the memories of nations
    For several generations
    With a tacked-on scene of vengeance.
    For years and years we have been deprived of air,
    Deprived of the music of the spheres,
    Deprived of the sweet cello strains of mourning.
    No human literature, no hymns.

We want exact retribution for our suffering:

For so much silence, so many chants.

FURIES I see what you are driving at, Poet. I, however, have the mission of striking straight to the heart. 90

This poet here is still thinking of one of those tribunes.

....

Tribunals!

....

No more tribunals; never again.

There's no condition as unbearable

As that of plaintiffs sent to court

When their tongues have been cut out beforehand.

....

On the side of my mouth there grows an exterior tongue 100

Which tells my complaint in my place

And does not know the taste of my pain.

Instead of my own seething emotion, I hear another, foreign, voice.

For my misery, there is no expression.

My eyes shed bitter tears

That are not listened to.

Pushed before the orifice of the court of justice,

In vain I lean forward to catch a glimmer.

I am nailed to the threshold, all is black inside.

Sitting on a bench, muzzled, substituted, 110

Aghast, I witness my own spoliation.

MOTHER Ah! We have all experienced that.

NIGHT So, we are agreed, no tribunal,

But, rather, a vast and audacious arena,

Where, not without proper ceremony nor an oath of truth,

The victim, who never spoke in the house of justice

Where my stars do not shine,

Will herself freely and loudly proclaim before us

The whole of her bereavement and her indignation.

Go prepare yourselves. 120

And come back as soon as possible to this portico.

Meanwhile I will send visions to

All those inside the city whom we will soon summon,

Since the characters in this story have not yet all

Gathered under my torches.

Those men without dreams, and thus without remorse,

Without remorse, and thus without dreams,

I want them all to feel that I, Night, exist.

[*Exit* NIGHT

CHORUS In vain do you look to me for salvation, 130

I'll have no compassion.

Yesterday, you acted as if you didn't see me,

I, today, have eyes that don't notice you.

Now suffer in your turn.

[*Exeunt* FURIES *and* CHORUS

MOTHER May my children's iron words
    Spill forth from my mouth and may those who died of sorrow
    Surge like flames out of their frozen tombs
    To give us strength.

AESCHYLUS I'll look for my dictionaries.   140
    Experience has taught me
    That pain needs numerous synonyms.

                                     [*Exeunt* MOTHER *and* AESCHYLUS

X1 Shadows, trash, refuse rebellious to reason and to law,
    Decrepit, sanguinary misfits,
    League of hysteria and senility,
    Association of madmen,
    Sordid pack of witches sick with cynanthropy,[38]
    Howl, you asylum fodder, you don't scare me!
    I wasn't born for doubt or trembling,   150
    But starting tomorrow, when the police
    Swoop down on you like a tide of plagues
    And clean up the entire cemetery,
    You'll mourn the time that's past,
    But you won't be able to bring it back.
    Today I seem small to you because I am in your hands,
    But tomorrow you will pass from the fallacious Night
    That makes you drunk with insane claims,
    To the sober logic of day,
    Which knows how to count, curb and retaliate.   160
    For some, it will be prison,
    For others, the madhouse,
    And you'll have only yourselves to blame.

Scene 8

                       Enter NIGHT, CHORUS *and* AESCHYLUS

NIGHT Let us now enter the Palace,
    Where everyone is nervous as the fateful Election approaches,
    Except for him, the King.
    The King has a secret and mysterious advisor,
    A very dangerous mentor, a very insidious old counsellor.
    Who do you say it is? No. No.
    The King's advisor is none other than the Grand Excuser,
    The leveller of hearts, who blunts our emotions.
    I am describing Time to you,
    The powerful gravedigger of human memory.   10
    No one has seen him.
    Yet one smells his odour in the Palace very well.
    Do you smell it? That sour scent?
    That acrid odour in the curtains?

We know it: it is the rottenness of kingdoms.

I smelled that smell once before, hundreds of years ago, in the cemetery at Elsinore.

If you come too close, it clings to your moustache,

To your coat, your gloves, your vest.

It turns into an ointment on your chest,

And then, for years to come,   20

It will stick in the pores of your skin.

AESCHYLUS An odour like that is a cry of alarm.

Sniffing this message, we all wonder:

This stench, where does it come from?

Of what opposite particles is it composed?

We all wonder: the King, who is he?

And the Queen, what does she say?

But there is the enigma: look.

Enter KING *and* QUEEN

KING Are you besieging me?   30

QUEEN I will be mounting a siege against you

Until the battlement cracks.

KING Speak.

QUEEN I had a dream bearing bad news.

I was lost in the immense Parliament

Teeming with people who were electing, or had just elected, whom?

Leaning by chance against a newspaper rack

Loaded with the day's newspapers, suddenly,

I see a big black headline on the front page:

"*Queen Dies* At The Children's Cemetery."[39]   40

It hit me hard. I, dead?

Had I read correctly? I lunge at the pile of papers,

I leaf through, tears overcome me, –

I feel sobs welling up in bitter swells,

Dead! I had to tell you, what ghastly news for my King!

Haggard, I search for you for hours, scouring the crowds.

Once, I catch sight of you from afar, as you disappear,

I'm going to tell the King, I tell myself,

But suddenly I stop – unless he already knows.

Wasn't the newspaper from the day before?   50

Of course! What you already know,

I hear it in the present of today

And too late! No, no, there's still time,

The end has not come yet!

KING It was only a dream.

We are quite alive, both of us,

And far from being defeated.

QUEEN It is a warning. Something in us is dying.

They're going to vote in two days,

Those who used to love us so   60

And now love us less.
You were among them like the Sun,
Everyone sought you out,
They adored your light,
And you, the Sun, you have set,
You let neon lights
Illuminate the land in your place.
Allow me to tell you about
The dead children.

KING I allow you.   70

QUEEN It's a very grave matter.

KING Grave, certainly, but not more than hundreds of others
Whose spectral faces I have seen sternly defying us
Before melting into the Ocean of events.

QUEEN It puts us in danger.
We will be thrown out without deserving it,
Just for failing to say, or do something . . .

KING We did exactly what had to be done.
What is it I did not do, hm?
You worry too much and you're blowing this out of proportion.   80

QUEEN Don't you sense that this misfortune is unsettling the entire Kingdom?

KING I do not sense what is not there.
Let's drop it. Besides, to act as if our fate,
The fate of our Nation and of all Europe,
Depended on a petty medical affair,
That's a great mistake. We are above that.

QUEEN A petty medical affair, no.

KING Yes. A medical affair. Yes. An affair of mangy doctors.
Mange is disgusting, but it's very easily treated.

QUEEN What if it were the end of your Kingdom?   90
A little scratch. A mere nothing.
But it bleeds. Bleeds. Bleeds.
Nothing can quench the blood any more.

KING Stop! Woman! You're speaking like a woman!
Nothing is more dangerous in politics than exaggeration.
A strong King must keep clear of snake pits.
If he falls in the pit, up close the snakes
Look like dragons.
Don't make the cut on a pinky look bigger than it is.
It's a wound, I don't deny that.   100
But in no way is it an historical event.
None of this will go very far. Let's forget it.

QUEEN Maybe, I don't know, I'm not an expert.

AESCHYLUS Queen, don't give up, fight back.

QUEEN But I sense what is there. The country trembled.
A deep sigh escaped from its throat.

AESCHYLUS Yes! Yes! Keep at it!

KING These earthquakes don't knock me down.

Three times already, three wars wreaked havoc in the world,[40]

Dismantling the country, my career, my existence.   110

We picked ourselves up pretty well, didn't we?

QUEEN Yes. Yes . . . Yes.

NIGHT But that's not it! He's changing the subject!

He's gaining ground!

QUEEN Don't change the subject.

I wanted to talk about this illness that is invading

The Palace, the Court, the Grand Councils,

This atrophy of nerves leading to the heart.

These people don't feel anything anymore,

They have no more images in their imagination.   120

Well may Pity attempt to display to their eyes

The most terrible acts committed

At this very moment under our rich windows,

They will not shed a tear.

Are they emptied of all their organs?

Is there an empty hollow in the middle of their chest?

The animal odour of hate that blows from the city

Into their faces should alert them,

If not move them. But their sense of smell is gone,

No ear, no eye, no nose.   130

Have they forgotten they are mortals,

Eligible, crushable, expendable? Detestable.

What must be done to wake them up?

What about you? You let your blind men run headlong to perdition?

You say nothing?

People have come to loathe these palace dogs,

And these liars, too. That's what people are saying.

Oh, I know, they don't do it on purpose.

When they used to say: "brother," "my brother," "brotherhood,"

"My sister," they were sincere.   140

And now, where have these words gone?

Their mouths are empty, like their hearts, like their heads.

KING You exaggerate. Some have changed, that's true.

But not everybody has changed.

QUEEN Lo! How changed we are too, my Lord,

As if we had changed gods

Without warning or saying so,

Without even admitting it to ourselves.

You should do something, fast, fast, right away,

Because, I'm telling you, if you don't immediately put back in circulation   150

Tears, feeling, what is called the soul,

Aspiration and blessed words,

We are lost.

KING What do you want me to do?

Because of one corrupt man, should I fire

All the ministers, all the cabinet secretaries?

May I not keep a single one?
Are my friends all rotten to the core?
One has never seen a more obliging King,
A King more corrupt, or perhaps more perverse,   160
Or again, more cynical, is that it?

QUEEN I'm not saying that!
It's not of you that I speak!
They're not all rotten to the core.

KING So, whom do I throw out?

QUEEN At least –

KING Whom do I demote? Who do you take me for?
I am neither blind nor ruthless.
I do not compromise on principle,
Nor do I refuse compromise on principle.   170
I am neither a monster nor a machine.
I am a veteran of reality.
If I eliminate all public servants
Who present a slight flaw, an impurity,
There will be no one left in the Palace, nor at my table.
Besides, I will not be there either.
Men are shady by nature,
It is my royal duty to take that into account.
And then, I am not the keeper of Cain and Abel, am I?
I can't spend my life eternally   180
Asking each minister, each cabinet chief
And each and every one: where did your brother go?
What did you do with your capital?
When I was born, men had already been manufactured,
Some a little straight, others a little warped,
Most of them crooked.
I can't recreate humanity,
I make do with what I have.
I have my reasons for not punishing.
It serves no purpose.   190

QUEEN I didn't say punish.

KING Then what?

QUEEN You have invited this week to your own table
The former prefect of the devil himself.
The King is having lunch with the man of evil law
Who filled my generation with bad memories:
Fifty years ago, he caused
Over 4000 children to be marched to the cauldrons
And ovens – an atrocious, coldly ordered destination.[41]
I doubt that will make for a good meal.   200
How will you make the people swallow it?

KING Precisely, I planned this lunch on purpose,
As a man of good example and conscience,
For I believe one has a right to change.

Nobody is criminal in essence.
You kill one time, and then never again.
All things have their season.
Today the hour has come for wiping the slate.

QUEEN Some slates cannot be wiped clean.

KING What, because memory howls,   210
    Time must stop its work,
    The past must eternally remain present,
    Eternally? What, it's the month of May and it's still December?
    When, then, will the cherry trees bloom again?
    If we don't start forgetting now
    We'll be like those madmen
    That memory chews up again and again.

QUEEN What, because this took place only once,
    We should forget the thousands of children thrown into nothingness?
    What, are these train loads of shadows,   220
    Herds of abstractions,
    Or simply five or six numbers standing
    Side by side, without a face, without a body,
    1, 1, 2, 3, 7. Eleven thousand two hundred and thirty-seven. Children.

KING With one foot in the grave, life must start again.
    Every man has a rotten side
    And a side of rebirth.
    I walk as best as I can, hobbling along.

QUEEN This lunch –

KING I don't want any more of your advice.   230
    My only vizier is Time.[42] Time and I,
    We are leading this country and we'll lead it even further.
    As for the ministers, they are our taxi drivers,
    Very good drivers.

QUEEN How you've become . . .

KING Hard?

QUEEN Cold.

KING Wise.

QUEEN Grey.

KING We are no longer in love.   240

QUEEN And yet the woman who loved you
    Still loves the man she used to love.
    It is she who speaks now
    And who worries.

KING For the cold king that I am?

QUEEN She can't help it,
    But I, I love you without loving you.

KING And you, with time, have become, altogether, a Cassandra.[43]

QUEEN Altogether? That seems a lot.
    I believe I am only a fragment.   250
    I am the handwriting on the wall of your Palace:
    "Belshazzar, beware!"

The hand without an arm, without a body,
Is all that remains of a vanished civilization.
It no longer speaks. But it still writes:
Beware! I await you at the election.
Unfortunately, you don't have Belshazzar's haggard look.[44]

Enter an USHER

USHER The Minister is here, my Lord.
KING Send him in. What time is it?   260
    Come on, let's be friends again.
    I cannot see with your eyes,
    But I like your gaze.
    Trust me.
QUEEN I trust you. But I am afraid
    That you will not be well understood.
KING I am not understood. But I do not care.
    We will not lose the election,
    And you will agree that I was right.

Enter MINISTER   270

    Come in, come closer.
    Why are you so pale? Another problem?
MINISTER No, no! Only impressions.
    Discouraging figures
    That I want to show you.
    And then, I had a dreadful nightmare.
QUEEN You too?
MINISTER I heard a crow caw in my ear:
    "The Minister has murdered Sleep!
    Nothing will ever wipe away the children's blood!   280
    You will never be President of the Council!"
    It was like a scene from *Macbeth*,
    And I was Macbeth. And yet,
    I am not guilty.
KING Ah no! That's enough! Enough raving. It's irritating.
    Don't read any more Shakespeare or Aeschylus
    If you have delicate little nerves.
    Go ahead, show me these figures.

                                              [NIGHT *puts out the candle*
    What is it with this candle?   290
NIGHT The King's crown was of glass, and it shattered.
    At that moment, the candle went out . . .
MINISTER Now we are in the dark.
KING That doesn't frighten me.
MINISTER Let's wait, the light will come back.

KING Usher! Usher! Where did the fellow go?

QUEEN I wanted to talk about the children and the mother.
   With all this election talk, I completely forgot them,
   Lost them.

KING It's not coming back.   300

NIGHT [*to* AESCHYLUS] What do you say about all this?

AESCHYLUS It's complicated. On the one hand, I'd say:
   You are not guilty, King,
   But you *are* guilty.
   You did not commit this crime
   But while you were King, this crime was committed.
   On the other hand, I might only say:
   "A sky so polluted
   Will not clear up without the help of a powerful tempest."

Enter USHER, *with a candle*   310

KING So, Usher, you had disappeared.

USHER I was looking for candles.

KING Candles? Where is the electrician? Go get me Maintenance, right away. I don't want to get worked
   up.

USHER It's just that . . . Maintenance isn't here anymore, Sir.

KING Not here anymore? Where is he? Come on, no secrets.

USHER He is at the cemetery.

KING Dead?!

USHER Oh, no, no! On the contrary.

KING How so?   320

MINISTER At the cemetery? He is with those people?

USHER He is.

KING Well then, call him.

USHER The telephone isn't working.

KING Send a messenger. I want him to come.
   He can't just leave like that, really!
   Well, go get him! Go!

[*Exit* MINISTER

   All of this is extraordinary!
   There is something in the Palace, in the furniture,   330
   In people's faces as well, something extremely strange,
   It's imponderable. Something in the way time passes, too.
   An hour just went by in a flash.
   [*Seeing the* USHER *sleeping*] And him sound asleep,
   And this wind striking and breaking me apart,
   And this oak suddenly shedding its leaves,
   My sap, my trunk. And this squirrel
   Sinking its claws into the branch
   And gnawing and gnawing. There too. The same thing,
   The same beast, gnawing and gnawing.   340
   You are all there, with a thousand claws in me!

Minuscule demons. Have I not fed you?
Are you changing sides? Are you falling out?
Ah, there's Maintenance . . .

MAINTENANCE *appears*

Well, old companion, you take off at night,
Leaving your friend without a light,
Without an explanation?
MAINTENANCE Sir, I couldn't stand
Repairing electricity anymore. I was too unhappy.   350
KING Why? You were in distress
And I wasn't told?
MAINTENANCE It should really be known
That in this Palace where light flickers,
The power has been going out every five minutes for the last three years,
Sometimes in a hall, sometimes in the sitting room.
It's not an electrician like me
That this world needs.
It needs a healing saint.
I was planning on leaving after the election,   360
But why linger,
To stay in the temple when one is disenchanted, that's a sin.
KING We've known each other for a good forty years
And you are telling me this now, all of a sudden!
With such drama!
Is this is in any way my fault?
Tell me a bit of truth.
MAINTENANCE The problem is the crumbling of beauty in this Kingdom,
Underway for some years already.
It is the petrification of living dreams,   370
The freezing up of energy.
I was under a spell between 1941 and yesterday,
I thought it was for life.
I'll tell you what I blame this King for:
For having said in the first scene: "I will do *this*,"
Then, for having done something else in the second scene;
Next, for saying in the third scene
"What I just did was exactly the thing I promised you in the first scene."
What I blame this King for
Is not having trusted me.   380
Forty years I spent at his side:
Did I ever leave him? I was the sword, the friend, the servant,
During each battle, before every city.
No need to lie to Maintenance.
This ruler here, I saw him from every possible angle.
What I blame him for is his failure to say:
"My friend, this year, no dreams.

I will not keep my promise.

No dreams for next year either.

I will take up arms again as soon as I am able to."   390

Would not Maintenance have stayed, then?

KING I should have spoken to you,

I never had the time. I didn't think of it.

MAINTENANCE For thirty years I was able to believe that we were going towards humanity.

And here he is, having lunch with the incarnation of inhumanity.

I see you giving medals to people who should already be in prison[45]

And I, your arm, your sword, your flank,

I, too, ate at your table, gave medals, made concessions.

You became more and more the King, I less and less my own thing,

Pursuing a bitter mission in the sunless Palace,   400

In dissension with my former gods.

This luncheon totally broke the spell.

Soon after I drew some conclusions.

Now, I share my thoughts and my meals

With the Society of Shadows and Refuse –

I would never have thought I could do that.

KING Well! Stay with them, then. Everything breaks down. Let's make an end of it.

An end to loyalty. Enough said! Too much heard!

I'm disconnecting. Cut the line. Cut off everything, everything!

This branch too. And the wind!   410

Bring all of this down.

A King has no friends! Cut!

Cut! I've been too patient.

Go away!

              [*Exit* MAINTENANCE

There was a time when such treason

Would have made my stomach heave.

But I have eaten this lethal dish so often

That like Mithridates, I have become immune to it.[46]

Abandon me, my last friend,   420

That is to say, my last betrayer.

The light comes on again as MINISTER *returns*

Ah, but I see that we have light now!

Who fixed it?

MINISTER I did.

KING You? Really, I am quite pleased.

Where were we?

MINISTER Discussing the polls. I was saying:

We've lost a hundred thousand votes in a few days.

KING Whose fault is that? No one's supporting the citizen,   430

Unthinkable choices are made,

And I'm to take the rap?

MINISTER You dare tell me that?

KING Let's quarrel elsewhere,
    Or patch things up.

                                                              [The electricity goes out

    And that, that's not you?
    I wish so much that discord no longer ate at our hearts.

                                                                     [Exeunt

AESCHYLUS It is wise to fear, in order to avert the worst,   440
    It is wise not to fear, so that the worst dare not show itself.
    Everything becomes very complicated.
    Whew! I can't wait to get back to the cemetery.
NIGHT Tell me, who is this Belshazzar?
AESCHYLUS Who isn't familiar with Belshazzar?! !
NIGHT I am not.[47]
AESCHYLUS One day, a king was eating up his land
    From gold and silver plates –
    I read it in the Bible –
    Then, their terribly furious God   450
    Sent him a hand that wrote on the wall . . .
    I'll tell you more on the way.

                                                                     [Exeunt

Scene 9

                    Enter SENATOR FORZZA *and* MONSIEUR CAPTAIN, *his attaché*

FORZZA Well, Monsieur Captain, you have a sparkle in your eye.
    Any news from the electoral front?
MONSIEUR CAPTAIN This one here, Senator: the mother of the murdered children,
    The one who retreated to the Grand Cemetery,
    She's getting ready to cause an extraordinary scandal.
    Here. I wrote a memo.
FORZZA Oh, this is great! This could not come at a better moment!
    How happy I am! A superb affair,
    We couldn't have done better. And it does not stop!
    There is always one more death. That moves people's feelings!   10
    Children, no less! And new developments!
MONSIEUR CAPTAIN Except for these doctors.
    Too bad they are on our side.
FORZZA Slander! That's what I say.
    As to you, young man, I'll give you an F.
    You should not be reporting this, even to me,
    At this delicate juncture.
MONSIEUR CAPTAIN Yes, you are right. Slander.
FORZZA But, tell me, was it you who urged the mother?
MONSIEUR CAPTAIN No, honestly, I didn't have anything to do with it.   20
FORZZA Well, this is very, very good.
MONSIEUR CAPTAIN Is it? I thought, Senator:

On all these gaping wounds
We could spill a hot spice that would make them scream.
Hatred would flame up.
Once the government was surrounded with accusations,
Our friends would break loose, we'd push . . .

FORZZA Stop! The winning ideas, here, it's Forzza who has them.
My idea, in this affair, is this:
What we'll do is: nothing. We keep quiet.   30
We don't move.
As you can see, the King and his party regularly get bogged down.
Meanwhile, from our camp stationed up high
We observe the others down below, sinking
On their own, by their own doing.
The people are disgusted, on their own.
"How much filth there is," people say to each other,
Going from one house to the next.
"Do you see this swamp?" they ask each other.
"It's their excrement. They who used to boast   40
Of belonging to a race different from the rest," says one,
"No dime, no grime,[48]
And a soul of better quality,
And yet, they are up to their chins in muck," says one.
And the other says: "They were like everyone else,
And they didn't tell!
What makes them less evil than those on the other side?"
And the other remains silent.
This is what people go around saying, of their own initiative.
Above all, let's not go and brag at the wrong time,   50
Now is not the time. Without any cost on our part,
This affair brings us one hundred thousand votes.
The enemy is working for us!
"The Benefactor In Spite of Himself," that's the title of the comedy.[49]
One never saw such a war.
I'm having a ball!
A war where our enemy, the poor thing,
Rises against himself, rushes against himself
And puts in our place and at his own expense
The very mines which blow him to pieces.   60
Go on, gentlemen!!!
Commit your blunders, practice your daily swindling,
Surely it's your devil, or perhaps our God,
Who inspires you. Cause a few more mishaps, gentlemen,
And you'll have carried us to the throne.
They are making us look virtuous and can't help it.
And meanwhile, they're undoing themselves.
Let me, therefore, give you the order of the day
To be taken to Headquarters:
As to the dead children,   70

The fire has rekindled itself. So, don't fan it. It's not worth it.
Let's not make coffins speak,
People will thank us for that.
Let no one forget Forzza's rule:
You must know how to want what you want,
And then you must go and get it, beg, borrow or steal.
Write steal: s-t-e-e-l.[50]
My advantage is to have grown up in the muck
From a very young age.
My father was in the military, my mother scrubbed floors,   80
So I learned about the world from the ground up.
Our life is a drama striving for the climax.
Whoever wants the State, follow me.
Mark my pace:
To reach the top, we make use of everything
We change with the wind, according to what's needed
We are men, snakes, or dogs,
We're not afraid of getting our hands dirty while climbing.
On the way up, we creep.
Once on top, we get hard.   90
So, in the first place, have no fear.
And second, have no shame.
Just look at those on the other side,
They are ashamed. We are shameless.
Look around Forzza:
Nothing but proud swindlers.
I am talking politics to you now.
Swindling is a very difficult job,
You can't bungle when you swindle.[51]
Every interested act you commit,   100
Just do it, period, and afterward clean up the mess.
Don't leave a single trace behind.
You must never get caught.
Appearances are essential,
They are what makes the difference.
Whereas our opponents are counterfeiters.
They ape us and at the same time they act disgusted.
That's why I hate them.
Getting back to the election:
This time around, we'll dress humbly,   110
In dull grey.
But if anyone among you
Discovers by chance a little something that's useful to our cause,
A little dirty trick that might grate on people's nerves,
Come and see me immediately,
Dressed in fog, naturally.
Let no one seem to be the source of these revelations – ever.
For example, Monsieur Captain,

Where was the Secretary of State on such and such a fateful date?

MONSIEUR CAPTAIN Right! We could talk the cemetery people into dragging the Ministers to the trial as   120
    well and, one thing leading to another, you see what I mean?

FORZZA The hostages must have thought of this.[52]

    One discreet helping hand, and it's in the bag.

    Well, young man, go tell all this to our team.

MONSIEUR CAPTAIN I'll do my best, Senator Forzza.

    Truly, I admire you, you are very strong.

FORZZA That's what my name says, I live up to it.[53]

MONSIEUR CAPTAIN If only your name had been "King"!

    It's a pity.

    I am leaving, Senator, and I'll serve you well.   130

[*He exits*

FORZZA "It's a pity!" Snot-nosed twerp!

    You'll see! I will make a very good king.

    Where do you think I am headed? For the antechamber?

    My name is pronounced ten times a day

    And yet you scarcely give me any attention.

    I am a very unknown familiar character.

    This is how your destiny advances, slipped into my silky envelope

    Until the day when this whole era

    Will bear my name.   140

    The clear-sighted people will all be astonished,

    But it's always like this,

    It's the lot of mortals:

    They don't see their master coming.

    Already you are in the era of Forzzism,

    You don't know it, but I'll teach you.

    Today, one among a hundred others,

    I wait, smiling, watch in hand,

    For the Hour that is coming.

    So, it was him that Time was hiding   150

    Behind its curtain![54]

    Until tomorrow!

[*Exit* FORZZA

Scene 10

Enter X2

X2 Everything tells me to make an end of it.

    I am telling myself, too.

    Am I not already a shadow of myself?

    Am I not the ghost still cruelly,

    Very cruelly alive, of the man I was?

    What are you doing, poor forked animal,[55]

    Still standing among the graves?

Yesterday, I was dreaming of honours,
I was being admitted to the Academy . . .

ECHO Demi . . .   10

X2   I wake up in infamy,
     They call me a murderer.
     For those of us in the limelight,
     How atrocious and brutal the public executioner is!
     Come on, lie down! And once I am dead, let them forget me.
     I want to sleep beneath a nameless stone.
     But you, academy of the dead, receive me without judgement,
     Don't tell me you'd have done better
     When I ask to be admitted.
     Tomb, whom do you hold?[56]   20
     Damned darkness, is this on purpose? I read with my fingertips . . .
     S-H-A-K . . . Shakespeare? Impossible!
     Why impossible? Why wouldn't the world also hatch beautiful fantasies?
     Shakespeare, I am sure *you* understand the wretched man
     That's sticking to me like skin to muscles
     And from this moment on pretends that I am him.

ECHO . . . sticky!

X2   I should not have done the deed that was done,
     But *when* it was done, I don't even know.
     If we knew what we do   30
     At the moment we do it . . .
     But in one act
     A hundred mysterious acts hide and simmer in secret.
     The man who did the thing I did,
     I do not know him,
     I am not that criminal.

ECHO . . . minal.

X2   The children . . . I could not prevent it.
     It happens like this: one misses the moment.
     A child is drowning: 40
     You don't throw yourself in the water,
     The child is dead.

ECHO You don't throw yourself in the water? Slaughter![57]

X2   But one can't live being one's own opposite.
     And I don't give anyone the right to debase me . . .

ECHO Base me!

X2   I am a man like you and me,
     And I, in any case, am not
     And have never been the sponsor of disaster.
     Had I been the captain,   50
     Never would such a shipwreck have occurred,
     But I was the second in command.
     Those who are given the second's role
     Are the most unfortunate
     Of all characters in all tragedies.

We are ordered to obey and disobey,

Nobody respects us and nothing benefits us,

Neither crime, nor triumph, nor attenuation.

But to stop the commander in chief, who ordered the slaughter,

I did everything a second in command can do on his own. 60

I remonstrated, I disapproved, I stomped my foot,

I slammed doors. All for nothing.

Maybe I should have killed him,

And escaped my state of subordination! Or left?

ECHO ... Killed him.

X2 I should have, I shouldn't have

Killed, not killed, I would have liked –

But what, how, oh – not to become crazy.

At the fork in the road,

I took the path that leads me away from the light forever. 70

Obscure forces hurried me along

On the heels of him I loathe,

And ever since, carried away by hurricanes surging from the depths of my soul,

I have been swept like a tiny speck of human dust

All around the planet, without rest.

ECHO Without ... rest.

X2 Forever I spin,

Myself against myself, divided to the core.

In my split chest,

Death and life clutch my arteries, 80

And with all their warring forces

Struggle, each tugging at this unfortunate man

Attacked in his very Personality.

It's in my interest to die.

What holds back my exit is fear,

Fear that the children lie in wait for me behind the door,

But as long as I am not dead, I dread.[58]

Yet to die today,

Not having enjoyed any of life's fruit,

Having lost everything on this side, 90

And going over to the other

Where there is nothing to win!

Who would wish for a premature death

Without the accompaniment of glory and fame?

ECHO Shame.

X2 I want that which I don't want to want.

I cannot want that which I want,

Neither to live nor to die.

At the end of my tether, I give myself ultimatums

That shatter me and that I reject. 100

ECHO Die.

X2 Die! No!

I denounce all denunciations.

No one has the right to push me to the wall of the last judgment.
One should look upon me from on high, to see that there are two of me
split, split, and therefore not guilty.[59]
I say all this out loud
And in no one's hearing.

ECHO No one.

X2 No one but the Gods for witnesses   110
And those who sleep underground.
Sssh! Someone is coming!
Ashes of my words, disperse!

ECHO Ashes yourself.

Enter X1

X1 I am truly happy to be with you again, my friend.

X2 You are not my friend, and I am not yours.
I never was.
I don't know how to repay you
For all the pain you have caused me.   120
I've never been of your kind.
I was doing science,
And you did business.

X1 Hey, poison snake,
Knock it off, you psycho, or I'll shoot!
He says "Science" with rosy lips.
False Jesus, slave driver, little slut,
Immaculate conceptionist!
"Science" in quotation marks, adorned with ruffles
And chastity shoes!   130
And myself, stirring the dirty brew, as black as a coal miner,
An untouchable? Who helped you, you fraud?
Priests that you are, who supports you, who protects you?
You're clean and we're tainted with excrement?
We're on the take, and you don't cash in?

X2 I am inviolate, all for science;
And you, all for greed.

X1 You are trying my patience, watch out.

X2 They call you Director,
Because you had that position.   140
But how can he direct the fleet,
Streams, rivers, canals,
All the vital circulation,
He who cannot read a map of our currents,
A man without letters,
A man of numbers. He speaks but one language,
And understands the words of no other person
Or nation.
This man goes to international conferences

| | Without a head on his shoulders.[60] | 150 |

Without a head on his shoulders.[60]
A man without memory, therefore without shame,
But with bottomless pockets.
Such a man gets his crooked way
By force. And who gave this force to him?
Who gave you this undue power?
Your unknown friends have
Exceedingly long arms.

X1 Finally, I understand
Who, for many years, has been stabbing me in the back.
While I defended our lines,
Who handed me over, betrayed me.
Who cut my hair while I slept,
Sold, and disfigured me?

X2 The one-eyed man sticks his finger in his eye.
I swear it, it's the first time I give words to my thoughts.
Can anyone say that I divulged terrible secrets,
Ever? Never!
This man here suffers from chronic venality,
Did I say that?
Gold persuades him that the bad product is the best,
Who can say I said that?
Corruption is his nature, and profit his guide,
Nobody ever heard me utter these frightful words.

X1 How could you have said that
Without bringing proof?

X2 The proof, I had it, the checks in your name,
The stubs, I held them
In my trembling hands.[61]

X1 Villainy, double villainy! You saw the checks and you said nothing!
You could have produced some nice testimony.

X2 You had helped me. My feeling of indebtedness to you stopped me, and today, I curse it.

X1 You wished for this corrupted man to go on feeding you!
No, it wasn't desire, it was fear.
Yes! I can picture the scene all right:
You accuse me, and I throw you
Directly into the swamp. I'll say we shared the profits,
I'll say we are exactly the same, fifty fifty.

X2 There is no proof.

X1 It will tarnish a reputation all the same.

X2 You horrify me. But at the same time, I horrify myself.
We are horrible.
Ah! I followed you too far! Too long!
It was then, at the very first step,
That I should have fled.

X1 The Friend was a snake!
Are you going to bite to death
The man that raised you up?

150
160
170
180
190

X2	Raised up!	
X1	Higher and faster than all your rivals.	
	You weren't much of anything	200
	When I hired you.	
	From the beginning of medical school	
	To the end of your medical practice,	
	Everything in your career has been trivial.	
X2	Trivial!	
X1	Everything! Your diplomas, trivial, the honours you garnered, trivial,	
	Your research, trivial, your findings and your knowledge, all trivial.	
	It was your good luck to have me.	
X2	You recruited a trivial person?	
X1	And turned him into an expert.	210
X2	This is a lunatic talking to me.	
	I am so discouraged	
	I won't say any more.	
	And now, to top it off, he cries.	
X1	Yes, I weep for us, you against me and me against you,	
	Friends yesterday, today adversity turns us into enemies	
	And transforms us into animals, both of us.	
	How much evil they have done us, these hounds,	
	Insinuating the evil spirit into us, these insidious ones!	
	I told you but one word,	220
	And this simple word took on gigantic proportions.	
	I was not even thinking it.	
	I opened my mouth, giving birth to alien ghosts.	
	You are the only man I could ever trust.	
	Do you understand me?	
X2	Ah! It's true, since these dogs have surrounded us,	
	I see claws and scowls everywhere:	
	Secretaries have hyenas' paws under their skirts,	
	Lawyers have cloven hooves,	
	My friends have a foul breath.	230
	I didn't know	
	How contagious hate is.	
	Insult strikes me in the heart	
	And its satanic sting injects	
	Abominable images	
	Into the very flesh of my life.	
X1	We are victims in the tragedy of errors.	
	God is a blind cyclone.	
	He was looking where to strike.	
	He fell upon us	240
	Instead of falling on the Palace.	
X2	One easily gets caught	
	Into this trap of guilt and accusation.	
	Stung by pain and rage,	
	One jumps on the first who comes along.	

When I was striking at you, I too was biting the wrong one.
After all, who started it?
Who named you leader?
Who entrusted to this man
The delicate, very delicate cargo, 250
So perishable? Barking endlessly behind the bars of my cage,
I came to forget that all faults
Were engendered by those powerful parents
Who now disown their offspring.
It's them, it's the King and his barons
That the blind God and his hounds
Should now assault.

X1   Are we reconciled, then?

X2   Of course.

X1   Then come, let's go prepare our joint defense. 260

[Exit X1

X2   I'm following you. Shakespeare, do you understand me?
I wanted to die, but the moment has passed.
Anguish returns, and so does fury.
What a fate to have this false twin, this ghastly double!
Ah, if only I'd never known him!
Let us unite in hatred![62]

[Exit X2

Scene 11

Enter the CHILDREN. *Song of the Incalculable*

DANIEL [*singing*] One more, help me, Benjamin!
How many are we, now?
BENJAMIN [*singing*] We need to do a new count.
DANIEL [*singing*] Help me, Benjamin,
I don't know how to do these accounts.
Should I add up only those who are here,
Or should I add
The dying children
To those who are already dead?
BENJAMIN [*singing*] That which isn't yet, 10
That which is more or less,
Do I add it
Or subtract it?
And am I still a person?
Let's sing the Incalculable.
DANIEL [*singing*] For months I have been counting for nothing.
One thousand three hundred and eighty
Plus me, one thousand three hundred and eighty one,
Plus those who won't be long,

Let's round it off and put it down . . .   20
Oh, if we could carry one.
When I was in school
The numbers were cool and round.
Now, we are all so weak,
I am no more than a tenth of what I was.

Enter NIGHT

NIGHT [*singing*] What are you doing, children, schoolboys without a school,
　　In such times without roots,
　　Counting and recounting that which has no end?
　　One child after another,   30
　　The scourge spreads.
　　This destruction will last a long time.
　　So come along with me to the cypress grove above.
　　For now is the hour of the new Justice.

Scene 12

All enter: CHORUS, FURIES, AESCHYLUS, DEFENDANTS, LAWYERS, MOTHER

NIGHT Stars, to your posts, flood this arena
　　With the serene light of eternities.
　　Servants of the Apocalypse,
　　Angels whose mouths bristle with sharp swords,
　　Blow into the air a transparency
　　Not to be clouded by any dubious word
　　Coming from any bench in this Assembly.[63]
　　You, the dead, who pass for dead and are alive,
　　Push off the tombstones that weigh so heavily on your faces,
　　Stifling your groans and moans,   10
　　Resume your place in the crowd, and speak!
　　It shall no longer be said that here the silent are mute.
　　Tonight, we inaugurate unheard-of opportunities.
　　If, in all the time that time endures,
　　Justice has one chance, just one, to be just,
　　It is now, and before us, that she will have it.
　　So, climb up here, Aeschylus, take the sceptre,
　　And invite the crowd
　　To the austere festival that will free their hearts.[64]
AESCHYLUS I take the floor   20
　　And I yield it immediately to the mother.
　　Come forward, cry out, and may the sorrows of all the mothers
　　Flow into your cry.[65]
　　The mothers who will never again be called:
　　"Mother! Oh mother! Mama!"

For the sands of time have
Absorbed the children's voices.

MOTHER .... Io ...

FURIES Louder! Take a deep breath, scream very loud
And ask for the desired mortal pains.   30

....

Well, you are not screaming? – She has stage fright.

MOTHER There, my voice is coming. Here goes:
[to X1 *and* X2] So, finally we meet, on my territory!
You forced us to leave the country
And to lure you here.
All I ask is this: two words.
These two words, I absolutely want them.
Two single, but all-powerful words,
Words that can interrupt the course of murder.   40

FURIES And what are these extraordinary words?

MOTHER "Forgive me."
These are the words I wish to hear
Coming from these lips here and those lips there.

FURIES Two words??! And you ask them of this murderer?
But what is the power of a word
Compared to a bloody expiation?
"Forgive me"! "Forgive me"! Anyone
Can pronounce them, those three syllables:
"Fooor–giiiive–meee"! It's easy!   50
No, no word can ever
Replace a sacrifice of oxen or pigs.

....

No. Punishment is the cure in such a case.

....

Yes, only punishment controls humans.
For their own Good, only punishment has power to heal.

MARGUERRE These words, let's say that we said them.
What then?

MOTHER Then, as soon as the words are said,   60
The ordeal comes to an end.
The great gates of heaven, the abode of mercy,
Which erases crimes and resentments,
Will open immediately, and all those
Who are, at that moment, armed to the teeth
In both camps, of one common accord
Will come out of the Hell
Where we've been boiling for so many years.

BRACKMANN We, utter these words: never!

MARGUERRE Is there anyone in this room   70
Stupid enough to take this bait?
Let's say we say the words,
I'll tell you what follows after that:

We'll be taken into custody,
Thrown into a cell, dragged before a court,
Found guilty, executed.
Because, in uttering these words, we'd confess
To a criminal act.
The woman is asking for the words that condemn!
It's a diabolical trick.   80
We think we are offering a hand, and the hatchet falls.
Forget it, madam, we won't fall into your woman's trap!

FURIES Good, that's the man for me!
You, the defence, don't yield one inch,
You'd deprive me of playing my role.
Be stubborn, never blunt your claws.

....

You, don't say those words
For if you said them, you'd abolish
The order of things in one breath.   90
On the other hand, if you could say the word "crime,"
I'd be thrilled, I need it for the victims.
Indeed, if one of you says: "I am a criminal,"
And the other echoes: "I am too" –

X2 Crime? Who's talking about crime?
Until now one said homicide!
Did I want to kill? Did he want to kill?!

X1 Did I ever touch so much as a hair on anybody's head?
I never administered cure or poison to anyone.

BRACKMANN Correct. Who can say and swear "he did want to kill"   100
And yet not lie?

FURIES Wantokill, there's a strange word!

....

Your sentences start out straight and finish crooked,
There is no rhyme.
But you won't get away from me. Fine, I take back crime. But I keep kill.
So, you have killed,
Even if you did not wantokill.
And what the killing consisted in, I'll tell you:
You did nothing to prevent our death.   110

....

Correct. And not to kill is not not-to-kill,
Not to kill is to do everything possible not to kill.
Did you do everything possible not to kill?
No. Did you *want not to* kill?

X1 No. Since it wasn't a question of killing.

X2 Why would we have done anything to prevent death, since there was no question of dying?

MOTHER ... Ah ...

FURIES Ah! Did you hear that?! He did not want not to kill. Therefore, he wanted to kill.

X1 Me, I wanted to kill?!   120

FURIES Wantedtokill. Yes. Since

You never wanted not to kill.

Isn't that a just statement? Answer!

MARGUERRE Don't answer!

You're trying to catch us with clawing words.

X1 I refuse to answer!

You want to snarl me up

In the nets of grammar.

FURIES Well, then, listen to this question:

All of our children were deprived of their bloom. 130

Your hands are covered with blood

And you keep saying that you didn't kill.

Whose fault is it, then?

Who will answer that one?

X2 1. There is no blood on our hands.

2. The fault is not ours. Moreover, it's no one's fault, there was no fault. There was only natural homicide.   Without any will behind it. That's life. That's science. That's the job. That's an accident.

X1 Idiot! Allow me!

If there was a fault, it was the State's, obviously.

The officers of the State are those who blaze the trail 140

Whose incline I follow submissively.

The State imprints its authoritative fingers on my brain.

I obey. Who elected, who commissioned us

For this transfusionary mission?

Who sent us on this boat

Rocked by violent storms?

Who, when our mast broke,

Left us in the lurch?

When our vessel leaked

And we asked to be bailed out 150

At 80, if not 100 per cent,

Who failed to answer us,

Thus taking the risk

Of letting our cargo perish?

I accuse the State from top to bottom

Of having manipulated me.

FURIES [*to the* CHORUS] You are not saying anything?

Help me. Invent irrefutable arguments.

....

With those metaphors of yours, you're trying to pull the wool over our eyes. 160

....

You, translate, in two words!

X2 It was the State's duty to forbid us to sell products tainted with uncertainty.

X1 *In case our products had been tainted with uncertainty*! It was the State's duty to forbid us to sell, and, having ruined us, to compensate us.

Watch your words, idiot!

FURIES You're saying the State is responsible for you?

X2 Yes.

X1 Therefore, had the State and its ministers only expressed their will, we would have obeyed.

FURIES [*to the* CHORUS] How do I answer this?   170

AESCHYLUS You answer: a doctor doesn't need an order not to kill.

CHORUS By definition.

FURIES That's it! So you're saying that unless you receive an order not to kill, in the normal course of things,
    you will kill?

CHORUS You are mechanical puppets
    That do everything according to the hand pushing the buttons:
    Kill, Don't kill, Forward, Back, Think, Shit?!

FURIES Good question! You, answer me!

X1 I say that I am a humble servant of the State.
    We are mere servants of Politics.   180

FURIES Back in our days, everything was simple.
    The guilty were guilty.
    Here, in your world, things are terribly complex,
    The guilty one is not guilty.

    ....

    I demand an explanation.

X1 I say that I am a humble servant of the State
    And that, for everything I do,
    I am accountable to my ministers and masters,
    And only to them. So, I am not guilty   190
    Because, if I were, first of all:
    My ministers would have proclaimed it;
    Second: I couldn't be guilty
    Because the origin and end of this affair
    Are entirely in the minister's hands.
    Third: you are taking the shadow for the king.
    Fourth: in conclusion, it's the State that I advise you to attack.

FURIES I already heard these things
    And I already crushed them
    Under the soles of my feet   200
    Armed with ripping spikes.

    ....

    You speak exactly like horrible Orestes,
    When he said to me, his fingers sticky with maternal blood:
    "It's not me, it's Apollo
    Who killed my mother."[66]

    ....

    Five thousand years, and that's all that comes of it?
    An aborted soul? Phew!
    I feel an ancient anger welling up in me.   210
    Do you feel it too?

    ....

    As for anger, look at me,
    You who are attempting to escape
    Down the rope of specious arguments.
    Behold anger rising in my eyes,
    Already my right eye is squinting,

FURIES And streams of boiling saliva

Collect in my mouth.

Watch out, I'll spit in your face.   220

You'd better confess the truth.

X1 Since I am innocent, I refuse to defend my innocence.

MARGUERRE You are tormenting a man

Whom everyone, from the highest to the lowest rung of the professional ladder,

Doubts is at fault.

BRACKMANN I say it loudly: we've had enough of this upside-down scene.

Who is suffering here? This man and that one.

X1 This is worse than killing me. I'd rather die for no reason than suffer this torture more painful than

death.

X2 Or, rather, continue torturing us,   230

Become executioners and let shame seize you!

MOTHER Executioner? I can't believe

He said what he said!

FURIES You there, repeat what you said.

....

Repeat! You said: continue and . . .

X2 And you will become our executioners.

FURIES What should we do?

....

We continue, naturally.   240

What was I saying?

....

Chorus, what would you say?

CHORUS Tell me, you there, if you are not guilty

Why don't you look us in the eye?

FURIES Ah! I've got it, I found the word!!

Conscience! That's the word I've been looking for

Since midnight! Conscience!

Conscience, do you remember?

In the past, oftentimes, people   250

Talking in their sleep, or in delirium, they say,

Would accuse themselves, and, wandering through the night,

Scrubbing their stained hands,

Would thus reveal their many hidden crimes.

Indeed, the heart was its own judge in our times.

What has changed in the Universe

Is the structure of the human soul.

....

But how so? That's terrible!

CHORUS The conscience of Europe was grievously injured   260

Fifty years ago.[67] Everyone knows it.

....

Since then, conscience is completely deceased.

Since then, everyone lies, deceives others,

Deceives himself, is deceived, reciprocally and equally.

Deceit is universal in Europe.

....

And everyone, unanimously,
Finds this excellent. Not once, in the past fifty years,
Have you heard the tiny trumpet of conscience,   270
Or have you?

....

You delude yourself!

....

Of course, but prove it.

FURIES What about faults, vices, sins, crimes and treasons?

CHORUS That's all over. Today, there are only errors and the unconscious.

FURIES Still, there must still be a tiny bit left? Of conscience, I mean?

....

Let's see.   280
At night, do you see yourself in your dreams
Being skinned alive, stripped of honours, of your shirt
And tailored suit, and then thrown
Into a cauldron of boiling water,
And then, still dreaming, do you hear
Your own heart telling you:
I am the cause of these tortures?

X1 No.

FURIES No? Stop looking at the ground
And look deep inside yourself.   290
Tell me, are there not in your heart any dead people
Who, waking up, wake you, too?
And since with your eyes you saw nothing,
Do you see nothing with your heart?
Stop looking at the electric wires
And look into your heart. Nothing? No.

....

There! What was I telling you?
There is the proof! I was sure of it.

BRACKMANN The proof of what?   300

FURIES The proof of their obstinacy in crime.
There isn't even room for the smallest dead person
Inside these shallow living people.

MARGUERRE That is precisely the proof of their innocence.

CHORUS You, the lawyer, don't you see you are leading your clients to disaster?
Do you believe yourself in a courtroom?
Don't you see we are under the stars?
Here we don't give a damn about the law.
What we seek is justice.

FURIES Who asked you to enlighten him? Be quiet.   310

....

You say that you are not feeling the lashes
Of an invisible whip?

X1   Bullshit!

FURIES   Bullshit? What does that mean?

MOTHER   No! You don't have children.

If you had children,
If, inside your body, breathed the lives of small creatures,
You wouldn't have these leathery hearts
Nor these dried up, empty eyes.   320
The idea of one day watching the death of
The child who inhabits your flesh
Would have made you bend under the ferocious wind of grief.
A groan escapes from the broken heart
At the mere thought, or fear, of horror!
What is a surviving parent?
A bloody stump, a ripped-open body,
Severed breasts, a soul with chopped arms.
No, you don't have children.
That's why nothing ever softens   330
The hard core of your hard-heartedness.
I was only asking for a thought, a sigh.
I beg you, don't turn these plaster masks
Toward me anymore. Give me a sign.
Don't even say the word, just give me a look,
And we'll find each other, you and me, sadly,
But together, on the same side of humanity.

X1   Madam, I have children.

It's difficult to talk, after so much violence,
But I insist on saying it, I am good,   340
And I feel no shame.
I swear on my children's lives
That I would have made the same decisions,
Had it been my own children.

FURIES   How many children?

X1   Two.

FURIES   Do you love them?

X1   Of course.

FURIES   Well then, expect that the lives of your children
Will be struck in their very bones by a plague   350
That we cannnot avert from
Him who dares thus perjure himself. . . .

        . . . .
        And will be snuffed out.

MOTHER   No!

FURIES   Let us speak!

        . . . .
        And you, do you have children?

X2   Yes.

FURIES   And you don't swear?   360

X2   I, at a tender age, swore to myself never to swear.
      It's a scientific position. I stick to it.
FURIES But you, you swore on the lives of your own beloved children?
      Crime after crime and lie after lie. It continues to add up.
MOTHER How can you do such a thing?
      To swear on your own children! We have evidence against you!
BRACKMANN Ah! You do, do you?! So, where is this evidence,
      And where are the witnesses?
      All I see here is a band of beggars
      And a bunch of demons.   370
      Where are the scientists? Where are the statesmen?
      Where is the Nation?
CHORUS What we want is the truth.
BRACKMANN The truth? Which truth?!
CHORUS The truest, the purest,
      The truth one cannot prove with proofs.
      Proofs are good for confounding liars.
      What the Mother and we want
      Is not much. An expression of regret.
      I'm not talking to you, Mr Attorney,   380
      You wouldn't understand it, you little runt.
      What does it matter to me, who wins and who loses,
      All I want is honesty.
      Why are they tanned, dried up and mummified,
      All these renegades of milky compassion?
      If this one were to say: Yes, I have sinned,
      I would say to him: Bravo! You're a hero!
      What's he risking? There is no judge here,
      There is no cop. Nobody here but the dead,
      And people without IDs.   390

      ....

      But the dead, especially the youngest ones,
      They want so much not to be killed again and again
      In punishment for having been killed once already.
      The dead, they want to make peace.
      But what am I doing?
      I'm speaking to foul slugs,
      Hoping to cure them of their slime,
      Of their lack of guts and spine.
      I'm such a fool! Why don't you stop me?   400
      Well, Mr Attorney, the proofs and witnesses,
      If you hold them so much dearer than the truth,
      I'll go look for them.
      Since you want your clients to pay according to the Law
      And not according to humanity,
      According to cowardice and not to humility,
      Since you prefer combat over consolation,
      I'll go get you thirty cubic feet of files

And a mass of scientists and academicians
Who will crush your lies   410
Under the treads of their powerful testimony.
Come, let's call in the most eminent physicians.

[*Exit* CHORUS

FURIES That will change nothing for us. To kill is one thing.
　　　But he who commits perjury by swearing on his children's lives,
　　　He's done for even before we light the fire.
MOTHER You shouldn't have sworn!
　　　You horrify me! To protect yourself in this way!
　　　But you, Furies, won't strike the children, will you?!
FURIES Of course, we will!   420
MOTHER To strike the father through the children,
　　　Inexorable sisters, I am against it!
FURIES Unless, having no other remedy,
　　　Pressed by our pursuit, feeling out of breath
　　　And out of strength, anxious for his offspring,
　　　The disgusting man surrenders to us
　　　And begs for mercy with tears.
　　　.......................
　　　I insist on that: with tears.
MARGUERRE Blackmail, villainy! To ask a harassed man,   430
　　　Surrounded and threatened on all sides, stripped of everything but his male dignity,
　　　To weep on command!
X1 Nails torn out, eyes rooted out
　　　Nose cut off, and so forth,
　　　Show me all your tricks,
　　　I won't budge. I stand behind my beliefs.
　　　The day is not purer . . .[68]
AESCHYLUS Ah! No! Silence!
　　　Or I, too, will soak and shrink you in vinegar.
　　　While we wait for the witnesses, take these creatures to the trough they deserve.   440

[*Exeunt* X1 *and* X2 *under the* FURIES' *guard*

MOTHER Will the Deluge not come?
　　　Will the globe keep turning and not stop?
　　　Will the sun not turn black,
　　　And the stars fall like petals
　　　Of the withered night?
AESCHYLUS Do not worry. Trust us.
　　　The hour will come.
MOTHER We are denied, thrown out, spat upon.
　　　So many months and years have burned before me.   450
　　　Let's make an end of this! I am tired!

Enter the CHILDREN

CHILDREN [*singing a duet*] Woe unto those whose houses have fallen ill.
　　　Sleep, mama, sleep,

Don't turn against me and my cries,

Don't wake up at my side with the sharp point of my dreams,

Don't spill your boiling tears on my eyelids.

Sleep mama, go nighty-night, my planet, and get up again.

Do not let me writhe in my chariot of brick and iron.

Sleep and wake up for a new assault   460

Because, still, we were assassinated.

MOTHER Yes, my children, cradle me,

Let me rest,

And I will take up the fight again.

[*Exeunt*

NIGHT To think that I announced this scene

With bugles, horns, and trumpets!

My hands, my wings, my wheels are full of eyes,

And all my eyes are full of tears.

[*Exit* NIGHT   470

Scene 13

Enter ABEL *and* ELIMINATE

ABEL I have but two eyes, but they could shed the tears of all the castaways in the world.

ELIMINATE Still, Abel, the time of our triumph will come.

I believe in revolution.

I feel it tingling in my spine and all the way to my fingertips.

For once, a sad story must have a happy ending.

And I'm telling you it will be ours.

ABEL All stories end badly.

Death and massacre sweep around the earth

And set up camp now in this country, now in the next.

It will always be like that.   10

ELIMINATE Look, haven't we won at least a hand?

ABEL Only one. And we remain one-handed.[69]

ELIMINATE Poor Abel, gloomy prophet! I, Eliminate, shall contradict you.

This day is coal-grey. Tomorrow the day will be crimson.

Justice and Punishment will enter the cemetery in great pomp.

And we'll be the heroes of this glorious moment.

ABEL While poor Eliminate daydreams,

The news is spreading quickly through the City,

It sweeps through the Palaces and reaches the leaders' ears. And suddenly,

Our case meets with an altogether different fate   20

Because of the approaching Election,

Which pits the citizens against each other.[70]

ELIMINATE Whether they vote or bloat,[71]

I don't give a damn

Since I'm no longer a citizen

Of their insane asylum.[72]
The City, I no longer need think about it.
ABEL That doesn't prevent it from thinking about us.
While it erects its stage for the war
And digs its trenches,   30
The two camps fill the newspapers,
Each with its own maledictions.
They sharpen tongues with knives.
It's pitiful: some people announce
That the Palace will be surrounded and besieged
Till death ensues.
Others utter prophecies
Of public floggings, pillories, and eradication.
On both sides the winds, carriers of infamy, have been released.
But what I saw there, in this ragsheet, is this: 40
No matter how separated, excluded, out of sight we are,
No matter how deeply hiddden underground,
We are caught in this whirlwind.
Despite ourselves – here, look – we are
Brandished about, disputed over, whore-mongered and dislocated.
Both camps grab hold of our case,
Each one proclaiming our blood to be on their side.
They despoil us, I tell you, they cling to us,
We are quartered, don't you see it?
Don't you see how they hoist our cadavers   50
Instead of victory flags? They throw at each other's heads
The skulls of our dead children.
Today, the cause of our suffering
Serves as their ornament of deceit.
Yesterday, before the election, we were welcome to croak.
Today, our victims interest them. They pillage our chests,
They pin our dead hearts on their lapels.
Deep down, they regret that more of us were not massacred:
They could boast about them and accuse each other in perfect reciprocity.
And you would like me not to tremble?   60
With anger, naturally.
I know them well, those oarsmen
And helmsmen of the State's vessels.
In time of Peace we are but flies for them,
In time of War we are ammunition.
We are never human beings.
If they believe us necessary to their victory,
They'll protect us.
If they deem us useless or nefarious,
They'll blow us up.   70
When I was a rat-man in the steel plant,
My task was to smell for gas leaks
Under incandescent heaters.

I worked in the coal bunkers of cathedrals of fire,
In the midst of steel rivers, on the edge of extinction.
Right now, I am smelling gas.
Just before or just after the election,
Everything can blow up.

ELIMINATE I see. All the more reason to hasten our plans.
Let's go urge all the characters in our story,   80
And may our desire outspeed the Assemblies of Schemers.

                                                    [*Noises are heard from the dam*

ABEL Do you hear that?

ELIMINATE Stop, dam!

ABEL As soon as we say "blow up," "explode," it starts to crack.
We should be quieter.

ELIMINATE Let's not be afraid. Come.

ABEL I'm not afraid. I'm worried.
In another life I'd like to be a Tibetan lama,
With my marrow and the marrow of the sacred tree   90
For my universe, and I'd know nothing
Of that which grinds and breaks in kingdoms without souls.

                                                                [*They exit*

CHORUS But I, sitting in this life, with my marrow of stone,
I don't see any sacred tree,
Nor any lama. Nor any doctor. I knew it,
It's not here, nor during this night, that something will finally happen.
....
I, too, see that nothing is coming.
....   100
Enough, you scarecrows! You, Aeschylus, who have read all the books,
What do you say? Will they come or won't they?
What do you think?
....
I, for one, will answer you!
I know them very well, the Doctors and great medical Lords.
They will come. . . . Or else they won't.
But if they come, it will be exactly as if they hadn't come!

AESCHYLUS Why do you say that? Listen.
I once knew a doctor: never did one see a more honest man, a brother to the deprived, a mother to   110
the sick, to those who drag on with a harsh sickness he was a friend all the way
to
deliverance.
And without the help of any god, he was a saint.
A venerable demeanor, a youthful face, severe and smiling.
Moreover, it was my father.[73]
On the other hand, I knew the opposite kind of doctor, who in every function of common life,
left something to be desired. An unsaintly man, chary of his care for the deprived, with a moderate
patience for the pangs of death, loving neither to comfort nor to help, but passionately fond of poker,
sporting a very cold eye and a flirtatious lip for the female patient. In everything, an enemy to human   120
friendship.

Moreover, it was my uncle.

So, as to the prognosis . . . (I have my reservations).

Enter CHORUS MEMBER

Ah! Here comes the answer. They are coming, aren't they? A whole troop of these barons,

You see!

And at its head, this respectable medical body has put the illustrious Professor Hornus-Maximus himself.

CHORUS MEMBER They are coming. But as a first step, they want us to clear the stage

And have it all to themselves. In order to examine

And probe each other's hearts freely and mutually.   130

AESCHYLUS They have ground for that. Let us withdraw.

Let the doctors examine each other.

Scene 14

Enter PROFESSOR HORNUS-MAXIMUS, PROFESSOR ANSELM, DR TWIN, DR BERTHIER,
DR BRULARD, PROFESSOR LION *and* MONSIEUR CAPTAIN, *prowling*

HORNUS-MAXIMUS Gentlemen . . . I have a message. It's about this abduction you're aware of.

They took our colleague and his followers and put them in solitary confinement.

They're getting ready to try them again in their own way (I am not sure which exactly), to degrade them in the eyes of the entire world – I am quoting.

It's enough to make you sick.[74] But let's move on: these people are now asking us, asking our National Council, for support. They want our Order to condemn colleague So-and-so and to express fully, and absolutely, with all possible pomp, a definitive indignation and reprobation. An historic testimony, they say. And a prompt one too.

They are counting on it before dawn. How will the Council respond to this request?

Anselm?   10

ANSELM Let's do it. Our colleague did very bad things, didn't he?

Beginning with a very, very big weakness for illegal money.

BERTHIER But after all, what did he do that was so bad, this poor fellow, I'd like to know. Profits? So what?

Let's not be prudish. If one can no longer say the words: merchandise, products, to sell, surplus, this is the end of medical research. The colleague was selling blood. Everything that sells brings a profit. Okay . . . Agreed, maybe he had a little too strong a weakness for unholy money, but is that so serious? Is that a reason to crucify him?

ANSELM First of all, he drew an astronomical salary, plus an indemnity a hundred times greater than those paid out to the patients who will die from his actions.[75]

BERTHIER Anecdotal.   20

TWIN The Ministry's business.

ANSELM I say he is a thief of blood and a thief of the Nation's public funds.

TWIN What a word!

ANSELM What, which word? Nation?

TWIN Thief! Thief! In that case, the entire world must be called a thief.

You sell: thief. You buy: thief. You earn money: thief.

You expand: thief. All the world's a market.

It's the law, it's the times, to gain and to bargain is not to steal,

Or else, do away with money and go back to your cave.

ANSELM What he did, would you have done it? And you, Berthier, in the name of the market, you'd have   30
continued to sell that blood? To make some dough?

BERTHIER What about it? Frankly, what was so terrible?

The entire world sells blood.

ANSELM Let's talk blood. You, would you sell me blood that carries death?

BERTHIER That carries death! But they didn't know it then.

TWIN It's true. We didn't know in those years that the blood was potentially dangerous.

ANSELM Not potentially. Not dangerous. Lethal.

TWIN Dangerous. Therefore, I, not knowing that, say he was wrongly indicted.

ANSELM You not knowing, but he knowing.

He knew, and he sold this deadly blood, exhausting his stock without batting an eye!   40

TWIN I don't believe it. Nobody knew. It was thought that there was a risk, a minimal one, that the blood
might cause an illness, and that this illness carried a risk, a minimal one, of causing death.

MADAME LION[76] It's simpler than that: he had stocks of blood carrying death and he wanted to sell
them.

BERTHIER He had stocks of blood but he didn't know that the blood was suspect.

MADAME LION There never was any doubt. He knew, and he wanted to sell it. Knowing, he sold. On the
one hand knowing, on the other selling. Wanting to. I knew. He knew. The halls knew. Everyone could
have known. Everyone should have known. You could have known. Everything was published.

BERTHIER Ah! Yes, but that was in the *American Review*.[77] What if people don't read English? He, this
Somebody, didn't read English, apparently. And I am not ashamed to say that I don't either.   50

MADAME LION How about French, do you read French? Because at that time, I wrote it all in French in
the seventh issue of *Médecine aujourd'hui*.

TWIN Now now, Madame Lion, a person can't always read everything at just the right moment. In any case,
in that winter, they didn't know yet, I read it in the papers.

MADAME LION Before the winter, as early as the spring, they knew.

And they sold their sinister seed.

That's when he wrote the following. Here, listen:

[*She reads*] "Our whole blood supply is contaminated. What should we do? If we stop distribution,
the economic consequences will be very severe. The distribution of the products thus remains the
normal procedure while stocks last."   60

These words were written in the spring.[78]

BERTHIER What? I don't understand. The words didn't find their way to my ears.

TWIN But who wrote that?

MADAME LION These are his own words. His words of granite.

It's his own memo. I'll reread it:

"Our whole blood supply is contaminated. What should be done? If we stop distribution, the economic
consequences will be very severe. The distribution of the products thus remains the normal procedure
while stocks last."

BERTHIER Let me see. Ah! So they knew?! But, I, no, I didn't! And I never knew that he knew!

Let me see . . . What . . . What . . . Words fail me.   70

MADAME LION But you, my dear colleagues, are not blood specialists.

TWIN Why was this not reported?

MADAME LION Not reported? But it was reported a thousand times since that year when infanticide was
for sale. How many thousands of times must one say the same thing so that it is said once and for all?

BRULARD It's just that such a thing is hard to believe.

BERTHIER I, personally, heard people maintain for years: we *didn't know*. I heard it repeated everywhere,
to the judges, to the journalists, and to the gods.

MADAME LION Those who deny truth are easily believed.

Lies have such a strange force. That's the enigma.

Stubbornly, Truth writes: it was known.   80

Right away, denial pounces on these words

And stamps out their light.

It wasn't known crushes *it was known* – an inexorable struggle.

Truth, driven out, gasps in hiding places underground.

Up above, deceit erects its monuments.

Obstacles block the fountain of truth.

And ignorance rewrites history every day.

TWIN If he knew, then I am at a complete loss.

HORNUS-MAXIMUS You speak of knowing, as if we knew what knowing is!

Do we know what we know? Do we know what we don't know? We don't know what we know. And   90
as our masters said, before knowing we don't know. Thus, to reach a fair verdict in this case, we need
to know on what day and at what hour we knew that we knew.

BERTHIER Since you knew so well, Professor Lion, why didn't you sound the alarm?

TWIN Good question.

MADAME LION I did sound the alarm. All the alarms.

For years and years, I sounded them, and sounded them, and sounded them.

Until the lines of reason broke.

One day, I said to myself: I will call So-and-so until he answers.

Ten times a day for ten days in a row I called the man in question and a hundred times he refused to
answer me. Refused, one hundred times in a row. I had told myself, I will sound the cry of blood a   100
hundred times, so piercing and so full of anguish that it will penetrate his shield. I did it a hundred times,
and then I did it again, one last time.

Without a single echo, ever. All my cries fell into the sea. My mouth filled with sand.

HORNUS-MAXIMUS Do you have proof?

MADAME LION Proof of telephone calls? No. I should have thought of that. One should never cry out in
cries, on the air, by telephone. Everything should be cried out by letter.

HORNUS-MAXIMUS Exactly. You should have written to us registered mail.

MADAME LION Honoured Sir, ten years ago, I went to see you, remember? I told you: it's as if we were
catching children with the bait of blood. You said to me, send me a four-page report.

HORNUS-MAXIMUS Did you send it to me?   110

MADAME LION I sent it to you.

HORNUS-MAXIMUS Did I respond?

MADAME LION You did. Thank you for your report, which I have duly noted. I am old, I am tired, I cannot
take care of everything. Take this up with the Ministry of Health.

HORNUS-MAXIMUS You only had to . . .

MADAME LION So I kept sounding the alarm at the Minister's office

Until I was told: go see the Professor,

Since he is our Expert.

Everyone was informed, yet no one knew anything.

What purpose did the deluge serve? Does no one hear Death rising?   120

Deafness, that's the problem.

HORNUS-MAXIMUS Madame, I thank you for that presentation.

So, he knew. Good. What time is it?

Time to get back to the business at hand.

I am old, said I, thus I am wise.

I am no longer my brother's judge.

That's why I refuse to testify against this man.

I believe he has paid enough.

I must add, too, that I am concerned for our Order.

Whether we want it or not, the defendant is a member of our corps.   130

As you know, when people are intoxicated with the fury of vengeance, the part and the whole are for them indistinguishable. We experience it already all over the country; the doctors in the provinces are complaining: since this affair surfaced, a wind of distrust blows through the hospitals, and in each doctor's office.

The patients show their teeth without patience.

I see scandals coming, persecutions hitting us one after another in our profession.

How do we remedy that?

Union. Join forces. Face up to them.

And we must end these outpourings of hate.

STOP.   140

And now what?

BRULARD What about the testimony?

HORNUS-MAXIMUS We'll refuse to give it, agreed?

ALL —

HORNUS-MAXIMUS But that's not enough. There was a wound. Let's write a letter that will stitch it up.

I see it, dignified, impressive. It condemns this feeding frenzy of which Mr So-and-so is the victim. It will say that the right to ignorance is also a doctor's right. And that a layman has no idea of the paths by which Science runs its prodigious course. It progresses even through Dr So-and-so. In short, this philosophical, ethical, and scientific letter must set an impassive limit to chaos. Each one of us must sign it. Our united great names will raise up a majestic mountain between us and this uprising.   150

Yes, Brulard?

BRULARD Sir, . . . still, our colleague, he did commit a sin. One can say that he didn't kill, but still, he gave death. In just a few years, he wreaked havoc in one of our Order's great strongholds. We may not always be saints, but we try to be doctors. He, however, is of a different breed.

HORNUS-MAXIMUS Maybe. But that doesn't change my position.

ANSELM You didn't respect him, you didn't keep company with him. One used to mock the "Emperor of blood" in your antechamber. I do not understand you.

HORNUS-MAXIMUS It is because I am speaking to you from beyond good and evil. Without passion. The individual does not interest me. My only concern is for the perennity of the Order. You'll see when you are my age.   160

ANSELM But the only thing that counts for So-and-so is him, him, him, him, and we should pardon him?

HORNUS-MAXIMUS Pardon? I prefer: let live.

MADAME LION Let live!? Whom?

HORNUS-MAXIMUS Anyway, my mission is not to attack, but to defend and assist.

MADAME LION Defend? Whom?

HORNUS-MAXIMUS Is there anyone here who feels he has the right to cast, on his own, the first stone at this wretched man?

BRULARD But, Sir, even so, did *he* think about us, did he?

And about all those whom the wheels of his beautiful Jaguar splattered with mud?

HORNUS-MAXIMUS How difficult these times are,   170

When we do not know whom to fear more wisely,

Whom not to offend more justifiably.

Mr So-and-so is repulsive,

He is a spineless, sneaky, solitary swine. Okay.

This is the private truth.

Open your eyes, dear colleague:

Should the fate of a rotten little fellow

Shake the immense destiny of Medicine,

Its honour, its immemorial image,

Its numberless victories, which are our foundation? 180

Are you going to jeopardize, for the sake of a nasty, but quite ordinary little swindler, that time will

sweep aside tomorrow with one gust . . .

What was I saying?

MADAME LION To jeopardize . . .

HORNUS-MAXIMUS Yes, jeopardize your privileges, your honours, your rights, your heritage?

Your fate is here, with us. Believe me. I see clearly.

BRULARD Ah! Sir, when you speak, you are so lofty,

But in my mouth the same words would, I am afraid, appear cynical.

HORNUS-MAXIMUS Must I dot all your i's?

Don't you see what lies in wait for you? 190

What broods in this sinister cemetery

Is the twilight of physicians.

Between us and the sick creeps the spectre of war.

Yes, I know, this is a bitter pill to swallow,

But I don't like to tell lies.

BERTHIER We listen to you and we learn common sense again.

BRULARD But I wouldn't want to feel guilty.

HORNUS-MAXIMUS Guilty? Of what?

Always the same old itch.

What are you? Jewish? Christian? No. 200

A doctor. All right, I take responsibility for everything.

And you, try and rise to the occasion.

MONSIEUR CAPTAIN Allow me, Sir . . .

HORNUS-MAXIMUS Ah, yes, Monsieur Captain . . .

MONSIEUR CAPTAIN There's a rumbling out there.

The populace wants its guilty parties. And rightly so.

Guilty parties, there's no lack of them.

But they're not here, they're at the Ministry.

And there are some big ones in every office, all the way to the top.

I can give you all the names. You have only to expose them. 210

HORNUS-MAXIMUS What you say is true, Inspector.

As for exposing them, do it yourself. I trust you.

As for us, we will follow the path of discretion.

It is time to sign. Dawn is approaching.

Professor Lion?

MADAME LION All right, then, I shall cast the first stone.

I will not follow you. I don't want to enter

This grey country where there is no mourning, no terror, no empathy.

I will not sign this letter, because

This man bought gold with children's flesh.   220
Gold and betrayal always walk hand in hand, a perfect couple.
This fellow followed the twin demons
Beyond the border of humanity.
Let's not absolve him.
I don't want to see him with eyes dulled by old age.
He is guilty, I see it with my own sharp eyes. Without timidity,
Let us reject him, my friends, and publicly so.
He who sees evil and says nothing,
What is his motive?
I will not sign.   230
I will not dry his hands
Smeared with the blood of children.
With my name, I give my signature
To the hundreds of dead children.

HORNUS-MAXIMUS What a ruckus! So much talk for such a small thing!
One could say, Madame, that you pile it up.
I know you are a good doctor,
But a prophet, what do we need that for?

BERTHIER That's right, enough posturing.

TWIN Enough! We want to bury this affair! What's your problem?   240
We will not be ordered about by a hysterical woman.

BRULARD . . . No . . . No . . . Continue.

BERTHIER Do you want to get yourself a moral facelift at our expense?

MADAME LION What can a Church be worth, if it's built on a child's corpse?
But who knows, maybe many small corpses have been ground up in our mill for years and years.
And we didn't even smell them!
Don't you smell anything? Ah! horror wells up in me.
Don't we already stink?
You don't smell your own stench, right?

HORNUS-MAXIMUS She is crazy!   250

MADAME LION Don't sign this letter, my friends.
We are going to make the wrong choice.
Believe me, everything can still be saved.
Let's write a letter. That letter will state our disapproval.

HORNUS-MAXIMUS It's my duty to oppose
This aberrant, deluded, unscientific speech with all my strength.
Pass my letter around.
Madame, you are upset. Get yourself together,
And you will sign it.

MADAME LION I will not sign your letter.   260

HORNUS-MAXIMUS Madame, if you leave this meeting
In this state of mind, you sign your own ruin.
You lose our support. You lose your friends,
Your colleagues' esteem, your reputation.
I don't know what will become of your career in such conditions . . .

MADAME LION There, you've convinced me.
Sign it, Gentlemen. I'm leaving.

I will let you burn me in effigy. Farewell!

HORNUS-MAXIMUS Farewell! We will henceforth consider you our enemy!

Farewell! And keep your patients!   270

Don't try to place them in our hospitals!

TWIN Get out, Don Quixote!

MADAME LION Don't you see that your life

Is fading with every reply?[79]

[She exits

BRULARD [*to* ANSELM] What should we do?

ANSELM I think we must stay. Don't you?

To leave is too easy.

HORNUS-MAXIMUS A woman! Just what I hate!

And under the pretext that . . .   280

In any case, it's not a woman's absence

That will weaken our cohesion.

A non-entity. A female she . . . Anyway, you never were

One of us, in no manner whatsoever.

We lose no one.

TWIN Here are our signatures, Sir.

HORNUS-MAXIMUS My friends, *age quod agis*: you've done the right thing.

Let's be vigilant, let's not panic,

And let's speak no more of this case.

Let's go to bed.   290

[Exeunt doctors except BERTHIER *and* ANSELM

BERTHIER He knew that his entire supply was contaminated. But . . .

ANSELM Don't think about it anymore.

BERTHIER But just the same, still.

[Exeunt BERTHIER *and* ANSELM

AESCHYLUS What a silence! No one comes to our shore

Peopled only by the ghosts of the children buried

Despite their cries of rage.

The people from the high-rises

Ride around in their air-conditioned, air-tight, sound-proof BMWs,   300

City people never step down from their chrome boxes,

In vain our winds howl at their doors.

MOTHER So, will all this continue?!

The doctors want to save the doctors.

Oh! Time passes over us,

Crushing our children under its rocky hooves.

Our little ones descend beneath the earth,

One after the other, one after the other.

Meanwhile, gold Ore rises

And in your Order, nothing is shaken.   310

We die, the doctors don't come to our burials.

Our dead will grow weary.

FURIES They took the murderer's side!

. . . .

Impious Order, you multiply iniquities

As if you yourself were the epidemic.
You betray your supplicants?
You heap indifference on top of indifference.
When you are sentenced, I'll pour
Streams of boiling blood upon your bald heads,   320
And there will be no compassion.
        ....
Once the meat is scalded,
The skin comes off without difficulty,
The cleaver then hacks the still raw flesh,
Chop, chop, chop, very fine,
Add a fresh onion at will,
Oil, mustard, capers,
Ketchup . . .

MOTHER What are you doing here,   330
        Dear dreadful friends?

FURIES You see: lured by the outbursts of injustice,
        We came to show our indignation.
        If it weren't for us,
        Who would shout horrified wails?

MOTHER What about the prisoners?
        Did you leave them all alone? Who is guarding them?

FURIES Well . . . but . . . usually . . . we have
        Dogs that bark, but . . .

MOTHER But tonight you don't have any.   340
        The prisoners could escape!
        Oh! the anguish! Quick! Quick! Run!

FURIES Yes. Let's hurry! Let's follow the trail!

                                        [*Exeunt* MOTHER *and* FURIES

CHORUS I feel like killing.
        ....
        One day I'll write a letter
        And address it to all the following popes:
        The royal pope, the presidential pope, the papal pope, the medical pope.
        My letter will read: 350
        Pope, what are you sowing on the surface of your State?
        Are you sowing the wheat of peace or the wheat of plague?
        Tell me which of us has crucified the other?
        What have you done, you son of a bitch,
        For the creatures without dreams, without means, falling apart at the seams?[80]
        Whom have you fathered with your peter of stone?[81]
        Do you know where those you forgot in your prayers make their homes?
        The cemetery is our pad.
        You are such a corrupted idea of God
        That He can never exist   360
        As long as the thrones of the earth are monopolized
        By impostors of your species,
        Whereas I am the aching incarnation,

The last of the godly tribe.
I am a tear that has fallen straight
From the lashes of heaven onto the face of this cemetery.
....

According to you, Aeschylus, are we infamous at birth or do we have a say?

AESCHYLUS It depends on the person, the genes, the day, and the sex, on one's ancestry, one's dreams, on
    currents in the air or in the sea.   370
    Everyone is so different.
    Numerous are the mortals who prefer appearances to being.
    This was once said in my *Agamemnon*.
    For an unfortunate person, all are ready to let tears flow,
    But rare are those who let sorrow
    Bite its way into their entrails.
    Empathy is expensive. Every man for *myself* [82]
    I don't want to suffer for you. Life is far too short.
    You need courage to share.
    I don't have time to stop. Even bread, I have a hard time letting go of it.   380
    In my antechamber I harbor a giant fear of never having enough.
    Ah! If only one could give without spending!
    But to go back to this variety of the human species called
    Medical, which you would enjoy slicing up . . .

CHORUS Blood-covered swine.

AESCHYLUS Don't cut up my words with your word-cutter.

CHORUS What! you don't like my hatred?

AESCHYLUS I like it well enough, but
    In a play where the just hopes to make itself justly heard,
    I would like you, if you don't mind, to say a few words   390
    To shield us from
    Whatever injustice might be mixed up with your just anger.
    There is, after all, this woman
    Who has now turned against the horde
    Her lioness's brow adorned with a crown of thorns.
        CHORUS But you say she's a doctor?
    Who can tell me that tomorrow she won't
    Turn back into her opposite and, stripped of her crown,
    Go crawling back like the rest into the horde and the herd?
    Life is so short, why exert ourselves . . .   400

AESCHYLUS Here the woman comes now.

Scene 15

Enter MADAME LION

MADAME LION Refusing to sign this letter means to me
    More than a retreat, more than a banishment.
    A door has opened.

This non-signature shines before me like a flag.
How alone I am! Farewell my brothers and masters,
I see you bolt away. All is fear and cowardice,
There is no love. The Night is so beautiful,
And they do not even watch it breathe.
I believe I am about to be born.

Enter DOCTOR BRULARD   10

BRULARD Madame, may I keep you company?
    I feel so alone.
MADAME LION Please do. You – ?
BRULARD I signed. But I did so love your words.
    I agree with you. But I am unhappy. I signed.
    I couldn't do otherwise. The Order is so powerful.
    My whole life would be devastated, my name would be crossed out, I would be banished from colloquia
    and professional meetings.
    I know these doctors. And on the other hand, the sick, they are no lambs either, are they?
MADAME LION "In the presence of the masters of this school,   20
    I promise and swear to be faithful
    To the laws of honour and probity."
BRULARD Excuse me? What are you saying?
MADAME LION I was reciting to myself the Hippocratic oath:
    "I shall use my profession neither to corrupt morals
    Nor to encourage crime . . ." And then?
BRULARD "If I keep this oath faithfully,
    May I enjoy my life
    And practice my art,
    Respected by all men . . ." And then?   30
AESCHYLUS "But if I swerve from it or commit perjury,
    May the reverse be my lot."
BRULARD That is terrible! One should never take this oath.
    We're so young when we do.
    We don't know what we are doing. We swear before the Professors.
    Already the next day, we perjure ourselves. Having done it once, we go on doing it.
    How can we possibly get out of this?
AESCHYLUS Bitterly beautiful are
    The swift words of the oath spilled onto the ground,[83]
    A noble drink for the dust.   40
MADAME LION For a long time I did give these masters . . . respect.

                                                                              [*They exit*

CHORUS Now, my feet are cold.
    If they had let me do it,
    I'd have taken the Horned One by the horns,[84]
    I'd have spun him in the air,
    I'd have flung him over the wall.
    . . . .
    Well, do it.
      50

Too late.
When my feet are cold, there is no more spring in them.

Scene 16

Re-enter FORZZA *and* MONSIEUR CAPTAIN

MONSIEUR CAPTAIN Take charge of the denunciation, they urged me.
FORZZA And so, you did!
    You should have done everything possible to let them do it!
    You should have led them right into the trial arena, and stayed outside yourself.
    You should have pushed, spurred and electrified them,
    Unhinged them and made their blood boil;
    You ought to have led to the circus a crowd
    That cheered each one of their verdicts
    And sustained their overly cautious efforts against our adversaries;
    Convinced them that the whole country   10
    Shared their ulterior motive;
    Whipped up their timid blood with adulation
    And promises of absolution;
    And, unbeknownst to them, turned these quacks into
    The foremost allies of our scheme!
    I gave you the powder, you failed to set the fire –
    And stand here listening to me! What are you waiting for!
    Make up for lost time, goddamn it!
    Tomorrow morning I want to see the papers on fire with these doctors' incendiary words.
    They must spread a fever through the country!   20
MONSIEUR CAPTAIN Tomorrow morning, but . . .
    That's in a few hours and . . .
FORZZA What? You're not ready?
    But it's been like this for five thousand years.
    What does the populace want? Victims! I mean, victory.[85]
    And magic tricks! Let's hurry.
    The city is combustible. One match, that's all we need.
    Courage, Captain, charge!
MONSIEUR CAPTAIN Action, lead me on! I'll follow you! Charge!
                                        [*Exit* MONSIEUR CAPTAIN   30
FORZZA How exhausted I am!
    An eagle, a fox, an eel,
    A pack of wolves, a computer,
    The great master and his own servant,
    I've got to be everything at once.
    I must guess the hidden leads, understand the recesses of the human soul,
    And be a great painter as well,
    Draw savage portraits of the enemy,
    Heighten the colours, and show him worse than he is,
    The very image of the terrors that haunt the population.   40

Scene 17

Enter the QUEEN *and the* MOTHER

QUEEN Madame! Wait! Let me talk to you for a second!

MOTHER I don't have time!

  I am grievously busy. Come back tomorrow.

QUEEN No! Now. Between tonight and tomorrow

  The abyss will grow deeper.

  Two words. One second. I beseech you.

MOTHER I am listening.

QUEEN I too lost a child.

  I know your suffering.

MOTHER A child – killed?   10

QUEEN No.

MOTHER In that case, it's a different suffering.

QUEEN All the same, a mother's heart believes all is lost

  And releases endless floods of tears all year long.

  I am waiting for the anguish to ebb.

  Streams of memories slowly flow from my eyes.

MOTHER Who would have thought there were so many?

  The wind blows past, the year will never blow past.

  My head's broken, I fear losing a piece of my brain.

QUEEN We'd like to forget it all   20

  And yet, never to forget.

MOTHER In order to forget, one must remember.

  Oh my children, my children,

  To die and live at the same time live die.

QUEEN This tiny perimeter, it's the whole universe.

MOTHER You know.

QUEEN And one morning a brutal uproar

  Raps on our tomb.

  While we are crying, the world turns rude and militaristic.

  An army of brutes marches in,   30

  The city puts itself under the intolerable yoke,

  The earth explodes in a million shards, life is running out.

  In the palace emptied of goodwill

  The Devil, smiling, dons the crown.

  No later than tomorrow,

  Astride the throne,

  Smiling, he will sign thousands of death warrants.

  Meanwhile, in all the public squares,

  Monstrous trucks, devourers of conquered citizens,

  Rattle and rumble ominously.   40

  This could happen to us

  If the spirit of contempt were to win out.

  In these last hours our fate

  Hangs on near-nothings.

MOTHER I am one of these near-nothings,
    I know it. But I haven't deserved this.
QUEEN Help me then.
    Let us, you and I, make an exemplary peace.
    Take my side as I take yours.
    We are strong.   50
    That would silence our enemies.
MOTHER You'd like me to keep quiet?
QUEEN Strike an alliance with me, I am kin to you.
    I shall not speak of your superhuman pain,
    But let me help you on this earth.
    I know the road of modest consolations.
    I am thinking of the children who are left,
    I could get a hospital, a foundation,
    An emergency service, I have ideas.
    And then one day, you and I,   60
    We could take all these shamefully stricken children
    To China, to India, to the Silver Isles.
MOTHER Enough! Enough! I don't want any of that.
QUEEN We could give them the world.
MOTHER I can't! I don't want to!
    I'm afraid to hurt the dead who have nothing left but me!
QUEEN What about all the others, the mothers, the children, the sick,
    The dying or perhaps surviving,
    Less known than you and your children,
    Since they are still alive.   70
    Won't you give your consent?
    I speak to you humbly. I beseech you.
    I will go to the limits of what is humanly possible.
    If I were you, I'd make the greatest sacrifices
    To avoid the worst.
MOTHER If you were me! But you are only the Queen,
    I had almost forgotten.
    The King's cleverness goes far indeed:
    To send you here!
QUEEN He doesn't know I am here.   80
    I dared to dream.
MOTHER He should have come himself!
QUEEN Am I not enough for you?
MOTHER I would have asked him
    Why, how, protected by whom,
    The child-killer was able to kill.
QUEEN The King didn't pick that individual.
MOTHER He didn't kick him out either.
    The sword didn't flash.
    When the just turns away from Justice even once,   90
    And only once commits Injustice,
    Justice is forever profaned.

The King lost the just.

QUEEN You're losing your head,

Asking for the Absolute.

The King is as good as they come.

If tomorrow Forzza rules, you will

Regret your obstinacy.

MOTHER I cannot regret. I cannot accept.

I cannot renounce.   100

QUEEN I, I, I, I, I, I! Who authorizes you to carry the sword of heaven?

There is more than one mother!!! Have you nothing more to say?

MOTHER I'll let you judge.

QUEEN Judge! Who is the judge here? I am a supplicant,

Because I am afraid for this country.

MOTHER All countries are but passers-by on the surface of the earth.

When countries have passed on, there will still be

Mothers to love Justice above all kingdoms.

QUEEN So you refuse?

MOTHER Madame, we are not of the same flesh.   110

I'll be on my way.

[She exits

QUEEN Terrifying woman! She held up to me an incriminating mirror.

I don't even know what she's waiting for.

And I? I am at a loss!

I am not persuading anyone.

Oh! Impossible woman!

No. It's the child that's impossible.

[She exits

Scene 18

Enter NIGHT, FURIES, X1

NIGHT He is pursued, no ground will bear him any longer,

Deprived of a fatherland, alone in the world,

Gasping, without a father or mother, without friends,

He runs skipping, and the whole planet bristles under his steps.

FURIES Go! Run! We are right behind you.

You know that we are here,

And we know that you know that we are here.

X1 I've had enough. Kill me and let's make an end of it.

FURIES We'd like very much to kill you,

But we promised the mother   10

That we would only wear you down.

She has a few words to say to you.

X1 Have I deserved such dreadful glory?

Have I betrayed my King more than he betrayed me?

Between me and the fate befalling me,

The disproportion is monstrous.
Have I deserved to be thrown
Into an interminable downfall?
If I must expiate for ten years,
Then all the others, from the smallest henchman,   20
To the highest minister,[86] should expiate
For hundreds of years.
I am not even talking of the King.
There is only one person in the world
Who suffers such extraordinary anguish, and that's me.
Why was I chosen and selected
To be torn apart, I, of all men in humankind?

NIGHT I will answer you.
To each mortal is assigned a unique fate
And an anguish without precedent.   30
To each his own hell and his own heaven.
Everything is tearing and heartbreak. This is the normal course of things.
I tear myself into two to give life to the day.
Earth tears herself to give birth to the sky.
The maternal entity is pregnant with itself
And with its opposite.
Thus are things ordained,
With a stable ground, but also an abyss
In constant turmoil, and below, a bottomless hole.
You too split yourself into thoughts and afterthoughts. 40
The time has come to let your afterthoughts
Come to the foreground.

X1 Who are you?

NIGHT I am the friend of truths.
I am the Night who unties the tongues of the dead
And the tongues of liars.
I am the mirror at the end of the hallway
Where the two lovers see themselves shining as one.
I am the root of light in the womb of Darkness. When people can't see anymore, I see.
I am here to see   50
Those who under the empire of passions no longer see themselves.
I am the mother who loves in spite of everything.
It is I who look at you in your entirety.
I've cast over you a net of gazes so tight[87]
That no thought, no face, no matter how secret,
Can escape me.
Standing before me
As though before a mirror, you are who you are.
Look:

X1 [looking in the "mirror"] Oh! I see the mother arriving. 60

NIGHT What!? You don't see yourself?

X1 Not at all. Look. Who is there?
The mother.

NIGHT Is that all? And there?

X1 There? That's all.

  And now the mother is walking towards me.

NIGHT And now, speak freely.

  Only this man and this woman are present here,

  Good or bad, peace or war,

  Let amity have its chance: 70

MOTHER Sir . . .

X1 If you ask me to beg your forgiveness,

  Let's stop right there.

MOTHER I do not ask that.

  Tell me about yourself. Let me get to know you.

  That's all I ask.

X1 I will speak of myself in all sincerity.

  On the one hand, I love money, it's just a direct feeling, it's very simple, I love to earn it, I love to feel

  my wealth swell voluptuously.

  Sometimes I get carried away to the point of raving. I feel superior to my peers. When a business deal   80

  comes up, I pounce on it, by instinct.

  Do you understand? It's nature, Madame. It's the prehistoric forest.

MOTHER I understand. But on the other hand?

X1 On the other hand, Madame, there is an impossibility.

  Where is the man who can say:

  Out of compulsion for profit, I caused thirteen hundred children to die – or I did not cause them not

  to die. Besides, it's not really thirteen hundred, its only two hundred and ninety who are dead at the

  moment. Besides, when misfortune stepped in insidiously, science was telling us that only one-tenth

  of those affected might succumb, that's to say, one hundred and thirty. But Madame, if I had done

  that, I would deserve death. That's why nothing in the world can ever make me confess. I'm not ashamed   90

  to say that money runs in my blood, but it doesn't run in my head. For me to kill, the word money

  and its ardent syllables would have had to cause convulsions in my brain. But I have a cool head. Look

  at my hand, I have white, straight fingers.[88]

  If I had done that, do you believe that it wouldn't show?

  Your friends there want to slit my throat.[89]

  If it were only my life they wanted,

  I would tell them: go ahead, cut it off

  – The thread of my life is already so dreadfully unravelled! –

  But only on the condition that I die innocent.

  If you presume me to be guilty,   100

  I will not surrender.

  I'd rather cut my own throat and bleed myself white

  Than deliver to the enemy one drop of my innocence.

  Finally, you should know, Madame,

  That if my head is cool,

  I myself am a mother under the ice.

MOTHER A mother?! How so?

X1 Like this:

  One day, while walking along a rising river,

  I suddenly saw children being   110

  Washed away by a flash flood.

They were about to drown and perish.
I threw myself into the water, and I saved them.
I was twenty. I was celebrated.[90]
Would this same man have sent
These same children, or others like them, to their deaths?
How could I do the one thing
And yet also do the other?

MOTHER I don't know. I cannot conceive it.

X1 That's what I was telling you: there is an impossibility.   120
Between this act and me there stands an immense wall.
There is no door, no gap.

MOTHER And yet, there is the murder.
How could you,
With the hatchet in one hand
And sweet white bread in the other
(Horrible coalition, I recoil at this man!),
Be at the same time the oil, the fire, the lamb, and the cook?
I fear a race whose hands fight each other.
How could you do what cannot be!?   130

FURIES It's not hard. He lies, maybe.
I'll explain it to you. With this hand . . .

MOTHER He's not lying. He believes everything he's saying.

FURIES If she listens to this rattlesnake,
It will circle around her head for seven days in a row,
And on the seventh day,
Our last trenches will collapse.
The cemetery will explode: for you it will mean disaster,
You'll lose all your stars.
As for me, I'll lose all my teeth.   140
I don't want to see that happen. I'll cover my face
And huddle in a crack of the sepulchre.

MOTHER I am searching in vain,
There isn't the slightest shred of a lie
Or truth stirring in his mind.
Only drawers, drawers, and more drawers,
All empty! Empty! Empty!
How terrible! How pitiful!
Neither cold nor hot, neither thinking nor remembering,
Neither to the right nor to the left.   150
His heart is mummified. Horrible is its immobility.
There is nothing left that was red or shiny.
In vain I dig into inert matter.

X1 There we are, starting again with the litany!

MOTHER I don't want to get angry,
But I sense an enormous rage
Gathering within my entrails.
Quick! Go away!

X1 Where is the exit?

FURIES Hey you! This way!   160

X1   You again!

FURIES But of course.

     You can't go around me as if I were a post in the road. There is an impossibility.

X1   It's a trap! [*To* NIGHT] You had told me: I am a friend! I believed you!

FURIES Believed! Yes. Deceived![91]

NIGHT Let him go.

     There is no one at the bottom of this phantom.

                                                          [*Exit* X1

FURIES Did you see this? Night tells him:

     Go and lean over this mirror   170

     And, full of sacred terror, behold

     The procession of the children, dressed in red, slain

     In all the famous slaughterhouses of tragedy.

     Behold the children sliced and diced,

     The children of Thyestes, the children of Agamemnon,

     Behold the children of Edward

     And black little Eli,[92]

     Behold the little ones carved in smoke,

     All the little smoky ghosts

     Flying around chimneys   180

     Above the – what do you call them?

     Ghettos?

MOTHER Concentration Camps.

FURIES That's it.

     And then, as you behold yourself

     Among the gangs of butchers in soiled aprons,

     Shudder with fright!

     He goes to the mirror, he leans over it,

     And then, nothing.

     He fails to shudder with sacred terror.   190

     How can you expect anything

     Of such a pathetic creature?!

     ....

     It's a grave error!

     The eyes of this man's heart are blinded.

     He steps with a profane foot into the land of pain

     As he would into a bar,

     And your words fall stone dead

     Before the man whose face has no opening.

     He knows neither terror nor pity.   200

     That is why your tragedy is so tragic.

MOTHER Ah! It's your fault, hope,

     If I wait, I'll wait for that which cannot happen.

     Because of this crazy hope which won't die.

     Nothing rekindles itself more obstinately

     Than this cruel spark that is born to die,

     Born to die

And in rebirth renews the suffering.
I push it back, it clings to me,
I cut off its fingers, they grow back.   210
Stop, hope, let me go!
Ah! You will die only with me!
I no longer want to hope.
NIGHT But you hope all the same.
FURIES You would do better to let us hope
    The way we always do. It would be less abstract.
MOTHER I don't want to want anything. Never again.
FURIES It would be very concrete.
MOTHER It is you who incite me,
    I dream, dream, dream.   220
    If only you weren't here!
NIGHT Do you want me to go?
MOTHER Yes! Yes!
NIGHT I am going.

[*Exit* NIGHT

MOTHER No! Wait! Don't leave!
    Don't run from me, goddess, don't run from me! Help! Help me!
    Hold her back by the fringes of her dress.

[*Exit the* MOTHER, *running*

Scene 19

On stage, AESCHYLUS, CHORUS *and* FURIES

CHORUS Is this going to last a long time, this combat of hope?
    What do you say, you who have seen worse,
    How will this end?
AESCHYLUS Very quickly, very violently.
    The hour is not far off, the end is coming.
    I already hear the axe whirring.[93] Do you hear it?
    Follow me to the final scene.
    It will be a very special scene.
    .... But what is this?
    What is this fanfare of car horns   10
    And these loud clamourings which, coming from the City,
    Reach all the way here?

Enter MAINTENANCE

MAINTENANCE Sound the alarm! To your horses! On your mopeds! Giddy up!
    My friends! Forzza is sweeping the election!
    Like a huge wave rising
    To the towers, to the Palace,
    To the throne, rising and spreading like a white night[94]

Above what was once the Kingdom,
So does this tide come on, the like of which we have never seen.   20
Listen!
FURIES That's the first round! The City is falling!
For us, it's quite excellent.
The vilest precede the slightly less vile!
It's a good sign! Everything will go from bad to worse.
CHORUS What will happen to us?
AESCHYLUS A messenger.

Enter a MESSENGER

MESSENGER A message addressed to the mother, on behalf of the new government.
CHORUS Give it.   30

....
Get out.

[*Exit* MESSENGER

....
A message from Forzza:
Madame, come back. You will be compensated. Forget the riffraff.
This affair does not concern them. They must clear the cemetery. Or else . . .
FURIES Well, finish reading.
CHORUS I have finished. That's how it ends: *Or else.*

....   40
Or else?! I really don't like this Or Else.

....
Or Else? What does this mean, this Or Else?

....
I know this Or Else: it's the tyrant's first word.
How does one respond
To a threat so vague, so vast, so absolute?
The spirit of resistance must invent
Ruses that keep the resister alive.
Should I keep watch over this noble cemetery   50
Magnified by all these events,
And risk losing my life here?
Or, to keep my life,
Should I abandon this cemetery
And look for another one further away?
FURIES Do not listen to tyranny, ever!
Under anguish let courage flourish!
If you bend, if you flee,
Then tomorrow morning, how many scourges,
How much repression, how much division!   60
How much dissension!
CHORUS Could you please stop screeching
For one second? And let us think? Just one second!
You are not from here! You don't understand a thing about this place.

FURIES Io! Screeching! Me ! Already so vulgar!

    Io popoï! Not from here! Why don't you call me a *metic*, an Arab,

    A resident alien[95]! If you do,

    I'll walk out the door and slam it behind me!

CHORUS Yeah, yeah, that's right, get out! Out!

                                                 [*The* CHORUS *retreats*   70

FURIES And you, stay inside!

    How could you possibly think, you tamed rabbit![96]

    Already I see everything shrinking! Walls rise up,

    Expulsion and repulsion flow back into the veins,

    The air smells of exile and incarceration,

    Snow piles up with dazzling speed.

    We would like to flee, but where to go?

    A road chases me, then another,

    At the borders, the thorny thickets thicken,

    At the mountain passes, the exhausted outcasts   80

    Give up their winded souls to the universe.[97]

    The world has become a clenched fist.

    Yet, who can really say who is from here

    And who is not from here?

    It is so dark in the brain.

    So you bar my bridges? You wall up my exits?

    You burn my ships?

    Are all the cracks filled?

    You never saw such a blockade.

    Though my wings are clipped, I still speak to you: 90

    Tell me, which one of us here is the least alien?

    There is no beyond. Where I stand is where I am from.

    Don't answer me.

Enter the MOTHER

MOTHER I, for one, am not leaving, I don't want to

    Abandon to terror a single one of the dark

    Familiar streets of this cemetery.

    Here the voices of my children gleam brightly.

    But my friends, I ask this of you:

    Do not listen to this sinister message.   100

    Open your eyes, and see: the whole world is looking at you.

    You are not foreigners stepping into

    My story with a light foot.

    Who among you could shove this cemetery aside

    With a pitiless kick?

    This bitter garden is more than my cemetery,

    More than a nest for my birds,

    More than a roof for my exile, more than your City,

    More than your ark,

    More than a boat for our dead, more than a camp bed.   110

It is our library, our archive, and our future,
Our hive with cells gorged with dreams,
The book we must write, it is the proof and pledge
That no one will be forgotten.
Let us make no error:
This strange and cruel story
Isn't just the business of one insignificant woman.
It turns its apocalyptic eyes toward you, too.
Other people, with other names, in other bodies,
Have endured and will endure it.   120
This is why I'm trying to change its course.
Don't let your eyes grow dull, don't turn your heads.
Hardly have you turned it, and the Beast
Takes a huge leap forward.
Keep watch! Keep watch! Don't move from the edge!
If you throw an arm, a river, a province, a little brother,
A woman maybe, into the mouth of the Beast,
Its appetite will increase.[98]

FURIES What do you think, Aeschylus, will your myrmidons surrender to the Beast?

AESCHYLUS That would be impossible.   130
But it's up to them to decide.
Already the darkness rises,
Colourless, formless, without dimensions.
The sky is shortsighted, I see no sign. How about you, Thessaloniki?

THESSALONIKI Nor do I, I see almost nothing
But I recognize almost everything.

MOTHER Water is stronger than rock,
Hang on and resist, everything wears away,
Fear, stone and I too wear away.
My body is worn out, but I know I am right, and that gives me strength.   140
It will hold on until the Or Else vanishes.
They'll resist, I'm sure of it.
And before our unexpected hardness, the Beast will stop in its tracks.

FURIES For me, it's clear, they will surrender.
I see what remains to be done. Return to the hunt.
Until now we have respected the free movement
Of bereaved souls.
But those who look at us
Should not believe that we'll follow the tamed rabbits
To the dark abdication of melancholy.   150
I will not go down a second time into the same grave[99]
Until I have poured out my anger on all the arrogant.
Arise, my angers, arise!
And may our smouldering story flare up with the wind.
We are its dénouement.

                                                    [*Exit everyone*

Scene 20

Enter the KING

KING Finally! I am released! Defeat is mine!
Welcome, evil hour, I have been awaiting you.
This is my deposition from the cross and from the rock.
This is the inevitable seventh day, the day of deserved rest.
Here ends the hard work of the King,
The long sojourn up there where there are no friends.
Enough seen! Enough suppressed! My eyes are worn out
From seeing everything in the crude light of power.
I've had my share of this passion.
People do not see you,   10
They invent you and accuse you.
If I am guilty, it's of failing to move mountains
With a mere breath at the behest of an impatient age.
He who'd pry into my soul
Would not find me guilty of destruction,
Vengeance, or hatred against other men.
But I have no witness.
I am the only one to know
How I loved you.
They think they are dismissing me, but I have much to win.   20
Descending from the rock, I escape –
Not for the first time –
The delirious dreamers who ask kings to be gods,
And gods to be the servants of their selfishness!
At last, all my leaves have fallen. Autumn, be welcome!
The silent tree, the season itself excuse me from the throne.
No more lies masquerading as wisdom and pity,
No more daily tribunal to
Arraign, accuse and condemn the King.
What was there in exchange for so many inevitable pains?   30
An uncertain glory and a congregation of hate.
Oh, my anxious friends, citizens dissatisfied by definition,
I kept watch for so long while you slept.
Without regret, I break my magic wand.[100]
I am restored to myself. It's my turn to dream.
But you, who will look after you?

[*Exit the* KING

Scene 21

Enter FORZZA

FORZZA Oh! My nation, my beloved!
　　Count on your loyal fiancé
　　To rid you of evildoers of all kinds,
　　Who think only of abusing you.
　　Your Forzza will never abandon you.
　　What, what is it?!

Enter MONSIEUR CAPTAIN

MONSIEUR CAPTAIN Mr President![101] They're not surrendering!
　　It's a chorus of no's!
　　They didn't want to listen to anything!　　　　　　　　　　　　10
FORZZA You suggested everything, right?
　　Amnesty, punishment, conciliation, expulsion, regularization, renewal?[102]
MONSIEUR CAPTAIN Yes! Yes!
FORZZA And their answer was sedition and rebellion.
MONSIEUR CAPTAIN Well, no. Not exactly.
FORZZA Yes, exactly! Just as I predicted!
　　As I hoped!
MONSIEUR CAPTAIN But why?
FORZZA Because I'm not going to squander the opportunity of a good cleansing, am I? You know me a little,
　　don't you?　　　　　　　　　　　　　　　　　　　　　　　　　20
MONSIEUR CAPTAIN Yes, Mr President.
FORZZA Well then. The cemetery, the scum, the vermin, the invasion, the chaos, all of it, I want it to be
　　only a memory tomorrow. And the day after, a mere bite in the gaping mouth of Oblivion. Let's take
　　advantage of the confused feelings caused by my election to carry out fabulous purifications.
MONSIEUR CAPTAIN How so?
FORZZA A tidal wave. A fire. I don't care. Let's be sanitary.
MONSIEUR CAPTAIN Sanitary?
FORZZA We'll scorch anything that swarms.
　　We'll disinfect the sanctuary.
MONSIEUR CAPTAIN Is it necessary?　　　　　　　　　　　　　　30
FORZZA It is sanitary, I said. Or better yet . . .
　　Where is this famous, ill situated, poorly constructed dam
　　That shakes on its foundation?
　　You know, the one that splits open a bit each year,
　　Isn't it up the mountain
　　That towers over the cesspool?
　　Well then!
　　It will be a whale of a flood!
　　Come on, my good man, we'll flood. Now.
　　Give the order.　　　　　　　　　　　　　　　　　　　　　　40
　　Tomorrow, when I make my entrance into the capital,

There will be no more agitation or disorder
Than at the entrance of Fortinbras.[103]

MONSIEUR CAPTAIN What about the hostages?

FORZZA They are corrupt. Give them up to chance.
Find me an end that is like a beginning.
What? What's the matter?
You've lost the gleam in your eye . . .

MONSIEUR CAPTAIN I've always wanted to please you.

FORZZA Well, continue. This is no time to slow down.   50
I want to hear from you before the curtain lifts on my reign.

MONSIEUR CAPTAIN Faster, faster, faster.
No time to think anymore,
That's how one becomes a four-footed animal.

[*Exit* MONSIEUR CAPTAIN

FORZZA Tomorrow, at my entrance,
The cold hearts of the people,
Rekindled like the hearts of children
By the return of an unhoped-for protector,
Will give out a single acclamation of joy.   60
I know what you want, ancient race,[104]
Too often deceived by frivolous leaders.
You want a man who loves you jealously
And who honours the marital bed.
With Forzza, there is no polygamy.
I will make you happy, since you elected me
To put an end to the intrusions
Which defile this house.
What time is it? You are late, Captain.

Enter MONSIEUR CAPTAIN   70

So, is it done? Is the order given?

MONSIEUR CAPTAIN Given. Yes.
From my own mouth, harbinger of destruction,
Sprang out your inflexible speech.
Ah! What power you have!
No sooner did I say three words
Than the dark message spread.
Nothing can stop the thunderbolt now:
Already, powerful Forzza's
Violent will is accomplished.   80
God, what a frightful power you possess!
I'd never have thought that annihilation
Could be executed with such ease and swiftness.
This man says: let darkness seize this neighbourhood,
And in the wink of an eye, the regiments of darkness
Surround the neighbourhood.
At that moment, just before the fatal collapse,

The cemetery's suddenly minuscule creatures
Start running around.
Cries break out, but the flood swallows them,   90
People rush towards the gates,
Torrents of mud have already engulfed the exits.
A tide of uprooted tombs overtakes the fugitives
And rolls the children, alive and dead,
Into the anonymous abyss.
Ah! If I could give the opposite order
And force the torrent back!

FORZZA Too late.

MONSIEUR CAPTAIN All will perish.
At this moment my life looks beyond   100
Its pitiful limits.
For the first time, the blind man I once was can see.
I see the carnage of the unfortunate flock.
This thing wasn't necessary, and now it's too late.

FORZZA I do what I say, I want what I want
But I certainly don't like the voice in your voice.

MONSIEUR CAPTAIN Ah! I am ashamed to feel nice and cozy inside my skin.
Like a beast, I obeyed a beast.
Yes. A beast.

FORZZA Are you raising your hand against me?   110
Are you less than a dog, don't you know your master?

MONSIEUR CAPTAIN I cannot stop the irresistible arrow that I shot myself.
They will all die.
But I can stop the cause of misfortune.
Forzza, you believed you had mechanized me: fast, fast, fast, fast!
But there is some blood left in me that you haven't corrupted,
I am against your deification.
I am going to denounce you, Mr President.
Tomorrow, the whole country will know of your crime,
I will not fall alone.   120
I will be your downfall! Down with Forzzism!
And since you poured in me the poison of murder,
I will destroy you with wild pleasure.

FORZZA No! Don't strangle me, don't kill me!
You would regret it.

MONSIEUR CAPTAIN True! Enough killing.
Enough deaths. Farewell.

FORZZA Halt! One doesn't leave Forzza, little snot!
Always the same mistakes, Captain.
Too bad for you, maggot,   130
If you didn't learn from my teaching.
How many times did I tell you:
Don't miss opportunities,
Take no prisoners,
There is no such thing as good pity.

You shouldn't have spared me.

I won't spare you.

I will sweep you away, you insect!

MONSIEUR CAPTAIN [*wounded*] All are dead.

[*He dies*   140

FORZZA From now on you belong to the party of suicides.

You are a thing of my past.

I have only to clear out.

Still, what I wanted you to do, you did it!

Come, I'll take you with me,

But you will not see me King.

[*He exits, carrying the body*

NIGHT This ending is too unbearable to be the final ending.[105]

We need an epilogue to give us back our breath.

Aeschylus, arise!   150

Prelude

DANIEL [*singing*] Let's hurry, Benjamin,

Let's throw the shining net

Into the violent current.

Let's hoist into our shining mesh

All our friends engulfed by the Flood.

THE CHILDREN'S VOICES Hello up there, send the clouds,

Come down, quick. I found mama again.

Quick, lower the celestial raft.

I wrenched mama

From the black water's jaws.   10

Ho! Heave ho! Hoist the clouds

Gently! And do not scare

This very tender load.

Bravo up there! Ho! Heave ho!

Epilogue

NIGHT All right?

Are they all here?

FURIES Almost

Not quite.

NIGHT Hurry up, my daughters,

Quickly fish out all our dear shipwrecked ones,

Wrench their desolate bodies from the black water's jaws,

And bring them dripping wet under our caring guard!

Move fast, ye clouds, assist them,

Because the next life is about to start!   10

FURIES Whew! I am as out of breath as an old exhausted seagull:

I flew, I dived, I fished, I pulled,
And here they are, all lying
On the shore, emerging from nothingness
Like newborn travellers.
Is it yourself you're looking for, Aeschylus?

AESCHYLUS My notebook! My pencil! I must note it down:
It's my first time dying!
There! What was I saying? The axe had just fallen,
Our thread was cut. It was like a thunderbolt.   20
A hole in Nature, wham! We were falling!
I said to myself: I'm dying.
At that moment, gasping, I woke up
– We woke up –
The sky was breathing in my ears; from everywhere,
Tails spread, bellies white, the shooting stars came, bread in hand,
And we seemed like dwarfish squirrels in the virgin space.
I see it, our terrestrial chronology has ended.
How brief death will have been! What beauty!
The speed surpassed all psychology: 30
A spin of the wheel and poof!! Life passed away, we have long since gone beyond death and begun resurrection.
Now is afterwards,
It's not at all what people imagine,
The heart still beats like a flag in the chest.
Here the decor is very sparing.
Everything has reached perfection. The sky? Absolute.
Space? I would say: an infinite black velvet.

CHORUS I know we are no longer on Earth,
But I'd like to know   40
Where we are? Where? Where are we going?
Who? How?

NIGHT You have arrived.
You are at home on my infinite continent.
Here are no angles, curves or borders, nothing but reflections.
This is the city of black velvet
That stretches between the Pleiades and red Aldebaran.
Only a few thousand centuries separate us from the next star.
The one you see going by there is the long-necked moon who smiles dreamily to herself.

CHORUS I don't see anything!   50

NIGHT Put out your candle, Aeschylus, and let us behold the whole Universe.

[AESCHYLUS *puts it out*

CHORUS Oh! There! I see the Earth glowing softly!
Earth! I see you! Earth, where I am no more!
Distant ghostly orange,
Such a sad wonder, such a wonderful sadness,
To see the Earth passing without haste under the portals of the constellations,
Like our former ghostly orange,
It's very blue sky blue sea blue vivid blue

And not at all yellow.   60
O distant sadness that no longer pains me!

....

To think that yesterday death hung over us from the shattered dam.
And we were ants wiggling
In its terrible cracks.
The flood came upon us. Exhausted, drowned, and disjointed
We died. Or rather we tried
To run. And now I don't at all think that I'm dead.

....

Nor I. Lighter than lightness   70
With my old and worn words in hand
I step barefoot into your immense City of black velvet.
Infinity does not intimidate me.

....

Had I known I was going to die,
I could have made a will
But what could I have left you?
All I owned was my blood and my thoughts.

....

O marvellous absence of sadness!   80
O Earth, dear magnificent orange,
I cast on your sphere handfuls of caressing gazes.
Yesterday I didn't like you, today I adore you.
Had they known what would happen to us,
They wouldn't have killed us.
The love of Justice cost us the Earth
But it earned us the warless High City.
It's all a question of one's point of view.
From here I see the Perjured City very well.
I never saw it so distinctly before.   90

....

Never did one see two Cities so unlike each other.
I would have loved to present to you, when I discovered it,
The City that has no other name than yours, Night,
But this will be for next time.
When you arrive here you will see:
She is a very noble dazzling rejoicing splendid joyous grand magnificent living lady.
Meanwhile, below, death is crazily active,
It is everywhere, stomping in the prisons, plazas and palaces,
I hear all the seams bursting.   100
The clamour of indignation grows every day
And reaches our glistening ears.
Each street, each car, each bus
Transports choreuts, who, still alive, declare their anger more and more loudly.
Some, getting ready to die, predict the truth:
This cannot last, they whisper,
Once suffering reaches the boiling point

In the City's entrails,
Nothing can stop it from erupting in dreadful lava.
Oh! Our two Cities are so unlike each other!   110

NIGHT   And you, the Mother, I don't hear your voice,
Here you are, triumphant, licking your kittens and nibbling at their chins.
Say something. If you don't, our friends will worry.

MOTHER   It's because I have almost nothing to say, only to caress,
To lick taste roll sniff my newly reclaimed little ones.
Now I'm crying. Now I'm laughing.
I've stopped dying. I've already begun to imitate the next life.
How delightful it is no longer to be a main character in a ghastly drama.
Yes, I want to resume the dialogue with the hours of time and all their colours
And to taste the eternal savour of my children.   120
I want to take my indistinct place among
The plants, the stars, the passers-by.
I'm going to eat the air and drink the light.
Yesterday I cried with horror, now that belongs to the past.
Now I cease to punish myself, wanting consolation,
And I cease to offend, wanting to forgive.
Because to pardon is such an offence.

AESCHYLUS   All of you,
Listen to the Mother,
Because after this you will never again hear   130
Joy speaking so clearly.
You, the Mother, speak more slowly, continue.

MOTHER   What is there to say?
The play is over. Here I am, sitting with my friends on rocks of gold and silver.
And now, I understand, we must be silent.
But for all of you who remain down below,
What can I do?
No, I have not forgotten. No, I will not forget.
No, there was no call for despair,
Only the pains of unbirthing and then of birthing,   140
But now suffering has become painless.
Later on, I will build for you
A temple with silence,
A tribunal with silence,
A theatre with silence,
But if I create all these silences
Who, among you, will cry out?
I'm going to put my words, my thoughts, my angers
Underground, beneath your feet.
But out of this earth pregnant with my secrets   150
The tree of cries must grow. Or else,
Never again will a human being with light-filled eyes
Come to maturity in this country.
Our play is over. May yours begin.
It is your turn to insist that what is just

Comes to pass justly.

In memory,

I leave you my story with its taste of tears and milk.

CHORUS P.S. And I, for one, advise you:

Do not let a bad captain steer a living ship. 160

NIGHT Come now, follow my gleaming steps

I'll take you to your rooms embellished by our incandescent care.

Come. Let's go. Don't be afraid. It's not hard to walk on the floor of the sky.

First lift your right foot in a delicate movement,

Then brush against the sky, swinging lightly.

Your left foot will follow weightlessly.

Then, move forward, stepping slowly and gracefully,

Such is the step of the celestial company.

[*All exit*

That's it! They're moving forward! 170

Do you see them high up, these microscopic sparks?

They are moving into the future.

But know that, however far they may be,

Their dreaming eyes never close.

THE END

Notes to *The Perjured City*

1 [Author's note] This play was written between December 1992 and September 1993.

   The events of this story took place between 3500 BC and the year 1993. Later, events came to pass, in real life, which looked like them.

   This is because the word of the Theatre, uttered in the present and the intemporal, is, by definition, prophetic.

2 [Translator's note] The following notes are intended to suggest the wide range of historical, poetic and theatrical resonances in *The Perjured City*. For the author's own reflections on her play and its inscription in the contemporary historical context (the affair of the contaminated blood at the end of the Mitterand presidency in France, 1992–3), see Bernadette Fort, "Theater, History, Ethics: An Interview with Hélène Cixous on *The Perjured City, or The Awakening of the Furies*," *New Literary History* 28:3 (1997), 425–56. For the intricate connections between this play and the *Oresteia*, especially in regard to politics, justice and gender, see Bernadette Fort, "Spectres d'Eschyle: La Ville parjure d'Hélène Cixous," in *Hélène Cixous, Croisées d'une oeuvre*, sous la direction de Mireille Calle-Gruber (Paris: Galilée, 2000), 443–6.

   This translation is a carefully revised version of the text I provided to Northwestern University Theatre for the English-language premiere of *The Perjured City*, directed by Craig Kinzer, on 21 February 1997. The translation is the product of arduous personal wrestling with the original text and inspiration provided at different stages by many students and colleagues at Northwestern. It started as a project in a senior seminar on translation I gave in 1996. The rehearsals and performances of the play were crucial to my refining of a text designed both to be performed, that is, *heard*, as well as read. I thank Christopher Herbert, for putting his impressive knowledge of the intricacies of both the French and the English languages at my disposal. Reginald Gibbons, an acclaimed poet and author himself, lent his expertise in poetic sounds and rhythms. Gerald Mead and Linda Matthews contributed sensitive comments and suggestions, and Sophie Herbert-Fort made sure I did not stray too far from current idioms. My greatest debt is to Hélène Cixous, who encouraged this translation at every step and, in two memorable sessions in Northwestern's Rose Garden, unveiled some of the hidden beauties of her text to me and treated me to her famed translingual limberness.

3 Cixous cites from her own French translation of Aeschylus' *The Eumenides* (Eschyle, *L'Orestie. Les Euménides*, trans. Hélène Cixous, notes P. Judet de la Combe [Paris: Théâtre du Soleil, 1992]):

   > Le sang [. . .], une fois sur le sol,
   > Il est bien difficile de le faire remonter, popoï!
   > Le rapide liquide qui est versé à terre, s'en va.

   In Richmond Lattimore's translation (*Aeschylus I. Oresteia*, Chicago, Ill.: The University of Chicago Press, 1953):

   > [. . .] blood spilled on the ground

can not come back again.
It is all soaked and drained into the ground and gone.

This leitmotiv also appears in Apollo's speech: "once/ the dust has drained down all a man's blood, once the man/has died, there is no raising of him up again" (646–8). Further citations from this play in English refer to Lattimore's translation.

4   Allusion to Lady Macbeth after Duncan's murder: "Here's the smell of the blood still: all the perfumes of Arabia will not sweeten this little hand" (*Macbeth* 5.1. 47–8).

5   Allusion to the French adage "bon sang ne peut mentir" (true blood never lies).

6   The French "à leur corps défendant," literally "against their own body," is more graphic and apt.

7   There lingers here a distant echo of Bernardo's words to Horatio about the apparition of the ghost: "Let us once again assail your ears / That are so fortified against our story . . ." (*Hamlet*, 1.1.31–2).

8   The anthropophagic metaphor recalls the ghastly banquet served by Atreus to celebrate the return of his rival brother to Argos. Atreus had Thyestes' two young sons murdered, their bodies cut into pieces and served to their father.

9   "The milk of human kindness," see *Macbeth* 1.5. 17.

10   This neologism was suggested by the author for "ailé kiloptère." (The caretaker, later revealed to be Aeschylus, is unfamiliar with this artifact of twentieth-century technology, and thus with its name).

11   In French, "le maquis" refers to isolated mountainous regions of France where members of the Résistance hid and fought during the German occupation in the Second World War.

12   Goethe, "Die Belagerung von Mainz," *Gesammelte Werke*, Weimarer Ausgabe, 33:316: "ich will lieber eine Ungerechtigkeit begehen als Unordnung ertragen." I thank Peter Fenves for the reference.

13   The kind of tortures inflicted by the Furies.

14   An ironic reminder of the ending of *The Eumenides*.

15   See Athena's words in *The Eumenides*: "sped on my weariless feet, I came, wingless / but in the rush and speed of the aegis fold" (403–4).

16   See note 8.

17   Aeschylus speaks here in character with the pacifist message delivered in *The Eumenides*.

18   Nazi criminals and French collaborators found refuge after the war in foreign countries (such as Klaus Barbie in Argentina) or hid in monasteries under the protection of the Catholic Church (such as Paul Touvier).

19   X1's real-life prototype, Dr Michel Garreta, was given an armoured car for his protection.

20   In 1993 archeologists recovered in a Greek port a ship sunk thousands of years ago. It was still fully preserved in the silt.

21   Wordplay on "sacré et massacré."

22   As tears also flowed from Clytemnestra's eyes for the murder of her daughter Iphigenia by Agamemnon.

23   This is the path followed by the Erinyes on Orestes's tracks in *The Eumenides*. The evocation of the hunter's speed and force recalls *Eum.* 372–6: "For with a long leap from high / above and dead drop of weight / I bring foot's force crashing down / to cut the legs from under even / the runner, and spill him to ruin."

24   See *Eum.* 916–1047.

25   See Athena's pledge to the Erinyes (*Eum.* 804–7): "I promise you a place / of your own,

deep hidden under ground that is yours by right / where you shall sit on shining chairs beside the hearth /to accept devotions offered by your citizens."

26 Cixous both cites and transforms the Eumenides' pledge of peace and prosperity to Athena (*Eum.* 938–42): "Let there blow no wind that wrecks the tree. / I pronounce words of grace. / Nor blaze of heat blind the blossoms of grown plants, nor / cross the circles of its right/place. Let no barren deadly sickness creep and kill. / Flocks fatten. Earth be kind to them, / with double fold of fruit / in time appointed for its yielding" (*Eum.* 942–6).

27 See *Eum.* 976–83: "This is my prayer: Civil War / fattening on men's ruin shall / not thunder in our city. Let not the dry dust that drinks the black blood of citizens / through passion for revenge / and bloodshed for bloodshed / be given our state to prey upon."

28 Allusion to the many methods of separation, fractioning and processing of blood for transfusion.

29 The play on the signifier is not translatable: "Le nom? Non! Le nom je ne le dirai pas." The refusal to name the criminal's name has aesthetic, ethical and practical reasons.

30 Anonymity is achieved with the ciphers X1 and X2 for the physicians.

31 See note 18. René Bousquet, another French Nazi collaborator, whose case was finally going to be brought to trial when he was assassinated in 1993, was director of the Banque de Suez. Swiss banks were privileged repositories for wealth and precious objects stolen by Nazis from Jews (see the revelations which broke in the international press in October and November 1996). Cixous's text is shot through with correspondences between money (gold), blood and criminality.

32 See Apollo entrusting Orestes to Hermes' guard: "Shepherd him / with fortunate escort on his journeys among men" (*Eum.* 91–2).

33 An instance of the constant play with time frames which is characteristic of Cixous's imagination and writing. Aeschylus, we note, has just quoted Shakespeare, who wrote 2000 years after him.

34 In French, the name Thessalonique harbours quite a few insults: "t'es salo(pe), (tu) niques" (literally, "you're a dirty fucking bitch").

35 Lagadoue in the original.

36 The French word "métèque" is etymologically related to the Greek word "metic" (foreigner, alien). The Furies are "metics." In modern French, however, "métèque" is a slang, racist word for North African Arabs.

37 In the *Oresteia* (as well as in Homer) the Furies are always associated with rumbling, grumbling and snoring noises (for example: "they snore with breath that drives one back" *Eum.* 53). See also Jacques Derrida on the rumbling of the ghost in *Hamlet*, *Specters of Marx: The State of the Debt, the Work of Mourning, and the New International*. trans. Peggy Kamuf (New York and London: Routledge, 1994), 5.

38 An hallucination in which the subject sees himself transformed into a dog. Among other animals, the Furies were associated with dogs in Greek mythology.

39 "Queen Dies" is in English in the original.

40 In the French context, these three recent wars would be the first and second World Wars and the Algerian Independence War.

41 Many former Vichy collaborators, such as René Bousquet and Maurice Papon, who had been cleared after the war, continued to be received at the Elysée Palace by President François Mitterand. Bousquet was police minister under the Vichy government and solely responsible for the ignominious roundup of Jews called "Rafle du Vel d'Hiv" in July 1942, during which over 4000 Jewish children were gathered and sent to death in concentration camps. The trial of Maurice Papon, also a high official in the Vichy government and later Minister of Finances

under Giscard d'Estaing, was delayed for many years by Mitterand and finally took place, after Mitterand's death, in 1997–8. Papon stood accused of ordering the deportation of 1690 Jews, among which 233 children, to Drancy, which served as an antechamber to Auschwitz.

42 Mitterand made frequent allusions to time. He used to say one needs to "laisser du temps au temps" (give time to time). Laurent Fabius, prime minister under Mitterand, wrote that in the course of the twenty-five years during which he shared Mitterand's political life, Mitterand's "sole obsession" had been death. See also Mitterand's preface "Comment mourir?" to Marie de Hennezel's *La Mort intime* (Paris, Laffont, 1996).

43 Cassandra predicts the death of Agamemnon in Aeschylus' eponymous play.

44 For the story of Belshazzar's feast, followed by the siege and capture of Babylon by Cyrus, see the *Book of Daniel* and Xenophon's *Cvropaedia*. Cixous alludes to the biblical story of Belshazzar as represented in Rembrandt's famous painting.

45 Mitterand awarded the prestigious "Légion d'honneur" medal to Garreta for "exceptional services" on 31 December 1989, although charges had already been brought against him in May 1988.

46 Mithridates had gradually immunized himself against poison.

47 Night is older than the Bible.

48 See the assonance in the French text: "Pas de sous, pas de souillures."

49 "Bienfaiteur malgré lui." A variation on Molière's *Le Médecin malgré lui*.

50 "Vous écrivez faire: f-e-r."

51 The French is very alliterative: "Faut pas bafouiller en fripouillant."

52 The hostages, i.e., the two doctors, X1 and X2.

53 Forza, in Italian, means strength. The name also echoes with that of "Fortinbras," on whose arrival *Hamlet* ends.

54 This is how some writers, among whom Stefan Zweig, pictured Hitler's stealthy arrival on the political scene.

55 See Shakespeare, *King Lear*, 3.4.107: "unaccommodated man is no more but such a poor, bare, fork'd animal as you are."

56 Echoes of the graveyard scene in *Hamlet*.

57 A typical Cixousian play on the signifier: "Tu ne te jettes pas à l'eau? Salaud!"

58 "Mais tant que je ne suis pas mort, j'ai tort."

59 Untranslatable play on signifiers: "je suis deux, coupé, coupé, donc non coupable" recalls with irony the notorious formula used by Georgina Dufoix, Minister for Social Affairs in 1985, to decline responsibility in the affair of the contaminated blood. She said she was "responsable, mais pas coupable" (responsible, but not guilty).

60 Garreta had attended an international conference where the heating of blood was shown to be a necessary measure against HIV contamination.

61 Allusion to Garreta's misappropriation of funds.

62 Journalists reporting on the appeals trial observed that Garreta and Allain presented this time a united front, their strategy being to dismiss the attacks of the plaintiffs' lawyers with scientific evidence. See, for example, *Le Monde*, 20 May 1993.

63 In *The Eumenides*, Athena opens the trial thus:

> Herald, make proclamation and hold in the host
> assembled. Let the stabbing voice of the Etruscan
> trumpet, blown to the full with mortal wind, crash out
> its high call to all the assembled populace
>
> (566–69)

64 Another subtle rewriting of the trial scene in *The Eumenides*, where Athena yields the floor to the Furies as responsible for the prosecution: "For it must justly be the pursuer who speaks first / and opens the case, and makes plain what the action is" (583–4).

65 On the liquid metaphor for the maternal element, see Cixous's "Aller à la mer," *Le Monde* (28 April 1984). In English, "Going to the Seashore," *Modern Drama* 27 (1984), 546–8.

66 See *Eum.* 465–8:

> Apollo shares responsibility for this.
> He counterspurred my heart and told me of pains to come
> If I should fail to act against the guilty ones.

67 1942. The height of Nazi rule in Europe.

68 Allusion to the famous verse in Racine's *Phèdre*: "Le jour n'est pas plus pur que le fond de mon coeur."

69 Wordplay between "gagner une manche" (to win a hand /a round) and "être manchot" (to have only one arm, or one hand).

70 The legislative election of 1993 was very hotly contested. It resulted in a resounding defeat for the socialist party.

71 "Qu'ils votent, qu'ils rotent," literally "whether they vote or belch." The word "rotent" is brought about by phonetic attraction.

72 Again, there is a wordplay between "ce dont je me fous" (what I don't give a damn about) and "asile de fous" (insane asylum).

73 Cixous's father was a doctor. She has poignantly written about the feeling of irreparable loss at his death. See, among many testimonies, *Dedans* (Paris: Grasset, 1969), *Photos de racines* (with Mireille Calle-Gruber) (Paris: Des femmes, 1994) and the moving meditation devoted to him in one of her latest books, *Or. les lettres de mon père* (Paris: Des femmes, 1996).

74 The French colloquialism "c'est empoisonnant" (literally, "it's poisoning"), comments ironically on the charge of poisoning brought against Garreta by the lawyers for the haemophiliacs.

75 Upon resigning on 3 June 1991, Garreta negotiated that the CNTS would give him a three-million francs indemnization, a bullet-proof Renault 25, and pay the lawyers' fees for the forthcoming trial.

76 Dr Yvette Sultan, professeur des Universités and head of the haemophiliac ward at Hôpital Cochin in Paris, was Professor Lion's prototype in real life. She was among the first medical experts to testify at the appeals trial in 1993. See *Le Monde*, 26 May 1993.

77 Both this article and the journal's name are fictional, as well as *Médecine aujourd'hui*, mentioned below.

78 In a note to Dr Jacques Roux dated March 1985, Dr Brunet wrote: "It is likely that all blood products prepared from pools of Parisian donors are contaminated." See *L'Evénement du jeudi*, 27 Jan.–2 Feb. 1994.

79 Cixous transforms the idiomatic expression "avoir la vue qui baisse" (to have declining/failing eyesight) into "avoir la *vie* qui baisse" (one's life on the blink).

80 In the original: "Pour les créatures sans rien, sans bien, sans mien."

81 "Qui as-tu allaité avec tes pis de pierre?" plays on the homophony of Pie (Pius, for a pope) and pis (udder). I kept the transgressive sexual play on the signifier with "peter."

82 The manuscript shows that Cixous first used the idiomatic expression "chacun pour soi" (everyone for himself) – before opting for the revealing lapsus "chacun pour *moi*" – (everyone for *myself*).

83 See note 1 for Cixous's epigraph to her preface "Our Bad Bloods."

84 "The Horned One," e.g. Hornus-Maximus, Head of the Order of French Physicians (CornuMaxime in French). The Satanic dimension is obvious.

85 The French lapsus ("Que veut le peuple? Des têtes . . . Des fêtes") has been adapted.

86 The French text, "du plus petit des sbires/Jusqu'au plus grand ministre," is a quotation adapted from one of Mirabeau's speeches during the French Revolution. For Cixous, it was a key moment in history when the responsibility *of the individual*, regardless of his position in a social or political hierarchy, was invoked as a moral imperative. See Cixous's interview with Bernadette Fort in *New Literary History*, 434.

87 The net is one of the recurrent metaphors in Aeschylus' *Oresteia*. It is by entangling Agamemnon at his bath in her net of robes that Clytemnestra killed her husband upon his return from Troy.

88 See *Eum.* 312–14: "We hold we are straight and just. If a man/can spread his hands and show they are clean, no wrath of ours shall lurk for him."

89 "Vos amies." The feminine gender points to the Furies.

90 Hélène Cixous said she took this anecdote from René Bousquet's life. See her interview in *NLH*, 435.

91 There is a wordplay in French on "cru" (believed) and "cru" (raw):

> X1: . . . Je vous ai crue.
> Les Erinyes: Cru! oui. Tout cru!

92 Famous instances of brutal children's murders. On Thyestes' children, see note 8. Atreus' son, Agamemnon, sacrificed his daughter Iphigenia on the shores of Aulis to propitiate the gods so his fleet could set sail for Troy. At the age of 12, Edward V and his younger brother, the Duke of York, were imprisoned in the Tower of London by their ruthless and ambitious uncle, the Duke of Gloucester, who had them smothered to death to usurp the crown. See Shakespeare's *Henry III*. "Little Eli" refers to *Eli, ein Mysterienspiel des Leidens Israels* by Nelly Sachs (1964), which stages scenes of the Holocaust.

93 On *la hache*, the axe, *une H*, and the initial of the author's first name, see *Three Steps on the Ladder of Writing*. trans. Sarah Cornell and Susan Sellers (New York: Columbia University Press, 1993), 3–4.

94 "Nuit blanche" also means "sleepless night."

95 See note 36 on the French insult "métèque."

96 For Cixous's use of animal metaphors to signify denatured humanity, see *On ne part pas, on ne revient pas* (Paris: Des femmes, 1991), 83–8 and passim.

97 A veiled allusion to Walter Benjamin, who committed suicide on a snowy Pyrenese mountain pass after a failed attempt to cross the French border over to Spain on his flight from Nazi Germany.

98 The Minotaur, the monster confined in the labyrinth built by Daedalus for Minos, received periodic offerings of young boys and girls in its gaping mouth until it was slain by Theseus.

99 See the ending of *The Eumenides*.

100 See Prospero in Shakespeare's *The Tempest* (5.1.54–7):

> I'll break my staff,
> Bury it certain fathoms in the earth,
> And deeper than did ever any plummet sound
> I'll drown my book.

101 Forzza has just won the presidential election.

102 Allusion to the laws curtailing immigration known as "the Pasqua laws," contemporaneous with the writing of the play; also to the various methods employed at the time by the French government to deal with illegal residents, or "sans-papiers."

103 Fortinbras (whose name distantly echoes Forzza) becomes the ruler of Denmark in the final scene in *Hamlet*.

104 "Ancient race," in the feminine gender in French ("je te rendrai heureuse"), underlines the sexual nature of Forzza's fascist political imaginary.

105 This concluding speech by Night was not in the original edition of the play. The Epilogue was added to close on a more harmonious note. See Cixous's interview with Fort in *NLH*, 450.

DRUMS ON THE DAM

In the form of an ancient puppet play, performed by actors

TRANSLATED BY JUDITH G. MILLER AND BRIAN J. MALLET

Characters (in order of appearance)[1]

DUAN, the soothsayer's daughter
The SOOTHSAYER
LORD KHANG
The CHANCELLOR
LORD HUN, Lord Khang's nephew
The ARCHITECT
The CHIEF INTENDANT
TSHUMI, the little court painter
The PALACE SERVANTS
The Chancellor's standard-bearer
HE TAO, Hun's lieutenant
WANG PO, the Chancellor's secretary
MADAME LI, the noodle pedlar
KISA, her servant
The MONK
The FIRST FISHERMAN
The SECOND FISHERMAN
The THIRD FISHERMAN

THE RIVER
The DRUMS
The PALANQUIN BEARERS
O'MI, the lantern pedlar
Her APPRENTICE
LIOU PO, he who warns of the breach
The ARCHITECT'S WIFE
The Chief Intendant's HENCHMEN
Hun's SERVANTS
THE FIRST GUARD
THE SECOND GUARD
The CHILD, Wang Po's brother
Wang Po's OLD FATHER
BAÏ JU, the puppet master
His WIFE
His DAUGHTER
His MOTHER
A DRUMMER

Scene 1 Dilemma at court

The SOOTHSAYER *and his daughter* DUAN *enter*

DUAN I who stand before you am named Duan. My father, the famous soothsayer of Quan Ze where Lord Khang rules, was visited by a dream last night which casts a terrifying light over the future of this kingdom. In haste, we have made our way towards the splendid palace, as it is told in the poems, and we have hurried so much that we are already here on the royal pontoon. The soothsayer wishes to speak and tell what he has seen.

SOOTHSAYER I saw the void. It was a time after the end of our world. You had all disappeared under the grey-coloured ocean. Only my intrepid daughter and myself were there, high up on the dune. What our eyes then witnessed was wretched. Oh, beloved countryside! Where are you? And the city of a hundred golden doors . . . Where is it? Where are the monasteries? Where is the Palace? Oh! Horror rises in our hearts. 10

"Look over there, Father!" Duan cries out to me.

Under our very eyes
A swoop of young children
Swollen like goatskin bottles,
Carried off by death
Powerful gallop, hellish gait
The face of a mother
Watches
The black hat of a scholar, floating lightly.

At the top of a pine tree 20
A family of monkeys
Embrace.
With one blow of its long hard tongue
The flood washes away
The wretched swarm.

Reaching out from the mud
A hand beckons, to what purpose . . .
That was my neighbour
The man knew the voices of all the birds.

Crouching on the dam 30
My daughter and I are
Remainders condemned
To make known tomorrow
The baneful news.

Not a breath. The water as immobile as a sleeping desert. You no longer existed, none of you. Once space has vanished, only the silt of time will remain. Listen, already the alarm hammers in our breasts.

[*The* SOOTHSAYER *exits*

DUAN I have seen enough! Trembled enough! Now Duan chooses and decides to act!

[*Exits*

LORD KHANG *and his advisers enter* 40

LORD KHANG "Once space has vanished, only the silt of time will remain." Chancellor, how long before the first rains?
CHANCELLOR The Western sky is already heavily veiled. It is raining hard over there.
LORD KHANG The seed of the will of gods . . . that is all we are.
CHANCELLOR The mud in the river has nothing to do with the spitefulness of the gods. For the past twenty years we have been cutting down all the trees to which the gods gave the task of holding back the banks.
LORD KHANG Am I the "we" cutting down everything to whom you refer?

CHANCELLOR My Lord, we are brutishly felling trees with our eyes closed. Our axes fly right and left. We will end up by cutting off our noses. 50

LORD KHANG You have come to importune me on such a day? You paint me like an old fool who ought to be locked up.

CHANCELLOR Noble Lord! I am only saying . . .

LORD KHANG Can one cook without fire? Of course not. So the State must cut. What else can I do on this earth?

CHANCELLOR First of all you should not have agreed to hand over the Purple Mountain Forest to your nephew. In all lucidity and sovereignty, you ceded your kingly right to an individual! All the West belongs to Hun.

LORD HUN And any trees that are left will forthwith feel the sweep of my great blade!

LORD KHANG That's enough, nephew! 60

LORD HUN [*bowing to him*] Dear uncle.

[*He exits, furious*

CHANCELLOR Not only has your nephew plundered the city . . .

LORD KHANG . . . For the corruption wrought in the city, I will deal with him severely.

CHANCELLOR . . . but he has also razed all your forests!

LORD KHANG . . . as far as the forests go, that is quite another matter. My nephew is a great visionary. Let us not confuse things.

CHANCELLOR But my Lord, what about the principle? We were in complete agreement about the principle.

LORD KHANG The principle? To destroy the least possible. The least is not nothing at all.

CHANCELLOR Razing the forests on the flanks of Purple Mountain is to lose the grip on the dragon! 70

LORD KHANG The forest grows back . . .

CHANCELLOR It took centuries! It will take centuries!

LORD KHANG Twaddle! Who is counting?

CHANCELLOR Your descendants will not survive your blindness!

LORD KHANG Silence! Jealousy leads you astray. I ought to banish you! A chill has fallen over our friendship. I do not want to see you again – for a long time. You are dust in my eyes!

[*The* CHANCELLOR *exits*

Architect, you who monitor the dams and all the other obstacles placed in the path of the river, please tell us what we have the right to expect and to hope for.

ARCHITECT My Lord, the two dams which protect our city, that of the North as well as that of the South, have both been strengthened through my efforts. When the river was last in spate, they held up very well indeed. 80

LORD KHANG That was a harmless swelling. They are announcing an unprecedented season. Will they hold?

ARCHITECT They are human creations. We cannot ask them to resist the will of gods. Is that not so, intendant?

CHIEF INTENDANT Ten years ago, when those very famous dams of our very powerful neighbour were submerged and broken in at least twenty places, it would have been wiser to make a sacrifice.

LORD KHANG What do you mean?

CHIEF INTENDANT By opening a breach in the dam. Then the liberated river would have devastated the neighbourhoods offered up to it and, once appeased, would have gone back to sleep. 90

LORD KHANG So we should blow up either the North or the South Dam?

CHIEF INTENDANT Yes. Yes, my Lord.

LORD KHANG How long for such destruction?

CHIEF INTENDANT A few barrels of powder. Not even the whole night.

ARCHITECT But we must first evacuate the population.

CHIEF INTENDANT That is the question.

LORD KHANG I had never looked at our city in detail. Chief intendant, what lies to the North?

CHIEF INTENDANT Your power base, my Lord. The port. Everything solid. And there, my Lord, since your nephew obtained from you the concession to the forests, he has built sawmills, workshops, factories, warehouses, shops, and businesses. In ten years this neighbourhood will be four times bigger. Soon nobody will remember what is laid out there today. 100

LORD KHANG And to the South, the Pleasure District?

TSHUMI Pleasures and the Arts, beloved Lord. There – the theatres for which I depict the world in my paintings. The celebrated Baï Ju stage . . .

LORD KHANG Baï Ju! I remember him! The puppet master! Does he still exist?

TSHUMI Yes, my Lord, but he is not doing well. There are your artisans, Lord – silks, jewellery, mirrors, colours, indigo! There is my hairdresser, about whom I have spoken. And right over there – the library.

LORD KHANG [*swaying back and forth*] Either this – or that. Either we flood temples, schools, theatres, artisans. Or we flood trading companies, factories, building sites. All these ideas make my head ache. I 110 who thought I was moving towards an old age which could boast a reign without accident. Oh! How ill I feel! To have to cut into my own flesh! I do not want to be my body without North or without South. The dice are rolling in my brain! Tshumi, come give a hand to your unhappy master. . . . Send the monk to my bedside. And find me Baï Ju with his puppets. I surely need another perspective. It is necessary to hesitate before deciding.

[*He exits followed by* TSHUMI *and his servants*

CHIEF INTENDANT Here we are floating in uncertainty. Is Lord Khang going to take a decision? What will he decide? When will he decide? Architect, are you at least really sure that our dams will hold for as long as it takes Lord Khang to think this out?

ARCHITECT Sir, I know these dams. I raised them to new heights according to your orders. At the first 120 fissure, I will be there.

The CHANCELLOR *returns*

CHANCELLOR Fissure?

CHIEF INTENDANT [*to the architect*] Idiot!

[*The* CHIEF INTENDANT *and the* ARCHITECT *exit*

CHANCELLOR The country is wavering on the brink of troubled waters. The left hand is getting ready to attack the right. Imminent disaster is stirring up into a fury brothers, appetites and desires. Each must choose. North or South, him or me. The virtuous man will be he who . . . And the countryside . . . The soothsayer has nevertheless spoken of it too, but no one heard him. Invisible villages, rice paddies, peasants. All the talk just now was of the city. It is so big. Some people spend a whole lifetime without 130 ever passing under the Dragon's Gate. It is so beautiful. Some people spend their lives admiring themselves in the infinity of its mirroring streets. What time is it?

A SERVANT It is so late, my Lord, that it will soon be very early.

CHANCELLOR This time no longer has any hour. Come, let us hear what the simple people across the river have to say.

[*They move away across the city*

LORD HUN *and the* CHIEF INTENDANT *enter*

LORD HUN Well?

CHIEF INTENDANT He is still swaying back and forth.

LORD HUN It is just like him to be short-sighted. The solution is here, under his nose. It strikes you right 140 in the eye, does it not?

CHIEF INTENDANT Yes. Maybe. Just what do you mean, sir?

LORD HUN It is that well-known story about Lord Kiou. You flood the countryside! It is upriver that the dams must be broken. You open a large breach, the city will be saved, and I will be back doing business better than ever.

CHIEF INTENDANT But surely you know that a thousand years ago 100,000 peasants perished with that solution.

LORD HUN So it will cost 100,000 yokels, that is all. One person's profit is another person's loss.

CHIEF INTENDANT But some of the courtiers have farms down there. Even I have some land. Others have livestock or family. And then Lord Khang would not want to drown his peasants, and the peasants 150
– I know them – will not want to be drowned! Lord Khang will never take that decision, I do not think . . .

LORD HUN Well then, I will take it for him.

CHIEF INTENDANT Are you thinking of some kind of conspiracy?

LORD HUN I swear to you, if I am allowed to take charge, the city will be saved.

CHIEF INTENDANT I have no doubt about it, illustrious Lord, but give us the time to breathe!

LORD HUN Do I have your consent?

CHIEF INTENDANT I will tell you tomorrow. Farewell.

[*He exits*

LORD HUN He has property in the countryside. He is going right off to denounce me to my uncle. I am 160
not going to wait around smoking my pipe enjoying the river view and then get caught! The quickest draw wins. He Tao!

HE TAO *enters*

HE TAO Yes, my Lord.

LORD HUN Keep an eye on the chief intendant for me.

HE TAO It is as good as done. And what about our plan, my Lord?

LORD HUN First I want to try to convince my uncle. I will remind him of the fable of Lord Kiou. If he does not listen to me, well then we will play it out without him. So get going and start recruiting all those down and outs and rabble routs whose only god is their stomach. We are going to need them very soon! The ideal thing, He Tao, is for my uncle to be on the throne and me commanding all the 170
machinery.

[*They exit*

TSHUMI *enters*

TSHUMI Too late! After holding council, those two vultures have adjourned and I never got to hear the agenda. I had better keep on their heels until I learn what they are up to.

DUAN, *armed for combat, enters*

Duan my lovely friend! Where are you going, all sternly equipped like a man of action!

DUAN I am going to join the drums which from now on, posted on the heights, watch over the mood of the river night and day. Come with me. Together, we will keep watch on the sky.

TSHUMI Me, join the drums? And take up arms with you against an ocean of perils? They say that where 180
danger increases, courage follows. But for me it is the opposite, it is my terror which is increasing! And, then, maybe I can be more useful here keeping an eye on some of the troublemakers. I will miss you.

DUAN I will miss you too, my best and most tender friend. Farewell for now. Watch over my father. I will send him all the news, even if it is dreadful.

[DUAN *exits*

TSHUMI The storm is threatening. Everybody digs their own hole and shores up, while only Duan throws herself into the fray. Contemplating the infinity of the fearsome universe, I shudder at the fate of the little court painter.

WANG PO *enters*   190

WANG PO Has Duan left?

TSHUMI [*almost fainting*] You missed her by a second, Secretary Wang Po. Duan has climbed the heights and joined the drums. In one leap she has gone from a golden childhood to the harsh figure of a human shield.

WANG PO Already? Oh! rue the day!

TSHUMI The Chancellor's secretary also seems out of sorts.

WANG PO Not at all! . . . It is just that . . . I can tell you Tshumi, I am dying of fright for her!

TSHUMI And I am dying of three frights. One for her, one for me, and the third . . .

WANG PO . . . for all the rest.

TSHUMI You could join the drums.   200

WANG PO Can I leave my Chancellor?

[*They exit*

Scene 2 At Madame Li's little inn

MADAME LI *enters hawking her wares, followed by* KISA, *then the* MONK

MADAME LI So, nobody eats any more?

MONK *All along the way*
    The monk dreamed
    Of a spoon
    And a bowl of noodles.
In this world of red dust, soup is a consolation.

MADAME LI Very honoured, I am. My name is Madame Li, the best noodles in the country. Take a seat, holy man. You look like you have seen a ghost.

MONK Coming from the heart of the woods, I feel quite surprised. The wild geese are leaving before their time. There are all kinds of odd things happening these days, without any explanations.   10

MADAME LI Odd people, too. Last night I served a man with two noses. And what brings you here?

MONK From the Palace came the order to the monastery. Lord Khang asks for a reading. They sent me.
The monk helps the lost cross to the other side.
    The bowl is empty.
    The monk is full.
    The pedlar wipes her brow.
    The wind begins to blow.
    Buffeted by the waves of time, I hurry to leave.

[*He exits*

MADAME LI Lord Khang wants a book?! Whatever for? Yet more unexplainable news! [*She utters her pedlar's*   20
cry] No body!

KISA Why not try the Pleasure District, Madame Li?

MADAME LI No, today is a day for politics. Madame Li holds her position on the pontoon in front of the Palace.

The CHANCELLOR *enters*

Oh! It's my Chancellor! I did not recognize you from a distance! So what is new?

CHANCELLOR And here? What is the City saying this morning? What are people talking about?

MADAME LI The dams. The North and the South one. Are they good?

CHANCELLOR Everyone knows already?

MADAME LI Everyone knows nothing, so we invent. Nonsense and nightmares. Me, too – the other night   30
I dreamed I was running from the flood on the back of a fish as big as a house, but with three flaps of its wings it slammed into the Palace wall and turned into a pulp. And you? Eh? What about it? Nothing to tell me today?

CHANCELLOR The moment is an ominous one, whichever way one looks.

MADAME LI That is all? Has worry tied the Chancellor's tongue? You should go and visit your mother. Right now she is rinsing her potatoes. Breathe in the smell of pigs in the rain . . .

CHANCELLOR Fishing in the rice paddies just before the flood . . .

MADAME LI You should get out of the Palace from time to time and mix with "the nothing special," as my grandmother used to say. Never forget where you came from, that is the secret. And now, secret for secret, what is his Lordship thinking?   40

CHANCELLOR If only he knew himself. The city is so fast! Lord Khang is so still.

MADAME LI You can tell me a little something. Come on! Be nice! The pedlar has to take care of herself. Very soon if we are not on the water, we will be under it. I will have to find a floating inn for my noodles. What should I do? Eh?

CHANCELLOR I really do not know . . . Buy a boat.

MADAME LI And who will pay for it?

WANG PO *enters*

WANG PO Chancellor! Lord Khang has changed his mind. He calls you back to the Palace! He adores you again and wishes to have your opinion, as soon as possible.

CHANCELLOR I will not go. For twenty years I have obeyed every wind. But now my sails have collapsed   50
. . . I will go later. Wang Po, tell my porters to get ready. Let us follow the advice of Madame Li. Let us go back to our beginnings and see my mother on Cherry Mountain.

MADAME LI But at least tell me one little thing!

[*The* CHANCELLOR *exits rapidly*

WANG PO There he goes – off in the wrong direction! Hun will take advantage of his absence. I should have kept him here, but how? All of us, whether servants or lords, are governed by resentments. At least I shall try to direct my master's path through the camp of the drums. There I will find Duan.

[*He exits*

MADAME LI So that is as far as we get! Tell me, frankly, who made the world like this? A firefly in the dark forest . . . She guides your way and you are very happy. But as soon as you have what you seek, you   60
step on her. Not even the tiniest bit of a secret! Stingy! Or maybe it is true that he does not know a thing? That man does not deserve us. But time is running out – for him, just as it is for the last of the poor fishermen. Let us go Kisa!

KISA Where are we going now Madame Li?

MADAME LI How do you expect a poor pedlar to know more than a Chancellor dressed in silk?

[*They exit*

Scene 3 The empty net

The FIRST FISHERMAN *enters, followed by the other two*

FIRST FISHERMAN The net is empty? They are saying everywhere it will be the flood of the century. The fish can already see death approaching and they are fleeing from here. All one can see in the water is the sad image of a starving fisherman.

SECOND FISHERMAN They say the river will tear down all the bridges and docks of the capital. And with them our miserable boats.

FIRST FISHERMAN And with our boats, us – who have always tended our flocks of fish with such care.

SECOND FISHERMAN I would rather die right now. A suicide on the Dam.

THIRD FISHERMAN Tonight the bowl will be empty again.

SECOND FISHERMAN Even Madame Li will not give us any credit. We could have a double suicide on the Dam.   10

FIRST FISHERMAN These pedlars – as soon as it is a matter of cash, they are ready to crush the little fellow. But I will not be starved any longer! I too can take in my hands the rebel's knife – and the pedlar will not have a word to say about it!! She had better not send me away again, eh!

THIRD FISHERMAN All we can do now is pray and beg the gods of our river . . .

FIRST FISHERMAN Stop your buffoonery! The river is deaf to all our prayers. Everything is already written: worries, turmoil, exhaustion. Tomorrow, just like today, I will be a beggar – and so will you!

SECOND FISHERMAN My cousin has fended for himself much better than us. Recruited by Hun, he is high up in the hills, where he cuts the forests. Those trees cannot run away.

FIRST FISHERMAN Exactly, and speaking of Hun, this morning He Tao, his shadowy lieutenant, made me an offer which this evening I can no longer refuse and which I am going to share. For us it would   20 be pure gold.

THIRD FISHERMAN Gold . . .

FIRST FISHERMAN We have an hour to accept.

THIRD FISHERMAN To work for Hun?! Up to now, I have always placed honesty at the top of my thoughts.

SECOND FISHERMAN Right! And you can see how far that has got us!

FIRST FISHERMAN Do you think I am interested in dying of honesty?! Stay put, if you want! But I am going to the feeding bins and cash in.

[*He moves away*

Are you coming or not?

SECOND FISHERMAN Why not! He is right . . . Let us cast hesitation to the winds!   30

THIRD FISHERMAN Yes, let us go! I am tired of missed opportunities.

FIRST FISHERMAN Tomorrow the fishermen will be rich and the peasants will be at the bottom of the water! And let nobody dare judge us. It is all the fault of that damned river!

SECOND FISHERMAN Oh, the times are terrible! We have been enlisted by calamity.

[*They exit*

THE RIVER *enters*

THE RIVER Who dares accuse me! The river! The river is as beautiful as ever. Where in the whole world has anyone seen a king more kingly than I? There is no respect here. They commit the crime and then they throw the blame in the waters of the river. They treat father and mother like garbage. And then they say the river is wicked! Big or small, all you inhabitants of this country are nothing but   40 a load of arrogant, ungrateful, and moody creatures. You are even more blind than the blind! Can you not see the end of the world? You will have the flood of the century, I promise!

[*He exits*

Scene 4 Lord Khang abdicates responsibility

LORD KHANG, *the* MONK *and the* SERVANTS *enter*

LORD KHANG What does the book say?

MONK The book says:

One: Keep from making the bad choice.

Two: Keep from making the good choice for the wrong reasons.

Three: Make the least bad choice possible.

LORD KHANG What does the book mean by that? The least bad?! How does one know?

MONK The book says: Let the future govern the days of the present.

LORD KHANG Monk, you are not making anything clearer! Your famous light is hazy and confusing! When
I was young, I delivered justice at the full moon. I cut to the quick and decided matters. It was always
clear-cut with never any postscript. All that is far away now. Today even a monk makes me doubt. How   10
to make the right choice?

LORD HUN *enters*

And you, my nephew, by your fault and in order to defend you, I have lost the very precious counsel
of my Chancellor . . . Even my intendant is not here today because he is so afraid of you! I do not want
to be another Lord Kiou and for *The Royal Chronicles* to say of me: "His long and superb reign ended
in disaster." Oh! If only one were able to sleep and, during this absence of the mind, if the agents of
destiny could carry out all that fairness and pity prevent us from doing. Oh! If only some fate were to
come to me at night and take into its hands the decision that my own poor will cannot bear to want!
But I am dreaming. Let us not speak about it any more.

LORD HUN On the contrary, my dear uncle, let us speak about it. In the thick of night, pushed by the   20
wind, rain, and necessity, my men, without fear and all of them devoted – on my orders, not yours –
steal in silence to the Cherry Mountain Dam and cut the knot that is strangling us.

LORD KHANG And everything is done by the time I wake up?

LORD HUN Everything is done.

LORD KHANG Let us not speak about it any more.

How pure the sky is! The city is gleaming in the brilliance of the morning. In the distance the
countryside bows its camellia head. And yet . . . and yet . . . If we escape the flooding . . . No, hope is
a temptation. Oh I tried in vain, but goodness does not make things right! Such fatigue overtakes my
soul! The Lord is going to bed. Monk, let us make peace and pray for me. Come, let us retire. I am
already asleep.   30

[*He leaves with his servants*

HE TAO *enters*

LORD HUN He Tao, he has yielded! He is going to bed to let us do the job in his place.

HE TAO He has yielded? Lord Hun? Are you sure?

LORD HUN My time had already come and I had not even noticed! From now on, I will be his secret,
I will dictate his desires, and what he is afraid to do will be done behind the curtain of his eyelids.

HE TAO And while we are at it, my Lord, we must make sure that the peasants, too, sleep like logs. Because
a peasant who wakes up with the drums means trouble, becomes crazy – and then the matter could
escape our control.

LORD HUN You are reading my thoughts. So . . . in a steely dark flight, we will cut through the night and   40 suddenly swoop down on Duan, the famous sentinel who is keeping watch with her drums on Cherry Mountain. You . . .

HE TAO Ahhhrgg, I will cut her throat . . .

LORD HUN As soon as it is done, I will launch our men into the attack. So let us go quickly and get ready, and before dawn, up there, the Dam will fall.

TSHUMI *appears, followed by the* MONK

TSHUMI I will come too then! Dear Lord, let me join the ranks of the brave who will destroy the Dam. Without anyone noticing it.

LORD HUN You? A player of paints and brushes? You want to take up arms?

TSHUMI You have awakened the warrior in my breast! The smell of powder! But enough of pleasantries! 50 I know these paths. I was born of this land. I will act as torchbearer. Please, my Lord.

LORD HUN Since you insist. Let us go!

[*They exit*

MONK Where did the counsellors go? Who will now enlighten Lord Khang? Betrayal and treason mark the hour on the city's clock. I have already lived through all this in another life, but I no longer know how it ends. Let us follow them. One or the other of them, whether he be good or evil, might have need of a monk at any moment.

[*He leaves*

LORD KHANG, *who cannot sleep, enters*

LORD KHANG Still no news from the Chancellor. I am neither blind nor senile. I can see everything that 60 is happening. I know very well why no one is here, neither Hun, nor the Intendant, nor the Chancellor. Not even poor Tshumi. I have been left alone with the fates. The author of all this story must therefore be me.

[*He exits*

Scene 5 The drums

DUAN *and her drums enter. They are on the lookout*

DUAN Such as you see me I have become the Captain of the lookouts. Camped out on the mountain, my men and I have the mission to watch over all the movements of the river. At the slightest change, it is our task to spread the news of the sky and the earth. You have here before you the best drums in the country. This is our system. For every situation, there is a rhythm. There is not a peasant in this patrol who does not already know them all. Listen to the first signal to attune your ears.

[*The first signal*

This alarm means: There is flooding in the North. Hurry, flee to the South!

[*They play*

There, on the other hand, is the signal to tell those in the South to fly to the North.

[*They change rhythm* 10

And this is for the worst situation: an unexpected breach.

[*A new rhythm*

The CHANCELLOR, WANG PO *and the* PALANQUIN BEARERS *enter*

CHANCELLOR You are going to spread panic!

DUAN On the contrary, Chancellor. In this way the people will know that we are watching out exactly as planned and there is not a single inhabitant who can be caught off guard. At enormous speed, the villages will pack themselves up and run to the city for safety.

[*The drums call out to* DUAN

It is true, we also have rhythms for courage, joy, swiftness, and imagination.

[*They play, then silence*   20

CHANCELLOR Allow me to continue on my way.

DUAN Farewells must be brief. Farewell.

CHANCELLOR Farewell.

DUAN My Lord, when you see my father, tell him the news.

CHANCELLOR I will give him the message. These are happy men. They alone know the secret: "Watch over those who sleep." An enormous feeling.

[*He exits.* WANG PO *stops near* DUAN, *kisses her and leaves, while the drums continue to play*

Scene 6 In the Chancellor's village

The CHANCELLOR *enters, followed by* WANG PO *and the* PALANQUIN BEARERS

CHANCELLOR We are lost, Wang Po. The paths of my childhood have changed so much. Everything has become foreign to me. In dreaming of my mother, I have lost my way. Let us rest a little.

[*They fall asleep*

O'MI, *a lantern pedlar enters*

O'MI *Lanterns! Lanterns! The sparks of ghosts!*
    Difficult to find your way
    Without the light from my lamps!
    Tonight, in the shadow of the forgotten mountain
    What will be shining and trembling in the wind?
    Neither the iridescent worm nor the star stitched to the sky's greatcoat.   10
    Lanterns! Lanterns!

[*The travellers wake up*

CHANCELLOR Oh! The river! The sound of oars! This is familiar to me! I have explored every one of your tufted ridges. My, the lake is full! You think you are safe but the wind prowls like a thief. The weather is treacherous here.

O'MI Neither the wind nor the river glistening at our feet catches off guard those who are vigilant.

CHANCELLOR Who is that woman?

WANG PO I can hear her clearly, my Lord, but . . .

O'MI The rising fog is not coming from the river.

CHANCELLOR She is so close to me . . . The swaying of her great sleeves . . . touches me. Who are you?   20

A PALANQUIN BEARER It is a lantern pedlar who keeps repeating the same story.

O'MI Between two lands, the river prays. Everyone is sleeping in the land to the West. The forests lament. Who is listening? In the land to the North everyone is nodding off – with their caps over their ears, those who have never known the shock of the great misfortune. And no one to say: remember the Grand Catastrophe.

CHANCELLOR What Grand Catastrophe?

O'MI Hundreds of years ago, during the deep secret of night, in order to save his city threatened by the waters, Lord Kiou, a very cruel Lord, had a treacherous breach cut in the spine of the dam protecting our countryside. At dawn, thousands upon thousands of peasants went to their inhuman deaths. The survivors were filled with such rage that they razed the city and killed thousands of city dwellers. One can understand them.

CHANCELLOR You are reciting some old myth. It is just a story people tell.

O'MI Even today, when turning over the soil of the rice paddies, the peasants sometimes find a skull, sometimes a golden hairpin. For the waters climbed up even higher than where we are now.

CHANCELLOR That is a story which happened more than a thousand years ago. It could not happen again today. And, besides, our drums are watching over you.

O'MI If it does not bite into the stone, the river churns itself up. What is the point of a sky as clear as a mother's heart, if there is no one to read it. You are as headstrong as ever. There is nothing I can do about it. Go, my son. Night will fall more quickly than you think. Take this . . . take it, my son, and look in every direction.

[*She gives him a lantern and they bow good-bye*

THE RIVER *Men are like lanterns*
Thrown upon the Ocean's swell, they float.
Moving apart, they dance.
Blinder than the blind, not once did the living son suspect anything.
He has unwittingly greeted his mother for the last time on earth.
And together master and servants trembled.
Ever fainter
Ever farther away
The spark flickers.

[O'MI *and* THE RIVER *exit*

WANG PO She said, "Go, my son."

CHANCELLOR Did she say that? She said, "The waters will climb up over the roofs."

WANG PO Did she say "will climb?"

CHANCELLOR I hope she is wrong. Even so . . . let us go back to the city.

WANG PO Are we not going to visit your mother?

CHANCELLOR We will go in the spring. For the sake of coming centuries and Lord Khang's honour, I will renounce my joyous reunion at the farm for the thirteenth year. My mother always used to say: "think about the people." She used to prepare stuffed fish. I do not know why I am speaking of Mother in the past tense. Let us be on our way . . . And why is Wang Po scowling at me? What is wrong? Are you thinking about your mother, too?

WANG PO My mother is dead, but my father is still alive. And by dint of serving and following my master, I had forgotten.

CHANCELLOR Well! What should we do?

WANG PO If the Chancellor would allow me to go and fetch him, I would shelter him in the city as soon as possible.

CHANCELLOR Go ahead, but come back quickly. I need you.

[WANG PO *exits*

Everything is so uncertain. I feel like turning back and going to see my mother.

PALANQUIN BEARER Back we go.

CHANCELLOR Stop.

PALANQUIN BEARER We stop.

CHANCELLOR I must take a good look. On this side, the city and its dams. I move up the river with my eyes.

And here, the countryside. And the majestic Dams of Cherry Mountain. In the shelter of that ancient shield the peasants sleep in huddled families. What is that cry?

PALANQUIN BEARER An owl!

CHANCELLOR An owl? Here? Should I sound the alarm? While we have been walking, Hun has been pressuring the royal brain. How long will it take to find Duan again?

PALANQUIN BEARER At least two days.

CHANCELLOR Two days!? Even so, I have to find her! You two, come here. Without stopping a moment, 80
return to the city and hurry to the chief intendant. I do not like him, but today I want him for an ally, because he, too, knows that anger turns a sheep into a tiger and peasants into rebels armed for three harvests.

[He writes a message

Take this message to him. And may the gods sharpen your wits! You understand? Go! Quickly! To the city!

Placed in a corner of my heart is a lantern. Who was that? Let us not think about it any longer. Let us go!

[The PALANQUIN BEARERS *exit, the* CHANCELLOR, *in turn, exits in another direction*

Scene 7 Madame Li sets off

MADAME LI *and* KISA *enter*

MADAME LI This city is going crazy. Out of fright, some people are turning into jackals, others into rabbits. At the market, they are fighting with knives over a grain of rice. The thought that the end of the world is nigh is troubling the firmament. People are losing their grip. At the North Dam, once honourable fishermen are now bandits, and without a second thought, they steal everything from the pedlars, and immediately sign up as assassins in the pay of the worst conspirators. There are no more boats. There are no more friends. Madame Li has nothing left, except her bruises and blisters. And Kisa, of course. Did you hear that? It is the cry of a frog being swallowed by a snake . . . If I could have, I would not have been born. Come on Kisa.

KISA Where are we going now Madame Li?

MADAME LI We are going up into the hills. Up there, thanks to the drums, we will be safe. 10

KISA If you say so, Madame Li.

[They exit

Scene 8 Murders on the Dam

LIOU PO *enters as the wind begins to rise*

LIOU PO I am Liou Po, the unfortunate stonemason fallen from the heights. Before my fall, I was the head foreman on the dams. When everything was finished, I discovered a defect. You can be sure they would have accused the foreman right away. The architect told me to disappear. And before I could be hanged, I did. But yesterday I am walking on the dam. And what do I see? It is seeping. I tap it. It sounds hollow. The defect is still there and with everything they are predicting, and the wind rising, our dam will never hold. I warned the architect. It is up to him now to decide the end of the story. I am escaping to the lookouts. Up there, I will be safe . . .

[He exits

The ARCHITECT *and* ARCHITECT'S WIFE *enter on the dam*

ARCHITECT Liou Poooo! Oh! That devil! A breach here! To tell me that now! What a monster! But why   10
accuse the stonemason?! I have walked in front of the dam a hundred times. I have never examined its
face. What are eyes for if it is not to see what you are afraid of seeing?! Ah! Twenty years ago, standing
right here proudly on my Dam, I embraced with my eyes the entire country which I promised to protect!
And right after that, the corruption began. Mud swamps my soul. We let ourselves be lulled by shame!
Ah! What a decline! I will drown myself: for me, all that is left is to disappear.

[He raises his sword, his WIFE *snatches it from him*

ARCHITECT'S WIFE What a fool you are! Give me that weapon! What are you doing? Adding wrong to a
wrong! Falling even lower!

ARCHITECT Let me go. Do not hold me back!

ARCHITECT'S WIFE So! You do not love me any more! You run away from your wife and you betray the   20
city! Would you let all the people perish – and all your family?

ARCHITECT What can I do? Everything is too late! I am damned!

ARCHITECT'S WIFE Gutless and selfish man! You give me your death and your shame as consolation! No.
No! Take hold of yourself. Listen to me. Go right now and throw yourself on the mercy of Lord Khang,
you will find him alone and bewildered, and tell him everything.

ARCHITECT You are crazy! They will kill me!

ARCHITECT'S WIFE Enough of that! Listen! There is still time to save everything! You throw yourself at
his feet, pale, on your knees. You tell him everything and then you immediately add: "Only I can repair
the breach. Let me save the city, for heaven's sake! You can punish me as soon as the city is out of
danger!" Then Lord Khang, once the city and all its inhabitants are saved, will forgive you, moved by   30
your repentance . . .

ARCHITECT But what if . . .

ARCHITECT'S WIFE If he condemns you, I will follow! If it is a matter of dying, at least let us die honourably.
And you will leave a glorious name behind forever! Confess! Do not be afraid! Lord Khang is
magnanimous.

ARCHITECT You think so?

ARCHITECT'S WIFE Follow my advice. Obey me! Take the right path!

ARCHITECT Yes, yes. The gods hear you. I am going. I am obeying. Oh my dear wife! To save the city
and stand up proudly again on the Dam as I did twenty years ago! I will obey you!

[He exits   40

ARCHITECT'S WIFE Go! Go! Life lies that way! But what do I see shining over there . . .? My husband's
sword! He has left without his weapon? Oh gods of pity! Watch over my husband! Where have I sent
him! Who will he run into on his way! With his swift gait, my husband parts the night! I speak to the
passing wind.

[She exits

The ARCHITECT, *tied and bound, two* HENCHMEN, *and the* CHIEF INTENDANT *enter*

CHIEF INTENDANT So, I caught you just in time. What were you planning on doing in the Palace at this
hour?

ARCHITECT Denounce us! Tell Lord Khang everything! Let him know about the breach. There is still time
to make repairs and amends!   50

CHIEF INTENDANT Just what breach are you talking about? What repairs?

ARCHITECT Traitor! And yet we had clearly agreed among ourselves to fill it in discreetly.

CHIEF INTENDANT Agreed? You and me?

ARCHITECT "I will take care of it," you assured me, "but it will take money." Those were your very words! So I gave you everything left in my account.

CHIEF INTENDANT Where is the paper?

ARCHITECT The paper?

CHIEF INTENDANT The receipt for the expenses.

ARCHITECT You said to me: "Honourable men do not need paper."

CHIEF INTENDANT No paper? When have you seen the chief intendant do business without paper? 60 Scoundrel! Who will believe you? You embezzled money and you are trying to draw the chief intendant into your hole! Bandit! Thief!

ARCHITECT Liar! Liar!

[*The* HENCHMEN *beat him*

CHIEF INTENDANT If you care anything about your life, architect, I strongly recommend you keep your mouth shut. The incident is closed, right?

[*The* ARCHITECT *escapes their clutches and begins to cry out*

ARCHITECT Watch out! Watch out! A breach! A breach! There is a breach in the heart of the city.

[*The* HENCHMEN *and the* CHIEF INTENDANT *beat him*

My dear wife . . . will you be able to make repairs and amends? 70

[*He dies*

CHIEF INTENDANT At least he will not have stolen his death! Like a nightmare, he has vanished. As for you two, one word about his foolishness and I will turn you into cadavers before your time. You understand?

HENCHMEN Yes, my Lord.

[*They exit, the* ARCHITECT'*s corpse is carried off*

The CHIEF INTENDANT *enters again*

CHIEF INTENDANT A breach! A breach! Little causes, enormous consequences! A tiny little hole in a dam 80 . . . And it is the door to the void! Will I be guilty forever? But no! There is a solution. I will go to Lord Khang. I will tell him everything. We will close it. The man who has the courage to confess is a new man. But what am I saying?! Confess! But why! Do I not have the architect! I run to Lord Khang and I say: "The architect confessed his crime in his dying moments." That is the solution. I will be the saviour! Oh, my life, you are immortal, I knew it!

The ARCHITECT'S WIFE *enters*

Over there on the canal – who is that who seems to be walking on water? Is that not the architect's wife? What is this all about?

ARCHITECT'S WIFE My husband entrusted me with returning to you at once what you gave him.

[*She brandishes a dagger, pounces on the* CHIEF INTENDANT *and kills him,* 90
then runs along the canal to follow his body

He has completely disappeared! Oh wondrous death, goddess of speed. In the wink of an eye, he has gone. Was there really a chief intendant here only a moment ago! Like the water, he flows noiselessly – and now begins his long descent under the multicoloured pontoons. His head will hit them mercilessly, desperately searching a way out. Soon the mist will rise over the silent water.

[*The* CHIEF INTENDANT *looms up out of the water and stabs the* ARCHITECT'S WIFE,
mortally wounding her. She struggles and decapitates him

Woe is me! Am I to die without revealing the secret! Who stirs over there? Someone? The breach! The breach! Sound the alarm! . . . There is a breach in the heart of the city!

[With her last ounce of strength, she beats out the rhythm for the worst situation   100

No one to hear me. The gods did not want me to make amends!

[She dies and is carried off

Scene 9 The Chancellor's death

MADAME LI *and* KISA *enter*

MADAME LI We have never seen so much meanness and evil roaming our neighbourhoods. The number
of criminals is growing every day. But soon we will be safe.

KISA Where are we, Madame Li?

MADAME LI We are almost at Cherry Mountain. The faces of the lookouts, when they see Madame Li
arriving with her sack full of flour, make me feel like laughing. You will see, Kisa, the world is not as
bad as it seems.

KISA If you say so, Madame Li.

LORD HUN, HE TAO *and* TSHUMI *enter*

*[MADAME LI *and* KISA *exit*

LORD HUN Let us separate here. You take the path along the crest. That way, you will surprise Duan by   10
swooping down from the heights. For my part, I will lead our men along the damp flanks of the Dam
until we reach its most vulnerable spot. There, in the darkest of the darkest of night, when your signal
tells me Duan is out of the fight for life, we will begin our sabotage.

The CHANCELLOR *enters and bars their way*

CHANCELLOR No! I have found you just in time! Your dark flight has been halted. Be forewarned, the chief
intendant is on his way, followed by a much more powerful army than yours! Go ahead – laugh! I know
what pitiful game you want to kill. But the situation has changed!

TSHUMI *[aside]* Noble Chancellor, listen to me.

CHANCELLOR Do not touch me!

LORD HUN So the chief intendant is coming, Chancellor!?   20

CHANCELLOR Yes, he is answering my call and will be here at dawn.

TSHUMI Noble Lord, flee, or else . . .

HE TAO Help! Help! The chief intendant is coming! I am afraid!

TSHUMI The chief intendant is dead, Chancellor. You had better follow Tshumi. I beg you, my Lord!

CHANCELLOR Dead?! Oh misfortune! The last defence of the realm.

HE TAO Yes, indeed! The chief intendant is dead, Chancellor. But let me take you to him right away.
Follow me.

[He stabs the CHANCELLOR

And that is how He Tao reunites friends.

LORD HUN The servant has served. His time had come. Monk, take care of the rest. The hour grows   30
impatient! We must fly like the wind!

*[LORD HUN *and* HE TAO *exit*

TSHUMI He should have listened to me!! Tshumi would not betray a friendship. Monk, do you not know
that? I am trying to reach Duan and the lookouts.

MONK I know that. Go, Tshumi! Go, go and save Duan! What are you waiting for?

TSHUMI I am afraid; but I am braver than myself.

[*He exits*

MONK In thought, I will follow you among the wild beasts. May the gods wish that this adventure so cruelly begun ends less savagely.

[*The* CHANCELLOR's *body is carried off*   40

No light at all, sky overcast. On high and down below, the lanterns are mourning. Take yourself away, poor monk, run and warn Lord Khang of the loss, now irreparable, of his best and most loyal adviser.

[*He exits*

Scene 10 The signing

LORD KHANG *enters, followed by his* SERVANTS

LORD KHANG [*to the* SERVANTS] Get away from me, all of you! The Chancellor is roving about. Lord Khang watches over the house. A shameless epoch. Still no news of the villain?

You can see I am in a bad mood.

SERVANT He is not back yet.

LORD KHANG That I can see.

ANOTHER SERVANT A message from Lord Hun. It is the list of the Gates of the City – for your signature.

[LORD KHANG *signs*

LORD KHANG I have signed. Everything drove me to do it, because there was nobody to tell me: "Lord Khang, you are mistaken." Of me it will be said: "He was left alone in his confrontation with the heavens. And so what did he do? Well, freeing his soul of doubts, anguish, and procrastination, and without even realizing how, nor if he were right" – I lifted this hand and . . . just like that . . . signed. And, now, things, take your course! And this hand has in no way changed. How easy it is to do the most difficult thing.   10

The MONK *enters*

Monk, whatever you want to say, do not say it. You have come too late. I have accepted my responsibilities. As of today, the countryside has been sacrificed and all the gates of my city are locked. It is now for the gods to speak, if they care about us . . .

[LORD KHANG *exits, followed by the* MONK, *then the* SERVANTS

Scene 11 At the gates of the city

[*A* GUARD *shoots an arrow through an official notice*

WANG PO, *carrying his* FATHER, *enters, along with his little* BROTHER

WANG PO [*reading the notice*] An edict from Lord Khang. "Henceforth, the 100 gates of our city shall be closed. No one, whether he be peasant or city dweller, shall be allowed to enter our walls before a new order has been issued from the lips of Lord Khang himself." Oh! a feeling of foreboding makes me tremble!

CHILD My brother, run to the Gate of Marvellous Longevity. For you, maybe it is not yet closed. You are the Chancellor's secretary, after all.

OLD FATHER My son, leave me here. I am slowing you down.

WANG PO Wait here for me. I will get those gates to open, even if I have to knock them down! Little brother, I leave our father in your care.

> [*He runs off. The* CHILD *and his* FATHER *fall asleep, then wake up and hear the guards enter* 10

SECOND GUARD I do not believe you! I do not believe you!

FIRST GUARD I am telling you it is true. He Tao's army! My own brother is part of it. They passed by here at the darkest point of night, while I was on watch and you were sleeping! According to my brother, they are supposed to reach the Cherry Mountain groves just before dawn.

SECOND GUARD You have no proof!

FIRST GUARD No proof?! I have the handwritten order my brother left with me.

SECOND GUARD Let me see it.

FIRST GUARD But you cannot read!

SECOND GUARD Seeing it will give me an idea, just the same.

FIRST GUARD Look: here is the character for "Des-truc-tion." That one is the character for "Fatal hole" 20 – which means "breach." That one says "Silence or Death . . ."

SECOND GUARD Silence or death?

FIRST GUARD In other words, if a single one of our men fails to keep this muffled up deep inside, the entire garrison will be wiped out immediately.

SECOND GUARD How terrible! Such a little stroke of the brush!

FIRST GUARD The entire garrison!

SECOND GUARD All right. But why are our gates locked?

FIRST GUARD Do you not understand? Go ahead and open the gates, open them! And as soon as the dam at Cherry Mountain is destroyed, we will have people up here everywhere. Do you know how many stomachs are ready to invade us tomorrow morning? Forests, flocks, packs, mountains of starving 30 people . . . So keep the gates closed and not one more word!

SECOND GUARD I get it: the gates – they are for my own good. But for my sister in the village, it is a shame! . . . I am going to fetch her.

FIRST GUARD Stay put, you idiot! Shh! Rustling reeds. Wild animals?

SECOND GUARD Throw a stone.

> [*He throws it*

FIRST GUARD Nothing moved. Bad luck. It is men! They heard us! You spoke too loud, imbecile! We have to catch them, or we will all be dead, you, too!!

> [*The* CHILD, *carrying the* FATHER, *flees, pursued by the guards*

WANG PO *enters* 40

WANG PO All the gates are closed. Dark soul of the Palace! Like Lord Kiou, you have therefore decided on chaos for our countryside; and for those unlucky ones who think you are human, you have delivered them to the abyss. Your house will offer neither help, nor protection, nor nourishment. In vain I have knocked; the guards chased me as though I were bringing the plague. And yet the evil is inside. Shaking with fear, I look for my father. Where are the child and the old man?

> [*The corpses of the* CHILD *and the old* FATHER *float by in the distance on the river*

Evening gives me back my father, morning takes him away again. My beloved father with my little brother pass on, torn to pieces, the first victims of a perfidious fratricide. But I swear on their bloodstained faces that I will obtain justice.

The GUARDS *arrive, joking* 50

Oh mist, enfold me!!

FIRST GUARD Look! The mist has lifted.

WANG PO Here your life comes to an end.

GUARDS They attacked us! They are the ones who started it! They were spying on us!

[WANG PO *kills them*

WANG PO You should not have returned so close to my sword. I used to be tender. Now I am a master criminal; such is heaven's will. Farewell Chancellor, I am leaving your service. Today I enter into a war which must not be questioned.

[*The bodies are removed*

Hear my declaration! 60

I, Wang Po, servant of no master and by virtue of our innate right to compassion and the duty to ensure its respect, take the peasants' fate into my hands. Betrayed and abandoned, we order Lord Khang to open the gates of our city to those whom he himself has condemned. If not, I swear we will tear the gates off their hinges and throw to hell all those who have treated their fellow humans beings like stray dogs. And now let us join Duan and her lookouts, without losing another minute.

[*He exits*

The BAÏ JU *family enters during a storm*

BAÏ JU Hey there! Keepers of the Gate of Universal Compassion! Open up! I who call you from this windy squall am Baï Ju, the puppet master. Come on! Guards! Hurry up! Lord Khang is waiting for us! We have an invitation! It is a mission! Hey, come on! To have come all the way here, across water, wind 70 and misfortune, to be thrown into the gale! What is the use of keeping my promise to a lord who calls me and then will not receive me?! What is the use of poetry, rights, intrepidity?! For Baï Ju, this is the last gate. I will never perform in this city again. Can you hear me, you deafmen?

For us puppet-masters
A gate awaits us on each voyage.
Oh you guardians of closed gates,
Our ill fortune like a hatchet
Will be planted in your padlocked hearts.

Half-turn, my troupe! Let us flee from this hostile city! Let us climb all the way up to Cherry Mountain. On our way we will have rain, burdens and cold. But in the end, up there with the drums, we will find 80 a haven of goodness, friendship and safety for everyone!

Scene 12 Battle on the dam and the end of all endings

BAÏ JU *or* LIOU PO *enters*

BAÏ JU *or* LIOU PO Hun's soldiers are surrounded! The peasants tricked them! The enemy knew our Dam had a fragile flank on this side! But warned by Tshumi, we were waiting right here for them, up to our knees in water. Wang Po and Duan led us to victory – and I with them! A few more blows and that will be the end of Hun. Only He Tao, Hun's right hand, still eludes us. If ever and wherever I run into him, I will give him such a fight that at the end of the episode he will descend under the earth without his head; that is what I hope.

[*He exits*

HE TAO *enters, threatening* TSHUMI

HE TAO I was sure I would catch you! You thought you could shake off He Tao, you brainless clown! Come on, you wretched creature, lead me quickly to Duan, or else I will chop you into a thousand tiny pieces. 10

TSHUMI Please do not kill me! Who would guide you? Come General! Come . . .

[TSHUMI *kills him by surprise*

HE TAO I do not believe it: man is such a poisonous species. Alas, Lord Hun, the peasants will rebel and I will not see your triumph.

[*He dies.* TSHUMI *remains transfixed in the icy water*

TSHUMI Here I am – completely out of danger!

LORD HUN *enters*

LORD HUN He Tao, our army is now only but smoke. Arms, gun powder, equipment, everything was ours, but raging waters and a muck of rabble led by a woman and a bloody-eyed Wang Po have routed us! All is lost! Everything has perished, except me. He Tao, my friend, the last of my men . . . 20

[*He sees that* HE TAO *is dead. He goes towards* TSHUMI *and pretends to believe that* TSHUMI *is also dead*

And you too are dead, poor juggler of brushes?

[*HUN *stabs him abruptly*

Yes, this time, you really are dead!

[*He exits*

TSHUMI [*dying*] I used to be a milk-toast, now I am a hero, an avenger, and a corpse! [*To* HE TAO] You are just a poor human being after all – you, too, like me, who does not understand anything. Nothing else to do than to make peace. Duan, I had wanted to tell you . . . my beloved . . . Now it is done. In the heart of the night, we have departed . . . 30

[TSHUMI *dies. It is dawn*

DUAN *enters and realizes that* TSHUMI *is dead*

DUAN Tshumi! Tshumi!

[*The waters carry his body away*

Go, Tshumi! First of the dead to weigh on my heart. Last night I saw war and how with one turn of the blade it slices away everything that made us close. Yesterday, we were all neighbours, and with one blow no more brothers. By Lord Khang's fault the Dam has become all our universe and men are dead, killed for this earthen rampart. Despite our victory, anguish will not let me go. If only I could stop hearing in this crystalline air the violent predictions of my father. River – mystery for living creatures – is it life or death that you hold in store for us? Oh, my heart would so like to leave this 40 story.

WANG PO *enters*

WANG PO Hun is dead! The dangerous nephew is no more. He will have done such damage for no purpose! On my hands, the perfume of his blood!

DUAN Wang Po!

WANG PO In all this blackness, you are still alive – Duan, first day of spring! Field of unripened wheat, arbour of roses!

DUAN Happiness surprises me in the midst of mourning. The colours of the sky change so quickly.

[*They kiss*

The MONK enters, followed by an escort of servants

Monk, you arrive very late to bless us.

MONK An unheard of event has occurred in the city. Last night, without there being any time to warn or evacuate anyone, the North Dam collapsed as though under the orders of some supernatural will. There are no more gates, neither open nor closed . . . Torrents of water are rushing towards the city, people are already fighting over the boats . . . The trumpets are deafening. It feels like a shipwreck down there. Thereupon, Lord Khang learns that the army launched to destroy our Dam has been crushed by your peasants. He immediately gives the order to send a second force, armed to the teeth, to do what you have been able to prevent so far. He has given me this escort, and entrusted me with the task of overtaking as fast as possible the army galloping towards you, and giving you his message: he begs you to ease the suffering of our city by blowing up as quickly as possible the Cherry Mountain Dam; for if it is not destroyed within the hour, the City will disappear forever. If by misfortune, you do not obey, the army will swoop down on you and give you no quarter.

WANG PO The gods have delivered their verdict. We will survive and it is the city that will perish. Duan my beloved, my valiant captain, once again we must mount the charge mercilessly.

DUAN Wait! It is not so simple now! There are no more gates! Things have completely changed! Of course we must fight back, but as for the Dam, what are we going to do?

WANG PO The Dam?

DUAN If we prevent it from being destroyed, the city, already half buried, will totally drown. Let us evacuate the villagers and let the waters pass.

WANG PO Let the city sink! Let her lie there in her muddy shroud. Completely swallowed up! Right up to the roof of the Palace!

DUAN Secretary Wang Po, the matter needs reflection. Lord Khang is not the whole city.

WANG PO All the city belongs to him. The end of his world.

DUAN Ransack everything? Do we not have cousins in town! Daughters? Is not your Chancellor somewhere within those threatened walls? My father lives down there. I was born down there. We too are the city by half . . . Think about it! Are we supposed to forget forever the district of the markets, the theatres, the temples, the artisans, the library?

WANG PO They treated us like animals without desire and without light. I have no other mission than vengeance, no other virtue than hate!

DUAN You want to kill a father for a father! I will prevent you.

WANG PO Viscera without virility! It is not some Duan who will halt my wrath. Let me go! I want to kill!

[They grab hold of each other. To free himself, WANG PO *mortally wounds* DUAN

That is not what I wanted. Arbour of roses. Last day of spring . . . Things are decided.

DUAN It is so soon . . .?

A DRUMMER [*entering*] Sound the alarm! We are being attacked. Lord Khang's army has invaded the Dam.

[The DRUMMER *dies*

WANG PO Call out the trumpets! Let sound the funeral music of all agonies. The night is red! I plunge and sink into it!

[He exits. The servants flee

DUAN I shall not see the void with my father. Monk, go and find the soothsayer and tell him . . .

[She dies

MONK Here I am, the keeper of all silences.

*[*DUAN'*s body is taken away*

This story began badly. There have been so many errors and mistakes. Men strike each other right in the heart. The bridges are destroyed. The moon makes its way alone, dragging behind a net full of corpses.

[*He exits*

MADAME LI *enters, followed by* KISA   100

MADAME LI The city is condemned, Kisa, otherwise the peasants will perish by the thousands.

KISA Woe to both sides!

MADAME LI As far as the eye goes, the space for salvation is disappearing. The entire country has descended to the bottom.

Let us flee even further, Kisa, we will find somewhere to shelter in the end.

[*They exit, running, while* THE WATER *enters*

THE WATER No, you did not expect me! You pretended to wait for me from the beginning of this story; but I was just a word. Water! Water! Well here I am, in reality. You have had enough fun playing with me. "Water," you said, "after all, it is not fire!" But it is to me since the world has existed that the gods have entrusted all beginnings and all endings. Today, I enter into all your affairs. You are all my ancestral   110 fish, and I have come to take you back to the original void. The earth was your ship and you scuttled it through the sin of negligence and the sloth of your souls. You had eyes for nothing. And yet, when the forests framed me, was I not a large enough mirror?

BAÏ JU *enters and tries to fish out his puppets from the flood waters*[3]

THE END

The Boatmen's Cycle

"The empty net" (Scene 3) is the last version of this story and the one that was finally performed. The following texts retrace a short part of the path that took us to the bare, spare empty net.

1) "The boatman's got the blues" (1 April 1999)
2) "Brief riches of Madame Li" (26 April 1999)
3) "Ephemeral triumph of the boatman" (first version, 7 April 1999), (second version, 12 April 1999, entitled "The two brothers").

1 The boatman's got the blues

CRIQUET, *the boatman, enters and runs up and down the canal*

CRIQUET The water belongs to everyone! The only thought of a boatman is how to catch his customers. There is nothing romantic about life. The early bird catches the worm. Me first, the others afterwards. All aboard. All aboard. First boat for Chenjiang.

The boatman MIZU *enters*

MIZU Clear out of here, you gnat – if you want to live, or else pity your widow and orphan.
CRIQUET It is not your big hands and big mouth which chase me away, it is your rotten smell! You stink of misfortune, you sack of dead fish!

[*He exits*

NARRATOR The moon is veiled. Clouds of mosquitoes hum in the reeds of the river and the boatman's thoughts grope their way through the thickets of the night.
MIZU Chenjiang! Nanjiang! All aboard!
MIZU'S WIFE Not a passenger! The empty boat is too light. Dismayed, my husband, the ruined boatman, scans the suddenly empty canal. Whatever happened to those lovely voyages of yesteryear? Everything is the fault of current events.
MIZU The way I am feeling I could put an end to my days.
WIFE And what of me?
MIZU We could commit a double suicide from the parapet of life.
WIFE We had better think about it.
MIZU Or we could leave this city.
WIFE With what money?
MIZU The money from the boat.
WIFE We sold the boat?!
MIZU Obviously. What else?
WIFE So, we buy ourselves a little farm

MIZU You take care of the field and I watch the animals.

WIFE Or the other way around. So things could not be better for us.

MIZU But, the boat, who could we sell it to?

WIFE Madame Li. You know very well that she wants it.

MIZU She will never have the money. And the rest – just a bunch of crooks. Oh! The moon is black. I am
losing hope. Everything is weighing on me. Nothing I wish for ever comes true. I am not going to sell   30
for next to nothing.

WIFE Oh! If only we could know the future! I sigh, I sigh and say: "If only we could find an honest buyer."
But who is going to do business under such a lowering sky?

MIZU What to think about all this? A sad thing to be born an honest man. Peaceful work has no place in
this city. Treacherous world. Better to turn into a wolf or a jackal. Come on! Chenjiang! Nanjiang!!
All aboard! I am the boatman Mizu, famous throughout the city. And this is the finest boat riding on
this cursed river.

THE RIVER *enters*

THE RIVER The river! The river is as beautiful as ever. As far as the eye can see the satin water stretches
out. The water flows noiselessly. The stars' reflections sparkle like silver tadpoles in the black water.   40

MIZU Well! Are you getting in or not?

[THE RIVER *gets into the boat*

WIFE Where are you going, my Lord?

THE RIVER Far away. I am on a journey.

MIZU That we can see.

THE RIVER Has one ever seen in the whole world a king more kingly that this river? The forests and cities
follow in procession. Pink rays tint the borders of the mist hanging from its enormous sleeves.

MIZU You see the river through your own lordly glasses.

THE RIVER And just what do you look through?

MIZU Through our miserable life as boatmen. What does the river bring us? Worries, upheavals, exhaustion.   50
With this river, we are fighting for our lives. I would not hesitate to call it a slut.

THE RIVER You should not speak ill of the river.

MIZU Why should I care? Listen, here is some more: The river crawls along from its insignificant source
to end up like a madman, ravaging India, China and us – and all the others.

THE RIVER What do you know about the river which fed you? There is no respect here. They commit the
crime and then they throw the blame in the waters of the river. They treat father and mother like
garbage. And then they say that the river is malicious. Big or small, all you inhabitants of this country
are nothing but a load of arrogant, ungrateful and moody creatures. Can you not see the end of the
world? You are even more blind than the blind! You will have the flood of the century, I promise!

NARRATOR Mountains of black water will explode from the tops of the heavens, waves as high as towers   60
will fall on palaces; and buildings will be erased from space. Finally, a torrent of corpses will surge up
from the horizon carrying away bridges and gates as if they were scarab shells. Roots in the air, trees
will rush towards the Gate of Hell.

THE RIVER It is over. Everything is calm now. Except for the gong of the monastery, you can hear nothing.

[He *starts to leave*

Do you want to know what I saw in the river's infallible waters?

MIZU The river's waters are deceptive.

WIFE What did you see?

THE RIVER A bushel of rice will quadruple in price. Yet, down at the docks, boats freshly decked out in
purple and gold sleep like shiny fat cats. Dressed in silk, the boatman watches the moon tremble over   70

the black waters of the river. I see a killing pass by right next to him. You will be rich before the year is out, Master Mizu. You may continue on your way.

WIFE But who are you?

[THE RIVER *exits without anyone being able to make out what it answers*

NARRATOR As the noble traveller disappeared noiselessly into an extraordinary night, its weighty words sank to the bottom of the boatman's soul, as if Fate had spoken.

WIFE He said: "I am the river." What do you think about that?

MIZU He did not say anything! I am not thinking what I am thinking and I will not say another word.

WIFE He called you "Master Mizu." He said you will be rich next year.

MIZU He said "this year," not next. Do not go looking for trouble. 80

WIFE I will not say another word. He frightened us. But apart from that he was not really so bad, that traveller, was he?

MIZU I do not know who you are talking about. And I advise you not to say any more about it.

Death will come.
She will embrace me.
She will lead me, shaken,
Into her palace under the water.
Chenjiang! Nanjiang! Last boat! Last trip!

[*They exit*

2 Brief riches of Madame Li

MIZU Chenjiang! Nanjiang! Last boat! Last trip!

WIFE Stop saying "Last trip!" You are frightening the clients away. Last trip! You are going to bring us bad luck before it happens. I hope the gods do not hear you!

MIZU I say what I want. There are no gods. Heaven laughs at us poor folk. Even the river lies. Do you see anywhere this "flood of the century"? So I am supposed to get rich before the year is out? But tomorrow, like yesterday, I will be a beggar. I have nothing to put on my back, except my honour – except my honour! There is not a customer in sight. Nobody will ever come again.

[*We hear* MADAME LI *in the distance: "Paid! Paid!"*

WIFE It is Madame Li.

MIZU She is so proud of herself! 10

MADAME LI I have been paid! Paid! Paid! The dragon smiled on me. Lord Hun has paid what he owed me! And I have managed to sell my stall. What do you see?

[*She shows off a shiny purse*

MIZU The rich are paying their debts. Something wrong with that! I bet you did it with the devil.

MADAME LI Here you are: this is for the boat, a thousand as agreed upon. And this is to thank you for everything.

WIFE It is too much. We could never take it.

MADAME LI Please . . . Take this small token of my thanks. Good luck which is not shared only brings shame and arrogance.

WIFE Well, if it makes you feel better. I am very grateful. But you ought to hide all that. There are so 20 many bandits around. Just looking at your face would make somebody want to rob you.

MADAME LI Oh, yes, I have thought about that. I am going right away to my hiding place. So for now, good night. I will take the boat tomorrow.

MIZU I have changed my mind. Now the boat is three thousand.

MADAME LI Three thousand! And what about your word?

MIZU I said what I said because I did not believe you would buy it. But if it is for real, then it is three thousand.

MADAME LI Then, I am calling it off.

MIZU You will not buy my boat?

MADAME LI I would rather put my money in a safe place. If you are not selling any more, you can stew in   30
your juices.

MIZU Get out of here. Too bad for you. Tomorrow, this boat will be worth ten thousand.

MADAME LI I am leaving. Good night.

[*She waits a bit*

MIZU These pedlars . . . as soon as it is a matter of cash, they are ready to crush the little fellow. But I will not let them rob me. The person who keeps me from enjoying what I have earned places the rebel's knife in my hand.

MADAME LI Fine, so I am leaving and you will never see my money again, right? . . .

MIZU That is right. Just be careful to hide your bundle.

MADAME LI So, for now, goodnight . . .   40

[*she exits*

WIFE She will be back. I am sure of it. We will have the three thousand yin.

MIZU Do you think I would sell my boat for three thousand yin? What would we do without our boat?

WIFE What will we do without any money?

MIZU We will find some. There are ten thousand murders a year. Why not me?

WIFE Oh no! Do not do something crazy that will get us into trouble!

MIZU The old man said it. Everything is already written. The times are terrible. The weak are being wiped out. It is eat or be eaten. The flood is on its way. Hand me that knife.

WIFE You will not have the courage.

MIZU Just you wait.   50

[*He exits*

WIFE Well, then, I am leaving too. I am sick to the bottom of my heart.

[*to her husband*] I am going home and I am taking the lamp with me! Are you coming? Think about the punishment!

[*to the public*] The man is losing his mind. This city is going crazy. At the market they are fighting with knives over a grain of rice. Out of fear, some people are turning into snakes, others into rabbits. I am clearing off . . . Oh for the love of Buddha! I wish I could faint away . . .

The BOATMAN *enters*

Luckily it is my husband who is arriving!

MIZU Do you see this? What did I tell you?   60

WIFE That is Madame Li's purse! Did you kill her? A curse on you!

MIZU I did just as I promised myself.

WIFE Ah woe, woe betide us!

MIZU Not another word! Watch out! I am an entirely different man now. Hurry up! You are looking for trouble! Once the first step is taken, why not the next? You had better watch out for your husband!

[*He beats her and forces her to leave*

MADAME LI *re-enters*

MADAME LI Such brief riches. All Madame Li has left are her bruises and blisters. She had a friend; her friend did her in. And that is how the imminence of the end of the world troubles the firmament.

Honourable and courageous boatmen become bandits near the North Dam, and without any regret. 70
Do you hear? – the cry of a frog being swallowed by a snake. I dreamed way over my head. And now
where can a poor ruined pedlar go? I will finish my days as a latrine sweeper. If I could, I would not
have been born. All the evil is in the city. My noodles and I would be better off higher up. I will head
for Cherry Mountain. Kisa! Kisa!

[*She finds* KISA *and they exit*

3 Ephemeral triumph of the boatman: first version

THE RIVER *enters*

THE RIVER Yesterday, a bushel of rice quadrupled in price. And yet the people in this city are slipping
into lethargy. You cannot hear a dog bark. Their blood slows down in their veins. The enormous bars
of the moon tremble on the black waters of the river. Ships, freshly decked out in purple and gold, sleep
like shiny fat cats. They think there will be no flood; they want to think there was never a flood in the
universe. Houses, palaces, temples, night and day watchmen, lookouts with tired legs, school children,
old people, animate and inanimate things . . . Everything is sleeping. You are sleeping! The world thinks
only of not thinking, but death thinks about all the world.

The boatman's WIFE *enters*

WIFE I cannot sleep either since my husband has become rich. Now, half of the city travels on our boats.
Tell me what boatman's wife would not be swollen with pride to see us transporting all the fine lords 10
and their fancy ladies? Well, me, for one. I cry all day long: my husband, once the most helpful man,
the most . . . Oh, there he is! I had better keep quiet.

The boatman MIZU *enters*

MIZU Who were you talking to? Go ahead, denounce me. What are you waiting for?
WIFE I was talking to myself, that is all.
MIZU You were talking to Madame Li. I heard you. I should have cut her throat! There is no way to be
happy. Go ahead! Call the police.
WIFE Oh misfortune! You are losing your mind. How could I denounce my own husband?
MIZU You had better make sure your heart stays faithful! Otherwise, I cannot vouch for your life. Do I
frighten you? Come on, I was only joking. Give me something to drink. The sun is rising. 20

HE TAO, *his* MEN, *and* TSHUMI, *lagging behind, enter*

WIFE Well, now look at the fancy military passengers who have made their way to us.
HE TAO I am the honourable He Tao, Lord Hun's intendant. You had better receive me as though I were
my master!
NARRATOR And the boatmen bow down four times.
HE TAO Nice boat. It seems you have others?
MIZU We have nine of them, honourable He Tao.
HE TAO Nine. That is really perfect. My master will be delighted. I will take the whole fleet. Let us see:
nine times nine new boats, right, in all that will make nine hundred yin – we will round it off to a

thousand. Boatman, you can go and get paid tonight at the castle. We are in a hurry: we must embark 30
right now. We are going to the countryside.

TSHUMI We are going on a campaign in the campagna! Ha!

MIZU I am not selling! I am not selling.

HE TAO Oh yes you are. You are selling.

MIZU My Lord, I cannot. You are taking the light from my eyes. I have slaved my whole life.

HE TAO If you refuse, you had better understand that a big disappointment awaits you in the depths of a
murky prison cell.

MIZU My Lord, be patient. I am losing too much, give me two days.

HE TAO I would like to, but we do not have the time, as you know very well. Think of yourself as
requisitioned. I have discussed the matter with you long enough. You are not a fool. So come on! Let 40
go! Let go I tell you. And you, woman, off the ship!

MIZU Do not do this to me, my Lord! I will not leave my boat! I will hang on to the rail! I will stir up the
whole waterfront!

[TSHUMI, *powerless to do anything, whispers some advice
in the ear of the boatman's* WIFE

WIFE My Lord, do not listen to my husband! He has been drinking! It is an honour for us to be requisitioned.

MIZU Go ahead, you whore! Denounce me! Kill me!

[*He beats her*

HE TAO Get over here, you soldiers, and put a stop to this repulsive show! Throw them in the water!

NARRATOR The intendant is still speaking when a dozen huge men surround the boatman and his wife, 50
beating and punching them without mercy, without even giving them the chance to cry out. They push
them along the dock and drag them to the edge.

HE TAO That will do. Now, get to the oars! They are waiting for us over by Cherry Mountain! Once up
there, we will unleash the dam. Like deer chased by dogs, the peasants will flee when they see you.
But you have served Lord Hun so well that I cannot stop your pillaging the granaries a bit. But hurry!
Then we can get back to the city saved from the waters. Let us go, men! Row! I feel my eyes glisten!

NARRATOR The nine new ships disappear in the morning mist. It is the most graceful disappearance ever
seen. Boatman Mizu does not take his eyes off the mist-shrouded silhouettes. Dying of pain, he
contemplates the end of his all too wondrous fortune.

MIZU They cost me my soul!! And I am defenceless. An insignificant earthworm. It is my children they 60
are stealing. Ah! My only destiny is injustice; the only tears are mine; and there is no other end to my
misfortune than death. I bid you farewell, my wife, this awfulness has lasted long enough.

NARRATOR The wife, moaning, grabs onto her husband's legs. He is her husband after all.

MIZU If you stop me from throwing myself into the water, you kill me! Let me go!

NARRATOR He screams like a disemboweled dog. Why prolong such a life! The wife obeys. He is her
husband after all.

WIFE All right! I will go with you. The rest is not worth it. Just give me the time to say a prayer.

MIZU Hurry! Hurry! Do not discourage me. All my life you have held me back!

NARRATOR Hurriedly, the wife says her many goodbyes. The tears on her cheeks form rivers. Secretly,
she sends a final message to the scene's great witness. The river receives her last words. 70

WIFE [*to* THE RIVER] My Lord, this is for Madame Li. Let her think of me without anger. I could not do
otherwise. At last, we are quits.

NARRATOR With their faces bathed in pity, the couple hold hands and slip into the bed that has been
awaiting them from the beginning of their poor existence.

[*The* BOATMAN *and his* WIFE *sink into the water*

The two brothers: second version

MIZU [*pulling out his money hidden in the water*] This money – I do not know what to do with it. You should give me an idea.

WIFE Just by thinking we are rich, I feel intimidated. Did you really have to steal Madame Li's purse? Since you took it, the money has been sleeping and we are the ones who cannot close our eyes.

MIZU It would be better if your mouth stopped moving.

WIFE I continue: we lost our honesty and what did we gain. Eh?

MIZU Go ahead! Denounce me!

WIFE Me – denounce my own husband! You are losing your mind along with everything else.

MIZU Give me something to drink if you want to go on living. I used to be sad, now I am becoming bitter. We can never be happy . . .

WIFE You are growing nasty. Every day you are more and more like your brother. Oh! If only I could wake up yesterday.

MIZU What is done is done and cannot be undone. We would be better off with an idea. For example, that little farm . . .

WIFE You are joking! I know that little farm. I take care of the field and the pigs and you do nothing. Except drink and drink. The rest of the time we would be bored. I would rather die of boredom in town. But what about boats? You do not want boats any more? You used to dream about a fleet.

MIZU This fleet – where would we dock it? All the docks belong to Hun. If you get his permission to drop anchor, within a week you become his slave.

WIFE Maybe you ought to give the gold to the monastery.

MIZU That money cost me my soul and now you want me to give it to the monk? While you are at it, you might as well tell me to give it to the devil.

WIFE Look at that, you hardly say his name and here he is! If it is not your older brother.

HE TAO enters

HE TAO Chenjiang! Nanjiang! All aboard! Ah! So how are you? From as far away as Lord Hun's palace, I was thinking about you, dear little brother, and in one flying leap here I am. I know things have been rough for you and your pockets are empty, so I have a little proposition. I will get straight to the point. Recently, I was given the job of planning the murder of the chief intendant. You are strong and agile, and I need your help . . . 2,000 yin – will you take it? What do you say? For once in your miserable life, you will have some money. And for your wife – ribbons, ten metres of silk, mother-of-pearl combs. What do you say? Eh?

MIZU Keep your silk, big brother. I am not the person you think I am. I have money. I do not even know what I am going to do with it. Ha! Take a look at this! Can you call me a beggar now?

HE TAO But what is that rattling there? Those are the arms of my master, Lord Hun! That is Madame Li's purse!

WIFE We found it, Honourable Big Brother!! We found it over there.

HE TAO You mean my own brother is the filthy bandit who stole the pedlar's fortune? Since then, she has been in a rage!
[*he yells to a patrol*] This thief . . .

MIZU Shut up! There is no thief on this earth worse than your master, Lord Hun.
[*Ashamed and angry, he insults and threatens his brother from a distance*

HE TAO This thief to whom I was going to entrust, out of love and friendship, a secret and delicate mission, and who boasts of his crime!

MIZU You want to see what I can do, you valet to a pile of garbage, you butler to a vampire?!! . . .

HE TAO Disgusting puppet! Come on over here! Come on! . . .

[he continues to insult him and comes closer again

MIZU If I do, you can prepare your coffin! You servant to a vulture! If your master could sell the fingernails of corpses, he would rip them off, he would pull down the stars from the sky!

WIFE No, no! Do not listen to him!

HE TAO I am listening to my own indignation! I ought to knock you to the floor and beat you to a pulp! 50
Give me that purse!

[He beats the BOATMAN

WIFE Please, I beg of you, do not beat him. Above all, do not kill him! He is my husband, poor man!

HE TAO Let him live so he can die of shame! I do not know you. Even more: I never had a brother. Do I need a thief to help me kill the intendant! *[To the* WIFE] And you – one word too many and it is death, once and for all.
Nanjiang! Chenjiang! Last boat!

[He exits

MIZU This world is not made for those who are not evil enough. I am dishonoured.

WIFE It is because you were drinking. Your brother is not a brother. It is not your fault. 60

MIZU He wanted me to kill a man! Me! Never! Follow my reasoning: did I kill Madame Li? I should have, but I did not. And now I have lost everything . . . Oh! My only destiny is injustice. The only tears are mine. The only solution to my misfortune is death.

WIFE Oh! How your words frighten me!

MIZU I bid you farewell, wife. This comedy of woes has lasted long enough.

WIFE Moaning, I grab onto my husband's legs. He is my husband after all.

MIZU If you stop me from throwing myself into the water, you kill me. Oh! Let me go!

WIFE Then I will go with you. The rest is not worth it. Wait. Let me say a little prayer.

MIZU Hurry! Do not discourage me! All my life you have held me back.

WIFE *[to* THE RIVER] This is a last message for Madame Li. 70
Let her think of me without anger.
I could not do otherwise. At last, we are quits.
[to her husband] Give me your hand and now let us slip into the bed that has been awaiting us from the beginning of our poor existence.

[They drown themselves

Notes to *Drums on the Dam*

1 [Translators' note] In the Théâtre du Soleil production (1999/2000), each character was played by an actor-puppet who, in turn, was manipulated by one or more actor-puppeteers.

2 [Translators' note] Here, in the Théâtre du Soleil production, Wang Po prepares to kill himself.

3 [Translators' note] In the Théâtre du Soleil production, as the waters rise, Baï Ju wades in and finds one by one the hand puppets which represent the puppet characters in the play. He and several of the actor-puppeteers position these on the apron of the stage, from where the puppets look out at the audience as the lights go down.

Premières

PORTRAIT DE DORA
Théâtre d'Orsay, directed by Simone Benmussa with film sequences by Marguerite Duras, opened 26 February 1976. A radio version was broadcast on France-Culture, "Atelier de Création Radiophonique" in 1972.

L'ARRIVANTE
Adaptation of *La* (Hélène Cixous, 1976) by Viviane Théophilidès. Théâtre Ouvert, Avignon, France, July 1977.

LE NOM D'OEDIPE, CHANT DU CORPS INTERDIT
Libretto. Music by A. Boucourechliev, directed by Claude Régy. Performed in the Cour du Palais des Papes, Avignon, France, 26, 27, 28 July 1978.

JE ME SUIS ARRÊTÉE À UN MÈTRE DE JÉRUSALEM ET C'ÉTAIT LE PARADIS
Théâtre Ouvert, reading with Michelle Marquais and Bérangère Bonvoisin, 7 June 1982.

AMOUR D'UNE DÉLICATESSE
Radio play. Radio Suisse Romande, Lausanne, Switzerland, 28 August 1982.

LA PRISE DE L'ÉCOLE DE MADHUBAÏ
Théâtre de l'Europe, directed by Michelle Marquais, opened 13 December 1983.

CELUI QUI NE PARLE PAS
Théâtre Tsaï, Grenoble/T.E.P., Paris, June 1984.

L'HISTOIRE TERRIBLE MAIS INACHEVÉE DE NORODOM SIHANOUK, ROI DU CAMBODGE
Théâtre du Soleil, directed by Ariane Mnouchkine, opened 11 September 1985. Tour, 1986: Amsterdam, Holland; Brussels, Belgium; Madrid, Barcelona, Spain. 108,000 spectators.

L'INDIADE, OU L'INDE DE LEURS RÊVES
Théâtre du Soleil, directed by Ariane Mnouchkine, opened 30 September 1987. Tour, 1988: Jerusalem, Tel Aviv. 89,000 spectators.

LA NUIT MIRACULEUSE
Film scenario by Ariane Mnouchkine and Hélène Cixous, dialogues by Hélène Cixous. Broadcast on La Sept, FR 3, 13, 15, 17 and 23 December 1989.

ON NE PART PAS ON NE REVIENT PAS
(La Métaphore) Théâtre National de Lille, reading directed by Daniel Mesguich, 24 November 1991.

L'HISTOIRE (QU'ON NE CONNAÎTRA JAMAIS)

Théâtre de la Ville, Paris, directed by Daniel Mesguich, opened 6 May 1994; (La Métaphore) Théâtre National de Lille, June 1994.

LA VILLE PARJURE OU LE RÉVEIL DES ÉRINYES

Théâtre du Soleil, directed by Ariane Mnouchkine, opened 18 October 1994. Tour, 1995: Recklinghausen Germany; Vienna, Austria; Festival d'Avignon, France. 51,000 spectators.

VOILE NOIRE VOILE BLANCHE

In English translation (as *Black Sail White Sail*), the Sphinx Theatre Company, directed by Sue Parrish, opened 6 September 1994 at the Gate Theatre, London.

ROUEN, LA TRENTIÈME NUIT DE MAI '31

First reading directed by Daniel Mesguich, Centre Culturel International de Cerisy-la-Salle, June 1998. A radio version was broadcast on France-Culture, 17 December 2000. Opened 18 July 2001, Villeneuve-les-Avignon, France.

AIL! (IL NE FAUT PAS LE DIRE)

Théâtre de la Tempête, June 2000. A radio version was broadcast on France-Culture, 17 December 2000.

TAMBOURS SUR LA DIGUE

Théâtre du Soleil, directed by Ariane Mnouchkine, opened 11 September 1999. Tour, 2000, 2001: Basle, Switzerland; Antwerp, Belgium; Lyon, France; Montreal, Canada; Tokyo, Japan; Seoul, Korea; Sydney, Australia. 154,000 spectators.

Theatre bibliography

1971

La Pupille, Cahiers Renaud-Barrault 78, Paris: Gallimard.

1976

Portrait de Dora, Paris: Des femmes; reprinted in *Théâtre*, 1986.

1978

Le Nom d'Oedipe, Chant du corps interdit, opera libretto, music by A. Boucourechliev, Paris: Des femmes. English translation by Christiane Makward and Judith Miller, *The Name of Oedipus: Song of the Forbidden Body*, in *Out of Bounds: Women's Theater in French*, Ann Arbor, Mich.: University of Michigan Press, 1991; re-edited in Christiane Makward and Judith Miller, eds., *Plays by French and Francophone Women: A Critical Anthology*, Ann Arbor, Mich.: University of Michigan Press, 1994: 247–326.

1984

La Prise de l'école de Madhubaï, Avant-Scène du Théâtre 745 (March): 6–22; and in *Théâtre*, 1986. English translation by Deborah W. Carpenter, *The Conquest of the School at Madhubaï, Women and Performance* 3 (Special Feature) 59–95.

1985

L'Histoire terrible mais inachevée de Norodom Sihanouk, roi du Cambodge, Paris: Théâtre du Soleil; new corrected edition, 1987. English translation by Judith Flower MacCannell, Judith Pike and Lollie Groth, *The Terrible but Unfinished Story of Norodom Sihanouk, King of Cambodia*, Lincoln, Nebr.: University of Nebraska Press, 1994.

1986

Théâtre, Paris: Des femmes.

1987

L'Indiade, ou l'Inde de leurs rêves, et quelques écrits sur le théâtre, Paris: Théâtre du Soleil.

1991

On ne part pas, on ne revient pas, Paris: Des femmes.

1992

Les Euménides (Aeschylus) translation, Paris: Théâtre du Soleil.

1994

L'Histoire (qu'on ne connaîtra jamais), Paris: Des femmes.

Voile Noire Voile Blanche (Black Sail White Sail), bilingual, translated by C. MacGillivray, with extensive editorial notes, *New Literary History* 25, 2 (Spring): 219–354.

La Ville parjure ou le réveil des Érinyes, Paris: Théâtre du Soleil.

1999
Tambours sur la Digue, sous forme de pièce ancienne pour marionnettes jouées par des acteurs, Paris: Théâtre du Soleil.

2001
Rouen, la Trentième Nuit de Mai '31, Paris: Galilée.